PRECISION
FRAMING

PRECISION FRAMING

MIKE GUERTIN AND RICK ARNOLD

The Taunton Press

Publisher: JIM CHILDS
Acquisitions Editor: STEVE CULPEPPER
Technical Editors: BRUCE GREENLAW AND JEFFERSON KOLLE
Assistant Editor: CAROL KASPER
Copy Editor: CANDACE B. LEVY
Indexer: HARRIET HODGES
Cover Designer: STEVE HUGHES
Layout Artist: SUZIE YANNES
Front Cover Photographer: WENDI MIJAL
Interior Photographers: MIKE GUERTIN AND RICK ARNOLD, EXCEPT WHERE NOTED
Illustrator: MARIO FERRO

Taunton
BOOKS & VIDEOS

for fellow enthusiasts

Text © 2001 by Mike Guertin and Rick Arnold
Photographs © 2001 by The Taunton Press, Inc., except where noted
Illustrations © 2001 by The Taunton Press, Inc.

All rights reserved.

Printed in the United States of America
10 9 8 7 6 5 4 3 2 1

For Pros/By Pros® is a trademark of The Taunton Press, Inc., registered in the U.S. Patent and Trademark Office.

The Taunton Press, Inc., 63 South Main Street,
PO Box 5506, Newtown, CT 06470-5506
e-mail: tp@taunton.com

Distributed by Publishers Group West

Library of Congress Cataloging-in-Publication Data
Guertin, Mike
    For Pros/By Pros®: Precision framing / Mike Guertin and Rick Arnold.
      p.   cm.
    Includes index.
    ISBN 1-56158-463-0
     1. Framing (Building) I. Arnold, Rick, 1955- II. Title.
TH2301.G84   2001
694'.2—dc21   00-049833

To Charlie, Bruce, Phil, Todd, Marc, Scott, and Mac.

Acknowledgments

In brief, thanks to the various employees and friends who over the years helped us hone our framing skills and techniques: P. Money, T. Money, Thumper, Chas, Magoose, Wee Wee Bald Head, Sir Charles, Scooter, Dunc, Moosa, Andrew Baby, Soup, Pumper, Momus, and the rest of the cast. Thanks to Carol Kasper for keeping us on track, for putting on a tool belt to learn what we were up to, and for arranging the B-heads and C-heads. Thanks to Jeff Kolle for polishing things up. Steve Culpepper deserves thanks for enticing us to write *Precision Framing*. Special thanks to Roe Osborn for teaching us everything we know about writing and taking photographs. And, of course, thanks to Kevin Ireton and the rest of the *Fine Homebuilding* magazine editors for bringing us on board as contributing editors, taking us to lunch, and making us twist a little more to the left.

About Your Safety: Homebuilding is inherently dangerous. From accidents with power tools or hand tools to fall from ladders, scaffolds, and roofs, builders and homeowners risk serious injury and even death. We try to promote safe work practices throughout this book, but what is safe for one builder or homeowner under certain circumstances may not be safe for you under different circumstances. So don't try anything you learn about here (or elsewhere) unless you're certain that it's safe for you. If something doesn't feel right, don't do it. Look for another way. Please keep safety foremost in your mind whenever you're working.

CONTENTS

Introduction	2

Chapter 1
TOOLS   4

Office Tools	5
Hand Tools	6
Power Tools	13
Pneumatic Tools	16
Staging	19
Other Equipment	21

Chapter 2
MUDSILLS   24

Sizing Up the Foundation	25
Laying Out for Mudsills	26
Checking the Foundation for Level	33
Installing the Mudsill	36
Using Shims to Level the Mudsill	39
Framing Walls on Drops	40
Ready to Move On	41

Chapter 3
CENTER BEAMS   42

Beam Basics	43
Planning a Built-Up Beam	43
Installing the Beam	45
Other Beam Materials	53
Installing Support Columns	55
Beam/Joist Configurations	57

Chapter 4
FLOOR FRAMING   58

Joist Layout for Conventional Floor Decks	59
Framing Joists for Conventional Floor Decks	69
Installing Subfloor Sheathing for Conventional Floor Decks	82
Framing Floors with I-Joists	88
Framing Floors with Trusses	95

Chapter 5
WALL FRAMING 98
- Planning Exterior Bearing Walls 99
- Laying Out Bearing Wall Plates 105
- Assembling the Walls 121
- Framing Other Bearing and Exterior Walls 140

Chapter 6
ROOF FRAMING 146
- A Stick-Built Roof 147
- Roof Trusses 166

Chapter 7
STRAPPING CEILINGS AND FRAMING INTERIOR PARTITION WALLS 184
- Marking Interior Partitions 185
- Laying Out and Installing Strapping 186
- Laying Out the Wall 190
- Measuring Stud Height and Prepping Wall Parts 194
- Framing the Partitions 195
- Finishing Up 197

Chapter 8
SPECIAL FRAMING DETAILS 198
- Special Details for Framing Interior Partition Walls 198
- Special Details for Roof Framing 206
- Special Details for Framing for Subcontractors 209

Index 212

INTRODUCTION

Framing custom homes was our bread and butter for 15 years. But, unlike most framers who learn their trade working on other crews before breaking off on their own, we used the academic approach. The framing chapters of a couple of construction books written in the 1950s and 1960s served as our mentors. But the text was short on the how-to's of getting the lumber cut and assembled to look like the drawings in the books. More words were spent expounding the virtues of running the 1x pine sheathing diagonally rather than perpendicularly to the framing members and handling a crosscut saw. Our lack of training, which felt like a curse at times, had a positive consequence—we were always looking for and trying new techniques to build a frame better and faster. We weren't stuck doing it "the boss's way" like so many of our employees who had experience working on other crews. We gathered ideas from many sources and adapted them to suit our style. New employees came with their own experiences. We talked with other framers and shared ideas. We read building magazines and books. And we experimented with our own ideas.

As our framing business grew and we began running several crews at once, we saw the need to develop a standard operating procedure (SOP). We needed to write down the systems we used so all the guys were consistent. Three months of biweekly meetings with our six core crew members were spent mapping out the best way to do everything from checking a foundation's level to standard interior stud height to the procedure for nailing on siding. The SOP kept changing as we experimented with new tricks and still does to this day. This book is the expanded version of our 10-page SOP.

There are no right or wrong ways to frame a house. Building codes tell us what the result of our effort must be, not how to get there. There are as many ways to frame a house as there are framing crews out there. Our intent with this book is to demonstrate the way we've found most efficient to frame a custom home.

For framers building track housing for which speed is supreme, there's probably little to learn here. But for custom home framers like us who strive for flat, squeak-free floors, straight walls, and labor efficiency, you may learn some procedures you can adapt and blend into your own framing methods. Novices who want to do it themselves will be able to follow our procedures step by step and complete a quality frame—provided you can read blueprints. If you get lost following an ordinary road map, you should hire a professional. For you, this book will give you a vicarious view into the general procedures your framer will follow.

While our careers have shifted from framers who build homes now and then to builders who frame their own homes, we have never stopped trying new methods and materials to get the job done better and faster.

Chapter 1

TOOLS

OFFICE TOOLS

HAND TOOLS

POWER TOOLS

PNEUMATIC TOOLS

STAGING

OTHER EQUIPMENT

Before we started writing this book, this chapter in particular, we emptied out the toolboxes in our trucks, searched through our garages, and strolled around our backyards. We got all our tools together, and if we missed anything, either we don't have it, or we seldom use it. If you're relatively new to the carpentry business and you don't have all the tools we list in this chapter, don't worry, you can make do like we did.

Eventually, your inventory should come close to ours in size and variety. Not because it's fun to buy tools (which it is) but because having a complete inventory of tools and equipment helps your jobs go quicker, with more precision, quality,

All of the hand tools necessary to frame a house easily fit in a pickup truck.

and safety. Which, of course, means more profit. (Some of the specialized tools we make for different framing procedures are discussed in the later chapters.)

Our businesses are located in Rhode Island and some of the things we do and some of the tools we use on the East Coast differ slightly from the way carpenters do things out West. We would never purport that our ways are better or worse; sometimes they are just different and different is often good because that's the way carpenters (and other people, too) learn.

Office Tools

Throughout the book you'll see that a good part of our technique for running a fast, efficient framing business is proper planning. The planning begins long before the first nail is driven, and it continues during the entire framing process. A "toolbox" of basic office tools will save you countless hours on the job site. A lot of these office tools also get used on the job as much as in the office.

Fax machine and e-mail Rolled paper, plain paper, or fax-modem: Even the simplest type of fax machine serves the function as well as the one with all of the bells and whistles.

With the multitude of decisions to be made before and during framing, and the inevitable change orders that follow, notes of every conversation between contractor and homeowner or contractor and architect should be jotted down and faxed to the other party for documentation. If one or more of the parties involved in the project doesn't own a fax machine, include it in your price and supply them with one. Furthermore, faxing orders to the lumberyard helps prevent the mistakes of an over-the-phone verbal order, and you can send it at your convenience during their non-business hours.

As more people get e-mail, it also will become an increasingly useful tool for contractors. It's immediate and easy.

Measuring scales A lot of preplanning and estimating is done in the office on the blueprints, which are drawn to a certain scale. For residential construction the most common scale is ¼ in. = 1 ft. This means that every ¼ in. on the plans equals 1 ft. in the actual dimensions of the house. For example, if a stairway on the plans is ¾ in. wide, in the house it will be 3 ft. wide. We use scaled rulers to measure, mark layouts, and size different aspects of the job. These rules use different ratios to determine measurement. An engineer's rule is scaled in a decimal fashion to

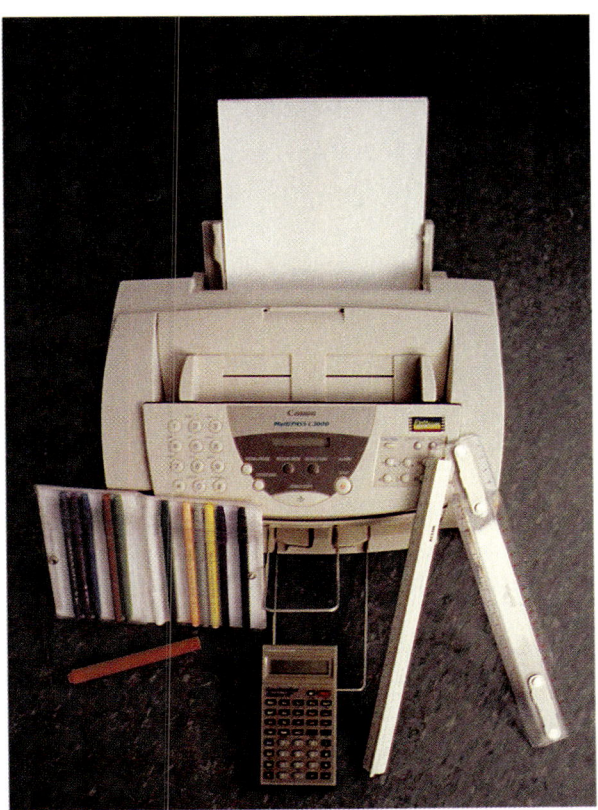

A well-stocked office can be as important to a precise and profitable framing project as a well-stocked pickup. Lots of work gets done in the office before the first nail is driven on the job site.

10ths and 100ths of an inch, while an architect's rule is scaled in fractions of an inch down to 16ths or even 32nds. These rules are generally 1 ft. long and have a triangular cross section so that they can have six different scales.

Roller scale Roller scales are hand-held penlike instruments with a small wheel or roller at one end. They measure in different scales, like the rulers, but are rolled on the blueprints. They are useful for adding up linear footage along many lines. They are available in different types; some give analog readings, some give digital readouts, and some digital ones can link to computers for dropping values directly into spreadsheets and estimating programs.

Calculator A couple of $5 disposable calculators with square root buttons are usually found in the glove compartments of carpenters' trucks, and they're a good backup to have in the office as well. The best type of calculator is one specifically designed for the construction industry. This type lets you work with feet and inches, which reduces the chance of errors made when converting from foot and inch measurements to decimal equivalents, as needed with standard calculators.

Colored markers Colored pencils, pens, highlighters, crayons, and markers are well-used office tools. We use different colors when laying out a set of plans to indicate placement and different sizes of framing members. Special details and mechanical layouts are also highlighted in color. Marking up a set of plans with color-coded lines and diagrams gives you an easy-to-follow guide while on the job site and keeps you focused on the important details.

Hand Tools

As the saying goes, "A carpenter is only as good as his tools," and this is where it all starts. Good, basic hand tools are essential to smooth, efficient work.

Belts and pouches On the job site, all carpenters carry around a lot of small tools. And they carry their tools in a wide variety of pouches, nail bags, and tool belts. These range from the canvas nail aprons given away by some lumberyards to the $200 synthetic material, multi-pocketed, pouched belt with suspenders and integrated back support.

This is a good example of "You get what you pay for." An inexpensive, imitation-leather pouch lasts about six months before the nails start falling through. And the belt it comes with is not easily adjustable.

We've found that a wide leather belt with a large buckle and a couple of multipocketed leather pouches is easily adjustable and lasts for years. The pouches are separate from the belt and from each other, so any part of the assembly can be replaced individually. Also, this system is versatile; you can quickly change between different types of pouches and tool holders to meet your tool-carrying needs. And you can slide the pouches along the belt in case you want the pouches in front, off to the sides over your hips, or in back.

Suspenders that clip onto the belts are available to help keep the weight away from the hips. Some tool belts even have their own suspender systems.

Hammers For framing, a bigger hammer is a better hammer. Check out the multitude of hammers at a well-stocked retailer. The longer and heavier ones are for framing. These hammers start at about 20 oz. and continue all the way up to 33 oz. The handles on framing hammers are longer than those on finish and utility hammers, and they are available in wood, steel, fiberglass, and graphite. We think that wood handles vibrate the least, but they are breakable. Solid steel shanks are virtually indestructible but they transmit a lot of vibration into your forearm and elbow. Fiberglass and graphite are somewhere in between. Many companies have built anti-vibration systems into their handles to help minimize the problems users can develop from too much vibration.

Hammer heads are available in various weights and different shapes. Framing hammers generally have straight claws but lighter-weight heads are

Hammers are made with a variety of head weights, head styles, and handle materials—and they all have advantages and disadvantages.

available with curved claws that make nail pulling easier. The striking face of the head can be smooth or ground into a sharp waffle pattern or other textured pattern. The patterned end bites into the nail head to keep the hammer from glancing off during those near misses. A smooth head is more forgiving when those misses occur. Patterned heads leave nasty blemishes.

Sledgehammers You don't need a sledgehammer that's heavy; a 6-lb. to 10-lb. tool is sufficient. They're used mostly for tapping things into position. A tap with a sledgehammer is very persuasive. We use them to drive the subfloor tongues into the grooves or to tap walls into position. Fiberglass handles are more durable than wood ones, particularly when considering that this tool spends most of its life exposed to the elements in the back of the truck. Eventually, though, sunlight can degrade fiberglass.

Tape measures Every couple of years we see a new and improved tape measure hit the market. Some make it, some don't.

For short to intermediate measuring look for a spring-loaded, self-reeling model with a 25-ft. to 30-ft. long, 1-in.-wide steel tape. It should have a strong spring with a locking mechanism to keep

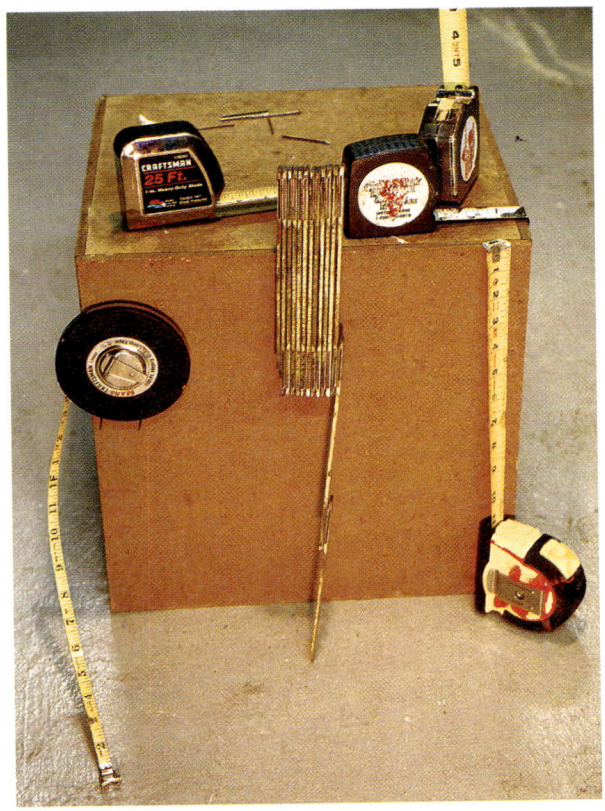

Look for a tape measure that's at least 25 ft. long and has a 1-in.-wide blade. To measure longer distances, you'll need a tape measure with a steel blade that's 100 ft. long and ⅜ in. wide. Having a backup for each is a good idea.

On the left is a wood-handled sliding T-bevel useful for duplicating and marking just about any angle. The large gold-colored adjustable square in the center also transcribes angles. The yellow-and-black combination square and the small triangular square mark 90° and 45° angles and fit easily in a tool belt pouch.

the tape extended when needed. And the important layout centers must be highlighted; usually 16-in. on-center increments in red, 12-in. increments with arrows or black marks, and the 19.2-in. centers minimally indicated with diamonds.

The hook on the end of the tape should be double- or triple-riveted to keep it from pulling off. And it should slide back and forth a little bit on the rivets so it can accommodate the measuring differences between getting hooked on the end of a board and being pushed up into a corner.

A tape should last a long time, and it will last even longer if you never let the hook snap back against the case as it reels in. Stop the hook with a fingertip and then let it ease back into the case.

For long measurements of 50 ft. to 100 ft., look for a ⅜-in.-wide manual-reeling steel tape. The on-center marks should be highlighted and the end tightly riveted with a fold-out tooth to bite into the lumber. The winding mechanism and handle will be less prone to breaking if they are steel.

Utility knives Razor-bladed utility knives are made for tasks like sharpening pencils and cutting string, but they take a lot of abuse. Every carpenter we know ends up using his razor knife as a screwdriver, a chisel, a prybar, and a metal cutter. They even work for digging out splinters. So it follows that durability is at the top of the evaluation list. A steel-bodied knife with an adjustable, fully retractable blade works best for us. We prefer the type that allows quick access to the extra blades stored inside the knife body and a quick-change blade feature that requires no unscrewing and opening up the knife.

Mini flatbar Mini flatbars take some of the burden off the utility knife as a jack-of-all-trades. These little tools don't take up much room in a pouch and serve many purposes during a framing project; for example, they pull nails, clear out bruised grooves in sheathing, help unscrew bolts, and scrape ice off lumber.

Squares The squares we are talking about here are the small squares used for drawing cut and layout lines on lumber. Adjustable combination squares are sometimes used by framing carpenters; but the combo square's foot-long steel blade can get caught up and bent while one is climbing around a framed structure. We think those squares are better suited for finish work.

Plastic or steel tricorner squares easily fit in a pouch pocket and have a variety of helpful markings. Inches are marked along one edge and single, double, and flat 2x4 stud widths are marked along another edge. Degrees and pitches are marked along an opening in the center, and the triangle is a true 45°. There are also rectangular versions of this type of square, which are primarily used as channel-marking patterns.

Chalklines Chalklines, a.k.a. chalk boxes, are one of the most simple and useful tools for precision-minded framers. They're used to mark straight lines on foundations, floor decks, ceilings, framing lumber, and sheathing. Most chalklines are teardrop shaped plastic or metal boxes that house a spool of cotton string and a reservoir of colored powdered chalk. The teardrop shape lends itself to secondary duty as a crude plumb bob.

Chalklines can also be used for stringing and straightening walls and beams. We keep several boxes empty of chalk for use as dry line string. The original cotton string eventually breaks to an unusable length and can be replaced with tougher nylon twine.

We like to keep a couple of chalklines in our tool pouches loaded with different colors of chalk. If a line is snapped in the wrong location, we pull out the other color line and resnap it in the correct location. Blue chalk will wash off easily when hit by the next rain. Red won't. This is important to remember, because sometimes you don't want to loose a chalkline and other times you do. Snap the lines for mudsill placement on top of a foundation in blue chalk one afternoon, and it won't be there the next morning if it rains during the night. When snapping a chalkline to guide the bottom of a white cedar shingle course, make sure you don't use red, or the owner will be looking at it a year later.

Metal or plastic box construction—it doesn't matter much; what is important is a gear-driven winder for rapid windups. Spend a little more for a good name brand rapid-winder type though, because cheap gears on inexpensive models seem to strip. Older chalkline model designs use direct-drive spindle cranks that are very reliable but are as slow as an old computer. A bonus to most of the rapid-rewind chalklines is that the crank can be depressed to release the line without its spinning around, as it does on direct-drive models.

Also, chalk refill ports that unscrew at the nose or opposite end of the unit are better than the types that have a sliding door on the side. It takes a little longer to fill the cap models; but, inevitably, the sliding door will eventually open while being knocked around inside your pouch, and the chalk makes a mess as it empties out.

Plumb bob The large 4-in. to 5-in. brass plumb bobs with replaceable points are common to framing and work great, but their loose, sharp point and awkward bulk usually keep them in a toolbox until they're needed.

A small 2-in. or 3-in., one-piece steel plumb bob, with about a 15-ft. string, tucks easily into a tool belt; and although it may not be as accurate as a big brass bob, it's a lot more precise than a spirit level. The great thing about a plumb bob is that it can't go out of whack. The point indicated by the end of the bob is always, absolutely, positively, with 100 percent accuracy, in a vertical line with the point from which the string is held, providing it's not windy.

Caulking guns Small caulking guns range from cheap disposable types to relatively expensive lifetime-guaranteed models. The more expensive ones are made with thicker gauge steel and are equipped with a built-in end cutter and an attached poker to break the seal of the tube. The cheap ones are just that, cheap. We've seen many pinched palms from pump arms that folded or broke into the handle when someone tried to push stiff caulk from a tube.

Large guns (to hold 29-oz. tubes) are used on framing jobs to deliver large quantities of adhesive to glue down subfloors. They, too, come in varying levels of quality.

Several more-elaborate caulking guns reduce the labor and effort of delivering gallons of caulk. Long-reach guns help lessen the fatigue caused by constant bending. And there are power-assisted guns that use a corded or cordless drill to squeeze out material. These work well during warm weather, but cold, thick adhesive has enough resistance that the drive gears can strip out.

Pneumatic-drive caulking guns are perhaps the most effort easing of the bunch, but they are the costliest and need a compressor to power them.

Levels A 6-ft. spirit level is ideal for framing. It gives a more accurate reading than the standard 4-ft. level and doesn't require an extra straight-edge. The 4-ft. bubble level is still the most popular on framing jobs, mostly because it is the longest one available that can be easily stored in a truck box or in the cab.

Levels are made from plastic, steel, aluminum, wood, or a combination of any of these materials. We favor the middle of the road as far as price goes; but, most important, as for many of our other hand tools, we prefer the brands that carry a lifetime guarantee. Drop your hammer, no big deal. Drop a cheap level, and it can go out of whack. Drop a level with a lifetime guarantee; and if it does go out of whack, you can get it replaced at no cost.

If you are going to be working with steel studs, a magnetized level is a must. It gives you that third hand you always seem to need.

Electronic units that fit within level frames are nice because they offer more options. Not only can they plumb and level like a bubble level but they can also read angles in degrees or pitches. The electronic unit can be interchanged between different length frames. But there's a problem with these sensitive electronic devices: One good fall off a roof and they're history. It would be good for a one- or two-person operation but definitely not for a large crew.

Another type of electronic level comes as a small boxlike assemblage and emits visible laser beams both horizontally and vertically. Used correctly, this can outperform a conventional level, but it's also more prone to damage and a rather costly investment.

A good level is critical to the quality of a house frame. It should be checked every day that it is put to use. Shorter ones work well if they are used with a long straightedge.

Prybars and nail pullers. When the first change order is issued, you'll see a number of different types come out of the toolboxes.

A good level is critical to the quality of a house frame and should be checked every day. To check a level, place it on a relatively flat and level or plumb surface and note the location of the bubble. Move it 180° end to end and place it in the exact same spot. If the level is true, the bubble will read as before.

Flatbars Flatbars, prybars, crowbars are all members of the same species and, in fact, the names are sometimes used interchangeably. For framing, the smaller flatbars and prybars (up to about 16 in. long) are most useful. Flatbars have a thinner profile and more surface area than crowbars or prybars. They can be used to gently pry and separate or to violently rip apart. Prybars are similar except for their profile. Their flat pry surface forms into a more round, rigid shank and cannot always provide just a light touch. Crowbars provide more leverage than the others because they are longer (2 ft. and greater) and are usually saved for the really tough jobs, like separating previously fastened headers or beams.

Cat's paws Whether from mistakes, changes, or just temporary fastening, a large part of framing consists of nail pulling. There are many different types of pullers available. The ones we look for have a set of claws on both ends of the tool. One set at a 90° angle to the shank, and the other set straight off the shank. The flatbar, prybar, and crowbar can also pull nails, but they require a lot more effort and digging to get at the nail head. Cat's paws dig beneath nail heads easily and don't tear the lumber up as much as the other bars.

Metal snips There are left-hand, right-hand, and straight-cut metal snips. For our purposes, one is as good as the other. We use snips to cut lumber banding straps and to trim small pieces of banding for various purposes during a framing project. This tool is not frequently used, but try to clean cut the banding straps without them.

Handsaws There is always a need for a handsaw at one time or another. An 8-point crosscut saw is always a good thing to have tucked away in the truck box. Keep a good sheath covering the teeth, because they bruise and dull easily in the bottom of a toolbox.

Framing squares We use our framing squares for the precision work of laying out rafters and stairs; and because of this, we think it is best to use a good square. Rust-resistant steel is fine, and there are lighter-weight aluminum models available too. The lines, numbers, and rafter tables should be easy to read and should be etched or ground in rather than just stamped on the surface. An instruction book that explains

The framing square (top) is a simple but precise tool used to mark out rafters and stairs. Look for a square made of rust-resistant steel or aluminum. A fixed-angle triangular square (bottom, shown with its instruction booklet) can do a lot of the same work as a framing square.

how to use the rafter tables comes with the better squares, so you're not at the mercy of your calculator's batteries.

Another type of framing square is the big brother to the small triangular square mentioned earlier. The design is the same, but the big ones are 12 in. long and can perform many of the functions of a framing square.

Framing squares are useful for more than just stair and rafter marking. As short straightedges and for squaring lines across wide framing lumber, they get a lot of use on a project. As with all precision tools, treat your framing square gently.

Stair gauges Stair gauges are handy little nut-like devices that clamp onto a framing square to ensure uniform layout during multimarking processes, such as laying out riser and tread cuts on a stair stringer.

Sliding T-bevels Although somewhat similar to a combination square, the sliding T-bevel (a.k.a. bevel square) has a blade that can be moved to match any angle and then locked into position. It is very useful for transferring and marking angles from one framing member to another when a template cannot be used.

Four-foot T-square Anytime you're going to be working with oriented strand board (OSB) or plywood, grab a 4-ft. T-square; it will save you a lot of time. You can measure for cut lines once; then draw a pencil line across the sheet, using the square as a guide instead of measuring the sheet along two edges; and then connect the marks with a straightedge or a chalkline.

Lots of measuring and marking of plywood and OSB can be done with this tool without even pulling out a tape measure. Because the blade of the T is a 48-in long ruler, you can hold the fence on either end of an 8-ft. sheet and mark out any increment. Then, sliding the T along the perpendicular edge of the sheet, line it up with the mark and draw a square cut line across the width of the board.

You can premark 16-in on-center lines for joist and stud nailing by lining up the 16-in. end of the fence and drawing a line along the 4-ft. blade. Then slide the tee over until its top end is lined up with the first line. The ruler is now at the next 16-in. on-center location. Draw a line and continue.

Marking nail lines on the sheathing after the sheets have been tacked into position is often necessary when using adhesives, because the sheets must be fastened before the glue begins to set. In this case, place the T-square across the edge with the 4-ft. blade set in the middle of the joist or stud and draw a line to guide fastener placement. T-squares can also help you easily mark rough opening cutouts when you're sheathing walls, floors, or roofs.

T-squares are made from different gauges of aluminum. We've had better luck with the thicker gauges.

Hammer stapler A good hammer stapler is indispensable for fastening tar paper, rosin paper, or any other type of building wrap. The force of your swing drives the staples on these models, and they're a lot easier and faster to use than the squeeze-type staplers. Look for one that will accept the brand of staples most popular in your area. You don't want to get stuck with one that uses an orphan size not readily available.

Multitip drivers Screwdrivers with exchangeable tips can be found at just about any checkout counter. The smaller ones take the place of about a half dozen tools and are made short enough that they are barely noticeable in the bottom of a tool pouch. The larger ones replace a dozen or more tools and fit in a neat little container.

Pliers A pair of slip-joint pliers or a pair of needle-nose pliers that cuts wire is all it takes sometimes to keep the whole crew going when a power tool goes south. Many field repairs on a generator, compressor, air hose, or framing nailer are possible with a simple pair of pliers.

Four-inch column cutter If you are doing a lot of framing, it pays to invest in a 4-in. pipe cutter to cut the Lally columns that support center beams. You'll see how well it works in chapter 2.

Nylon twine An average job takes a couple of small spools of dry line. Nylon twine can be pulled very tight to help avoid sagging over long runs and movement in the wind. It can also be reused many times. And if you need to replace the line in your chalk box, it's handy to have an extra ball of string. These loose balls of string are in addition to the dry chalklines mentioned earlier.

Power Tools

In this section, we explain the common power tools used on a framing job and what they're used for. For consumer information on the different brands and types available and for help selecting a model, we recommend you read the tool reviews published by the trade magazines like *Fine Homebuilding*.

Circular saws Circular saws do 99 percent of the cutting on framing jobs. There are two types of circular saws on the market: sidewinders and worm drives. The motor armature on a sidewinder circular saw spins parallel to the blade arbor, and the motor is mounted off to the side. On a worm-drive circular saw, the armature is positioned perpendicular to the rotation of the blade, and the motor sits behind the blade. On a worm-drive saw, the motor's power is transferred to the blade through a set of gears. Here on the East Coast, the most common circular saw is the 7¼-in.-blade sidewinder. The maximum depth of cut is 2¼ in. to 2½ in., and most saws can be adjusted to cut up to a 45° angle. The more expensive models have electric brakes that stop the blade from spinning when the power switch is released.

The two most important things to look for are high power (expressed by a high number of amps) and light weight. The power—we like 13+-amp saws—is important for the long rips through dimensional lumber and for cutting through three or four pieces of sheathing at once. Light weight is important to reduce fatigue as the day goes long. Most sidewinder circular saws are made for a right-handed user, but there are a few manufacturers that make left-handed models.

Worm-drive circular saws, preferred by some framers, particularly out West, perform all of the same tasks with a few pluses and minuses. Because of their heavier weight and different balance than the sidewinders, these saws are not for novices. It takes a bit of practice before you can easily and accurately cut using one hand. Most models put the blade on the right-handed user's side of the machine, so it's easy to guide the blade into a cut, especially on bevel cuts. Most worm drives will cut bevels beyond 45°, which makes off-angle rafter cuts easier.

Both types of circular saws have small and large versions. Smaller ones use 4-in. to 5-in. blades and are meant more for cutting trimwork than dimensional lumber. And many cordless models are available. Exterior trim is often done up on

Circular saws do the majority of the cutting on a framing project. Clockwise from upper left: standard-blade sidewinder, large-blade sidewinder, standard-blade worm drive, small-blade worm drive.

Reciprocating saws are great for reaching tight spots and for cutting apart something that needs to be changed. Sometimes they're the only tool that can do the job effectively. Reciprocating saws are invaluable for remodeling work.

To cut lots of pieces the same size, especially small blocking, a power miter box is an indispensable, but expensive tool.

staging and sometimes while hanging off a roof. These smaller, lighter saws are a lot easier to maneuver in awkward positions.

Larger saws, with 8½-in. and even 10-in. blades, are great for cutting through thick lumber or stacked lumber and for reaching through steep bevel cuts. Some saw models come with larger guards and blades ready for service or as after-market kits you add onto a standard-size saw.

Reciprocating saw When you hear "change order" think "reciprocating saw." These saws have long, straight profiles and long, straight blades. They are often the only saw that can even reach where you are trying to cut. They can cut through a double top plate, down in between the header and king stud, and out through the jack stud, nails and all, without trashing the blade. The blades are quickly changed and come in a wide selection of lengths and designs to cut a variety of materials. From 4 in. to 14 in. long, all in different gauges and tooth pitches, blades are available for cutting wood or metal, and there are combination blades designed to cut through wood *and* metal for those times when, for instance, you have to cut 16 in. off that nail-imbedded header because someone decided to change the size of the bathroom window.

Reciprocating saws are available with a variety of features, including single speed, dual speed, and variable speed; elliptical- or fixed-blade cutting action; screw-type or quick-release blade holder; and fixed or detachable power cord. We look for two-speed or variable-speed models that accept generic brand sawblades and that are convertible from straight to elliptical blade motion.

Power miter box You could get by without a power miter box, but some framing projects require repetitive cutting of a lot of small pieces. Perhaps the house has many windows and, therefore, many cripples, both above and below the rough openings. In these cases, we pull out the power miter box and set it up on a platform or table. Stops can be set at measured locations on the table so cripples can be cut production style. By preplanning and developing a list of the needed cripples, we set up the miter box only a couple times during the project.

Because this is a somewhat big-ticket item, a little research into the tool reviews is needed before investing in a unit.

Drills Drills are used a lot in the beginning of the project to drill holes through the mudsill plates for the anchor bolts. And then we use ours if we need to set up sidewall staging brackets, but after that they are rarely used. If you have a lot of other uses for one besides framing then do some research and buy a good one. Otherwise, save some money and get a basic model. Many of the available features—such as variable speed, reversible direction, and keyless chuck—are not concerns if all you're going to use it for is framing. Look for a ⅜-in. or ½-in. chucked model in the 3.5-amp to 5-amp range.

Battery-operated tools

Most power tools have a battery-operated counterpart. And although not all the different sizes, types, and options are available, they do come pretty close to the full complement. Every few years, a new generation of either the tools or the batteries is introduced.

We don't find much use for them on a project until we get to the trim and siding. But because we do everything from frame to finish, we have a large collection. What we try to do is stay consistent within a brand, so the batteries are interchangeable among tools.

Electric cords

Cords supply life to all of the power tools, and if the wire gauge of a cord is too small, the cord can shorten a power tool's life. The gauge of a wire is classified by numbers. The lower the number, the larger the diameter of the wire. Most of the on-sale extension cords in retail stores are 16 gauge or 18 gauge. They are too small for proper operation of most power tools and should

Extension cords. Heavy-duty, large-gauge cords—the lower the wire number the higher the gauge—and splitters are important. Skinny cords and bad connections quickly take their toll on your power tools by robbing them of needed amperage.

be left at home. The 14-gauge cords are good up to about 50 ft. and provide plenty of power without being too bulky and cumbersome. The 12-gauge cords are good up to about 100 ft. We usually run one of these off the service panel, then put a three-way splitter on the end, into which we plug the 14-gauge cords that connect to the power tools. For runs longer than 100 ft., use a 10-gauge or thicker wire. You can do this a couple of different ways.

The first option is to buy a long length of rubber-coated three- or four-conductor 10-gauge wire at an electric supply house and connect the proper plugs to each end. You could wire a junction box directly to one end, giving you a gang of outlets, but because the cord will be moved around daily, the box is prone to breaking unless it's made of very heavy-duty parts. Another method is to put a single plug at the end of the cord and then plug a splitter into it.

The second option for making a long cord is to purchase a roll of 10/3-gauge or 10/4-gauge underground-feeder (UF) wire and connect it directly to the ground-fault circuit interrupter (GFCI) breaker inside the service panel. Connect a

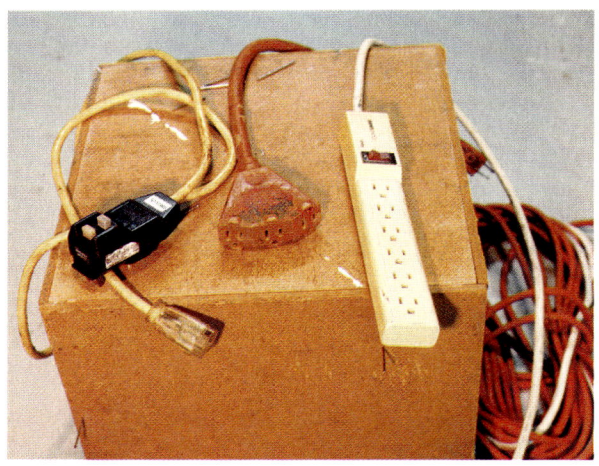

GFCIs and splitters for extension cords are available from many manufacturers. GFCIs (left) should be used at all times, especially if you're uncertain about your power supply. A molded three-way splitter (center) is hardy enough to survive most of the abuse that occurs at the busy end of the extension cord. An outlet strip (right) containing a circuit breaker, plugged in at the end of a long main cord, can save a lot of running back to the service panel every time a breaker is tripped.

four-gang junction box to the other end, and just leave it on the site until it's complete. It's a good idea to have your electrician do these tasks for you. Ask him if what you want him to do conforms to all electrical codes. Also, remember to turn the breakers off at the end of each day and to protect the junction box from inclement weather.

GFCI protectors By code (and common sense), all temporary service panels must have GFCI protection. Either the circuit breakers or the service outlets will be GFCI units. If the service outlet is a GFCI unit and not the breaker, and you hard-wired a main cord as explained above, the breaker must be replaced by a GFCI unit. But an experienced electrician already knows this.

When you connect an extension cord into power that is not GFCI protected, first plug in a GFCI pigtail with a reset button. These aren't as good as hard-wired GFCI protection, but they serve the purpose.

Breaker junction boxes For those jobs where there are long runs of extension cord from the temporary service panels, you want to invest in an outlet strip with a built-in circuit breaker. If you put this at the end of the main cord where you split off, it can save a lot of walking out to the service panel, particularly with a large crew operating a lot of tools at the same time. The breaker in the strip will usually trip before the one at the service panel. If you are using power from a neighbor's house, this is a must. If you don't use one, you know the minute the neighbor leaves for the day, the breaker inside the locked house will trip off.

Pneumatic Tools

These days, it's rare to see any framing crew without pneumatic, or air-powered, tools. In such a competitive field where labor is at a premium, it just makes sense to use pneumatic tools. One person with a pneumatic gun can shoot as many nails as at least three of the best hand-nailing carpenters on any crew. Even on small jobs, pneumatics soon pay for themselves.

The heart of a pneumatic tool arsenal is the compressor. Whether it has an electric or an internal combustion engine, the compressor has to provide enough air pressure and air volume to run the number of tools you use at any one time. There are many factors to consider before purchasing a compressor, including motor size, tank size, compressor type (oil or oil-less), number of pistons and cylinders, output at different pounds per square inch (psi), and adjustment controls. These should all be balanced according to how many air nailers you plan to be running at once.

Electric compressors Electric motors for compressors run from about $1\frac{1}{2}$ hp for hand-carried compressors to 5 hp for portable wheeled compressors. Generally, the higher the horsepower the more air the compressor can deliver. If you're working with a large crew of five or more, you'll need a compressor with a quick recovery rate. The larger motors push the larger

Gasoline or electric powered—that's the key question when choosing an air compressor. If you're always near a power supply, then buy a compressor with an electric motor (left). If your jobs are frequently started before the electric service is installed, you are better off with a gas-powered compressor (right).

compressors but require a lot of power. This is usually not a problem on a job site if there is a temporary electrical service panel set up. The compressor should be directly plugged into the service outlet mounted next to the panel. This eliminates the voltage drops experienced when you use a long extension cord. You may need an extra length of air hose, but that's preferable to a constantly popping circuit breaker and the damage an electric motor suffers from operating on the reduced current supplied through an extension cord.

There are models that have constant-running motors. As long as they are turned on, the motor runs. When there is a call for more air, a valve opens, and the pistons recharge the tank. The benefit to this is that it eliminates the initial power draw needed when an electric motor kicks on. It's that draw that pops the breaker on intermittent-running compressors.

Tank sizes are matched closely with the horsepower of the motor. The smaller ones have tanks of about 4 gal. (which, product literature boasts, can supply two framing nailers), and the larger compressors have tanks up to about 20 gal.

Again, your compressor purchase should be based on the size of your crew: The larger the crew, the more storage capacity you want so the compressor can handle multiple nailers simultaneously.

Gas compressors If there is no temporary electric service planned and you'll be working off the neighbor's outlet or a generator, it's best to go with a gas compressor.

Some crews prefer compressors powered by internal combustion engines regardless of what type of power is available. The crew can keep the compressor close to the job, without worrying about power headaches or outages. Plus, a large-horsepower gasoline engine can easily keep up with the air demands. Gas compressors are available from about a 5 hp with a 15-gal. air tank on up.

The down side to gasoline-powered engines is the constant noise they generate. When picking one out, decibel level should be considered along with the other factors.

Framing nailers The first thing to check when choosing a framing nailer is the type of nail that's accepted by your local code. Nailers drive two types of nails: full round head and clipped head. If your code does not allow clipped-head nails, then that eliminates more than half of your options. If it does, then you have a clear field of choice.

Any type of pneumatic framing nailer is preferable to hand nailing. The type of nails they can shoot and their safety features should be at the top of the checklist when considering a purchase.

There are two basic types of framing nailers: stick and coil. These terms refer to the collation of the nails.

Stick, a.k.a. strip, nails are packaged in one of two ways. The first type packages one nail behind the next in a line of 60 to 75 in a straight stick formation. The nail heads have small crescent-shaped pieces clipped out of them, which allow the nails to be grouped like this. Most stick nailers use the clipped-head nails. The other type of stick nails have full round heads. Plastic collation material spaces the nails apart so the driver doesn't hit the head of the next nail when it's driving the one in the chamber. These strips hold fewer nails because of the space needed to allow for the full round nail heads. Stick nailers have long, straight magazines that hold the nails and feed them into the chamber.

Coil nails are collated with spaces between them like the full round head stick nails, but come in long rolled coils of about 200 nails or more. The coil guns have round basket-type magazines that hold the nails while they are fed.

The stick nailers tend to be more balanced because the magazine and nails are spread more uniformly across the tool, but they need frequent reloading. The coil nailers are a little more clumsy to use, but you reload the nails about a third as often as you do with a strip gun.

Other questions to ask when selecting a nailer are whether the size and type of nails are locally available and if the tool accepts generic brand nails. You don't want to be stuck with a nailer that shoots only one specific brand of nails. If the local supplier closes down or moves away, you're in trouble.

Here are a few other things to research and consider when choosing a gun: Sequential or contact trip triggering, weight, adjustable depth gauge, removable magazine, rotating exhaust port, nose guards, wear guards, grips, warrantees, safety features, and service. Believe it or not, price should be toward the bottom of your list.

Staplers On a framing job, staples can replace nails (if allowed by code) for a couple of procedures. They can fasten sheathing to walls and furring to floor and ceiling joists. Staples are much cheaper than nails, and the staplers are a little easier to handle when fastening overhead because they are lighter than framing nailers.

Sizes and availability of staples and tool service are the main factors when selecting a pneumatic stapler.

Hoses We have a system to manage our compressor hoses that works well for us. We run a ⅜-in. inside diameter (ID) main line from the compressor to the house's foundation. It's usually a long run, because the compressor is out at the electric service. We join all the hose sections in this main line with threaded connectors, rather than snap-together quick-disconnect fittings. (An exception to this is the quick-disconnect fitting where the hose meets the compressor.) The quick-disconnect ends restrict the air flow more than the threaded coupling and are a prime blockage area during winter icing conditions.

Once the main line reaches the foundation, we snap on a ¼-in. quick-disconnect, four-way splitter. This allows three ¼-in. hoses to feed off the main line. The ¼-in. hoses are preferable for reaching the tools because they are lighter and easier to maneuver.

For long runs of hose from the compressor to the building, threaded hose couplings are less restrictive to air flow than multiple quick-disconnect fittings. (Photo by Roe A. Osborn, courtesy *Fine Homebuilding* magazine, © The Taunton Press, Inc.)

Pressure regulators A convenient gadget to have handy is an in-line pressure regulator. This gets set up with the same ¼-in. quick disconnects as the hoses. It can be placed between any disconnects in the line. The regulator allows you to reduce the air pressure in one line while keeping full pressure in others.

For example, nailing sheathing requires a controlled air pressure so the fasteners aren't overdriven into the sheathing. Nailing dimensional lumber requires a higher pressure to drive the nails completely in. With an in-line regulator, both jobs can be performed at the same time at the correct pressures off the same main line. The in-line regulator on the sheathing hose allows you to modulate a reduced pressure in that line only.

Repair kit Inevitably on a pneumatic system, accidents happen—a gun gets dropped, a coupling gets smashed—or parts wear out. A simple repair kit can keep the crew going, hardly missing a beat.

The kit should contain extra hose ends (disconnects and outlets), hose couplings, hose clamps, Allen wrenches, multitip screwdriver, Teflon tape, an extra compressor belt, oil, and antifreeze. (In cold-weather climates, we add

A five-man crew can come to a grinding halt for the lack of a simple part. A well-stocked repair kit is a necessity when using pneumatic tools.

about ¼ cup of antifreeze to the compressor tank to prevent water condensation from freezing up the lines.)

Staging

In this section we cover many types of staging we've used. You should always take the extra time to make your staging as safe as possible. The Occupational Safety and Health Administration (OSHA) has strict guidelines regarding staging and fall protection. We strongly recommend you contact them to get the pertinent publications.

Pump jacks Pump jacks provide a staging platform that's easily adjusted up or down. The metal pump jacks fit around a pole made from doubled 2x4s. An arm folds out from the jack, providing about a 2-ft. support area for staging planks. Wall brackets support the top of the pole at the correct distance from the building. There are attachments to the pump jacks that provide a platform for a work table and safety rails. Pole bases are sometimes needed to keep them from sinking into soft earth, and retainers help stabilize the bottom.

There are other types of pump-jack systems that use aluminum poles and staging planks. Properly used—following the manufacturer's set-up instructions—pump jacks provide the most versatile and safest staging found on most framing jobs. Using pump jacks, two carpenters can set the staging for a whole side of a house in less than half an hour.

Through-wall jacks Through-wall jacks are good for a quick setup of a work platform at a fixed height. For each bracket, drill a hole through the wall, insert the staging bolt from the outside, and screw on the holding nut with a 2x stock supporting block. Reinforce the point where the leg contacts the wall with a scrap piece of sheathing and you're ready to throw down some planks and get to work. There are guard-rail attachments available for these as well.

Staging planks Staging planks should be certified for use as staging planks. The stack of 2x10 spruce planks at the lumberyard may or may not be certified. Make sure it is.

When you need solid staging at only one level, through-wall jacks can be quickly installed and removed. A threaded rod on the upper arm of the jack is inserted through a hole in the sheathing and held fast against 2x blocking with a large nut.

Pump-jack staging systems are the most versatile for a residential framing job. Some pump jacks use wood poles (shown here), and others, aluminum poles.

Staging planks are available in wood or aluminum. If you can afford the sticker price, aluminum is the best choice for safety.

When you're selecting a plank, be picky. Avoid large knots and other noticeable defects. When you are considering a plank, ask yourself if you want to stand on it, 20 ft. from the ground.

The better option is to buy the OSHA-approved aluminum staging. It's expensive but worth it if you use staging a lot.

Other Equipment

The longer you are in the framing business, the bigger your "other equipment" inventory becomes. Here are some basic items that make framing easier.

Leveling instruments

There are a variety of different leveling instruments available. We've used them all and continue to, depending on the job, the site, and the conditions.

Water level A low-tech water level is the most accurate and cost-effective level. A water level is nothing more than a clear plastic ⅜-in.- to ½-in.-ID tube filled with water (or windshield washer fluid in the winter). For $10 to $20 you can buy a 100-ft. roll of plastic tubing. Back your truck over a laser level, and you have a pile of junk; drive over a water level and you have two water levels ready for duty. A water level is accurate to within ¼ in., and most of that is from operator error. By taking advantage of the fact that water seeks its own level, you can wrap the tube around corners and over obstacles, and the level of the water at both ends of the tube will be the same. (For information on using a water level, see p. 35.)

Builder's level A builder's level sights lines on a horizontal axis only. It is used strictly for shooting level lines. It's a relatively inexpensive tool, $200 to $300; and because it doesn't have many moving parts, it is pretty rugged.

A drawback to a builder's level is that it takes two people to operate: One to sight through the level, and the other to walk around to the different locations with a measuring stick of some sort. A builder's level should be calibrated every year, which will cost about $100.

Laser transit/level There are two basic types of rotary lasers—infrared and visible beam. Both types have electronic sender units that get mounted and leveled on a set of tripod legs. The units rotate 360° and emit a laser light beam. The visible beam unit emits a light beam that shows up on a surface as a red dot. On a very bright day, it can sometimes be hard to see the dot outdoors. The infrared unit emits a beam that is picked up by a small hand-held laser-detector unit that beeps when the beam strikes it. As the detector is moved up or down, the beeps become a single tone when it is dead level with the laser on the tripod. As the receiver is moved out of level to the emitter, the tone returns to beeps. The receiver unit mounts easily to any type of measuring stick.

There are variations on both of these types of transits, each offering different features. Some can

At about $15 to $20, the water level (center) is the most efficient leveling instrument, and it never needs calibrating. A $100 to $200 builder's level (left) works almost as well, but budget $100/year to recalibrate it. The laser transit (right) is expensive ($500 and up) but allows you to work alone.

be turned vertically so they can also indicate plumb. The most important feature is the one that shuts the unit off if the sender goes out of level. This adds about $400 to the $500 price tag, but one bad job because of a bumped tripod leg can easily cost more than that. The benefit of these units is that they can be operated by one person.

Framing supports

A framing job can be accomplished without manufactured framing supports, but if you are committed to framing, they're worth the investment. They make the job safer and more precise while also saving labor.

Form aligners We call them turnbuckles, but they are sold as form aligners. They are used by concrete form companies to align their forms before and during a concrete wall pour. We've found them invaluable during the entire framing process, from bracing and straightening the center beam, to straightening walls and plumbing the gable end of the roof. They eliminate the need to use adjustable, site-built spring braces (see p. 35).

Form aligners are about 2 ft. long, and any length 2x4 can be nailed to them. They are used for bracing and straightening anything that needs it. They install more quickly than any type of temporary wood bracing, and they can be tweaked at any time with a twist of the wrist. It's one of those tools that once you use it, you wonder how you ever did without it. They range from about $10 to $15 each.

Wall-lifting jacks Wall-lifting jacks allow a small crew to build and lift a long wall in one piece. They allow a large crew, to lift it more safely.

Before lifting, the bottom of the wall should be secured so it doesn't kick out off the deck (we

One person can do the job of two by using a turnbuckle to brace and straighten any framing member.

detail this in chapter 4). The bottom of the jack post should be placed over a joist and be well braced so it doesn't kick back.

The jacks should be placed equally along the wall so they lift equal weights, and they should be located so headers and other obstacles won't get in the way of proper operation. The wall should be lifted evenly.

Several brands of jacks are available and operate differently, so review the instructions carefully.

Truss spacers (made by Truslock, Inc.) are worth the investment if you will be doing most of your jobs with trusses. (Photo by Roe A. Osborn, courtesy *Fine Homebuilding* magazine, © The Taunton Press, Inc.)

Heavy-duty screw jacks safely support heavy loads until they are ready for the permanent columns. The jacks also adjust loads very easily.

Truss braces If you're going to be using roof trusses on your framing jobs, it pays to invest in a couple sets of truss braces. With one hand and one motion, they temporarily lock the roof trusses into position until the sheathing or permanent bracing is installed. They speed up the truss installation process, thereby reducing the cost of labor and the cost of the crane.

Screw jacks Many retailers and lumberyards sell temporary adjustable columns with pins that slide into holes in two telescoping sections of thin-gauge pipe. These work fine for temporary support, but the loose separate parts and small support plates are kind of a pain to keep track of. A better option is heavy-duty commercial-grade screw jacks made of heavy-gauge steel with large support plates that are welded to the column ends. The threads that operate the jack are an integral part of the column, and they offer a wide range of adjustment.

TOOLS 23

Chapter 2

MUDSILLS

SIZING UP THE
FOUNDATION

LAYING OUT
FOR MUDSILLS

CHECKING THE
FOUNDATION FOR LEVEL

INSTALLING
THE MUDSILL

USING SHIMS TO LEVEL
THE MUDSILL

FRAMING WALLS
ON DROPS

READY TO MOVE ON

The mudsill, made of rot-resistant wood, provides a square, level, and dimensionally correct nailing base on which the frame is built. The mudsill is the transition between the wood frame of the house and the concrete or block and mortar of the foundation. It also gives the framer the opportunity to make adjustments for the defects in the foundation.

It's rare to start on a foundation that's perfect, that is, one that has dimensions that match the plans and is level and square. In this chapter we'll describe how to lay out and square up chalklines to guide the mudsill placement. Then we'll take you through the process of establishing a level reference line around the outside face of the foundation used to level the mudsill. Finally, we'll demonstrate how to install the mudsill properly and how to shim the mudsill to correct defects in the foundation level. Along the way, we'll show you some equipment and methods we've found useful on our projects and how to handle foundation drops and the problems they present.

You need at least two people to perform the layout and leveling tasks, but you can keep a trained six-man crew busy by dividing up the tasks. But before too many tools get pulled out, the foundation must be checked, sized, and compared to the plans.

The mudsill is the transition between the wood frame of the house and the foundation. It gives the framer the opportunity to make adjustments for the defects in the foundation. The mudsill also provides a square, level, and dimensionally correct nailing base on which to frame the house.

Sizing Up the Foundation

Begin every framing project by checking the foundation's overall dimensions and comparing them to the plans. Foundations are seldom built or poured with incorrect dimensions, but occasionally it does happen. Sometimes mistakes in the foundation are the fault of the foundation subcontractor, and other times it's the designers' fault that the first-floor plan doesn't match the foundation plan. In either case, by the time you, the framer, arrive it's too late. There's a chance that the dimensions may be off in small increments; and by discovering this in advance, you can adjust the layout of the mudsills to compensate. Deviations beyond 2 in. should be brought to the attention of the contractor and the foundation sub, because the size of the frame may need to be altered. A resolution between all parties affected is needed before proceeding.

Next, check the foundation details like beam pockets, piers, etc. Occasionally a detail will be missed or it will be in the wrong location on the foundation. This usually can be corrected quickly, so these types of mistakes are not a big concern at

It's important to size up the foundation before laying out the mudsills. Check the overall dimensions of the foundation and critical features. Here, a beam pocket was installed in the wrong location and a new one had to be chiseled into the foundation.

this point. Missed beam pockets can be chiseled in and post pier locations can be repoured. Record any changes or variations on the plans. You'll use this set of annotated plans during the layout process.

MUDSILLS 25

Ordering Mudsill Materials

We like to order the mudsill materials in advance so they'll be on-site when we arrive to begin framing. You can estimate the order from the set of plans or during a preliminary visit to the foundation to do the dimensional check. You'll need mudsill lumber, sill seal for draft stopping, nuts and washers to anchor down the mudsill, and nails to fasten parts together. In some areas of the country, the building code requires that a termite shield be installed between foundation and mudsill.

Before you order stock, decide whether you are going to use a double or single mudsill (see "Choosing a Mudsill System," on p. 36). Measure the linear footage of the foundation and divide by the length of mudsill stock you plan to use. We usually order all 16-ft. lengths of lumber and cut shorter pieces from crooked ones. The most common lumber used for mudsills is 2x6 pressure-treated wood. The mudsill size of choice may be different in your area, so order accordingly. Order a couple extra boards just in case the stock varies a lot in width or some pieces are too warped to use.

Sill seal foam usually comes in 50-ft. rolls. Order that last roll even if you'll need only 5 ft. from it. We hang onto the end of leftover rolls from the last job to make up the balance when a foundation needs say, four and a half rolls.

Usually the foundation installers leave nuts and washers that fit the anchor bolts they installed in the concrete. Check to make sure and order some if you need to. To hold the mudsill straight to the line between bolts use 2½-in. or 3-in. concrete nails.

You'll need shims to level out the foundation; we make them from pieces of OSB, plywood, and hardboard of various thicknesses that are left over from previous jobs. You can either order sheets to rip up or raid another agreeable framer's waste pile. Some 7/16-in. or ½-in. and some ⅛-in. stock is a good start. Different thicknesses can be stacked to make up for deviations in all but the worst foundations.

Laying Out for Mudsills

Once you've got the materials on site and you're ready to launch into your framing project, you'll need to start with a mudsill layout to translate the blueprint information onto the foundation top. Our goal is to install the mudsill straight, square, and dimensionally proportioned to match the house plans. To install it accurately, we snap chalklines on the foundation and set the mudsill to the lines.

The process of snapping accurate lines is broken down into three steps. First, establish a baseline and one parallel line to measure and square all other lines from. Next, use diagonal measuring techniques to mark a perpendicular line and a parallel mate to create a self-checking rectangle. And then measure parallel lines from those lines to finish the layout.

Establishing and marking a baseline

The baseline is the reference you'll use to locate all other lines, parallel, perpendicular, or otherwise. But before locating the baseline, review the plans and compare the actual foundation measurements to find any deviations or changes. The goal is to set the mudsill to the exact dimensions of the first-floor plan. This means the mudsill may not match flush with the face of the foundation if the foundation is incorrect. Plan to install the mudsill to correct the errors in the foundation. For example, if the foundation is 1 in. too wide, the mudsill can be held in from the edge of the foundation ½ in. front and back to make the adjustment. Or if the foundation is too narrow, the mudsill can overhang a bit. If the foundation is off more than 2 in. or 3 in., then simple adjustments cannot be used to remedy the problem. Either the frame size changes or the foundation must be altered.

Pressure-treated 2x6 stock is the standard mudsill in most regions. The boards measure 5⅜ in. across their width, and that's important. The chalklines are snapped to indicate the inside edge of the mudsill. So, given that the foundation is true, the chalkline will be 5⅜ in. back from the foundation's edge where the baseline will be snapped. Check the mudsill stock. If it varies in width or if you're using different width stock, pick an average measurement to use before starting and discard stock that deviates by more than about ¼ in. in width

The best foundation wall on which to snap a baseline is the longest wall. Using the longest wall will make it easier to measure subordinate parallel chalklines later on. At each end of the longest wall, make a mark 5⅜ in. from the foundation's outside edge, then snap it with a chalkline. We use blue chalk first, in case we discover an error as we progress. That way we can make changes using the indelible red chalk. Everyone on our crew knows that if there are two lines, the red line trumps the blue one.

Mark the opposite parallel wall next. One person holds the 5⅜ in. mark at the end of a tape exactly on the already-snapped baseline. (Remember that you're using your snapped lines, not the edge of the foundation, as the indicators for the positioning of the mudsills.) A second person stretches the tape to the opposite and parallel wall and makes a mark on the foundation exactly 5⅜ in. back from the dimension of the building as indicated on the plans. For example, if the plans indicate that the foundation dimension is 30 ft., you would make a mark on the opposite wall at 29 ft. 6⅜ in. Make similar marks at each end of the wall and snap a line between the two marks.

This method, rather than that of just subtracting the total width of two plates from the building's dimension, reduces the chance of math errors. It's important to hold the tape measure perpendicular to the baseline; if it's angled, the mark on the opposite wall won't be accurate.

Creating a self-checking rectangle

Rather than continuing to mark and snap the rest of the parallel chalklines, locate a couple of perpendicular lines with the goal of creating a rectangle. With a rectangle, you can measure the diagonals to check that the perpendicular lines are set at perfect 90° angles before proceeding with the entire layout.

There are several different ways to square up perpendicular lines for mudsills. We've used the Pythagorean theorem ($a^2 + b^2 = c^2$), 3-4-5 triangles, and calculated diagonal measurements with success. But we're partial to the process outlined below. It can be easily taught to any crew member, is less prone to math errors, and doesn't require measuring multiples of 3, 4, and 5.

Marking the first two corners Start along the baseline and mark in 5⅜ in. from the edge of the foundation. The starting edge will be the one 90° adjacent to the one you marked for the baseline. Have a helper hold the tape at the 5⅜-in. measurement on the new mark and pull the tape along the baseline to the opposite edge of the foundation. Locate the plan dimension on the tape, count back 5⅜ in., and make a mark across the baseline. If the foundation wall is too long or short, adjust the two marks back or forth in the same direction to split the difference. For example, if the foundation is ½ in. short, relocate both marks back ¼ in., so when the mudsills are set they'll overhang the foundation by ¼ in. off each edge. These two marks on the baseline indicate the first two corners of the rectangle.

Finding the center of the opposite wall The opposite two corners on the parallel wall are located by first establishing the center of the parallel side. The process involves making equal

MUDSILLS **27**

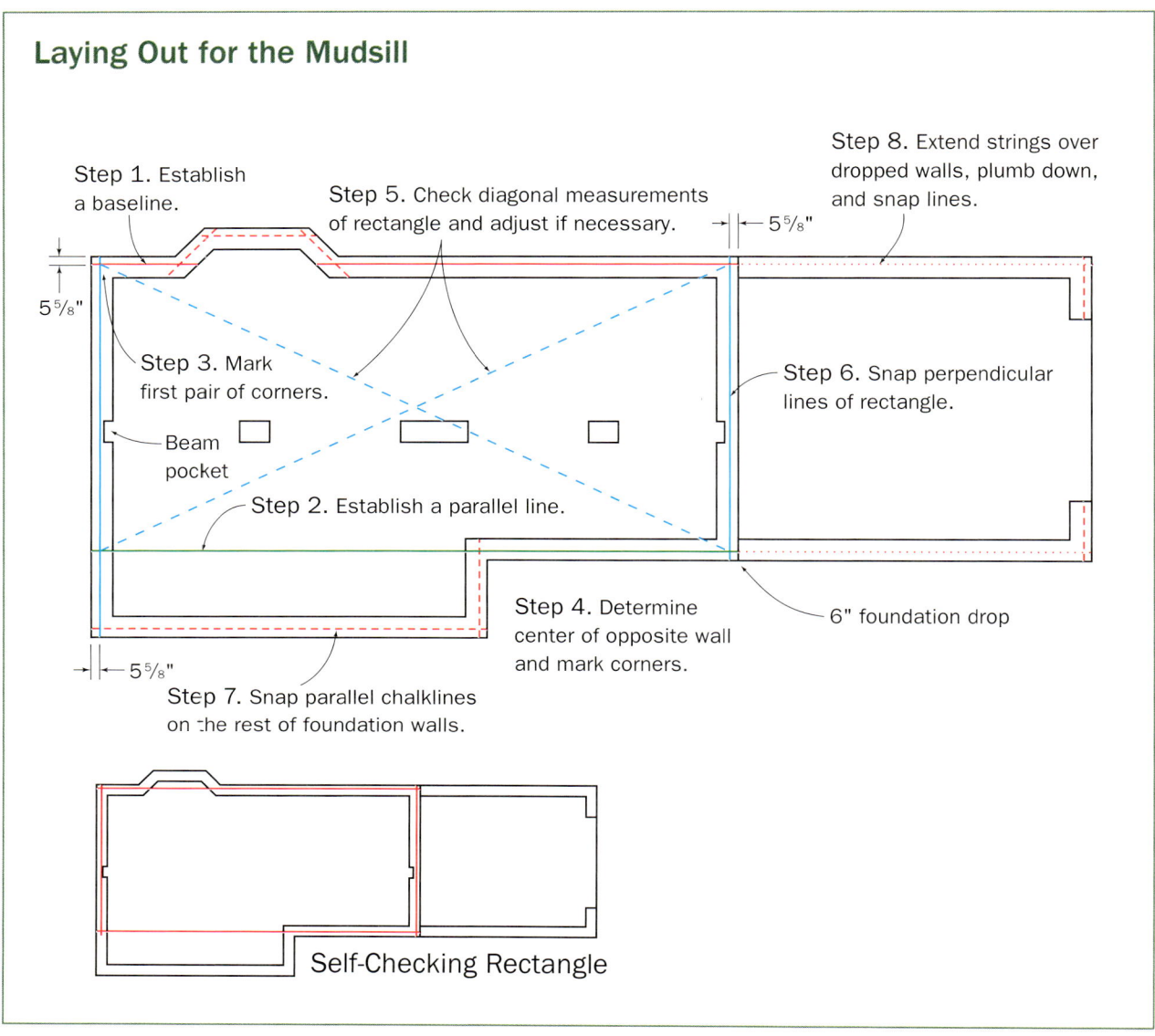

Laying Out for the Mudsill

Step 1. Establish a baseline.
Step 2. Establish a parallel line.
Step 3. Mark first pair of corners.
Step 4. Determine center of opposite wall and mark corners.
Step 5. Check diagonal measurements of rectangle and adjust if necessary.
Step 6. Snap perpendicular lines of rectangle.
Step 7. Snap parallel chalklines on the rest of foundation walls.
Step 8. Extend strings over dropped walls, plumb down, and snap lines.

Beam pocket

6" foundation drop

Self-Checking Rectangle

diagonal measurements taken from the first two corner points you established on the baseline. You can accomplish this with either a one-tape-measure method or a two-tape method. The one-tape method takes two people to execute. The two-tape method is quicker but requires three people.

For the **one-tape method**, have a helper hold the tape measure on one of the corner marks you just made across the baseline. We hold the 2-in. mark on the tape at the pencil mark rather than the end of the tape. This is more accurate than indexing the tape's end, which can move on the rivets, and it gives the helper some tape to hold on to when the tape is pulled tight across the foundation hole. Take the business end of the tape measure to roughly the middle of the opposite wall. Arbitrarily choose a measurement; the nearest full foot mark is easy to remember. Scribe a mark where the chosen measurement crosses the chalkline.

Have the helper go to the opposite corner mark on the baseline and duplicate the process, marking the same measurement across the second

Square up the foundation by first finding the center of the opposite wall. Start the process by stretching two tape measures from the corners of the baseline you established and cross them at equal measurements over the chalkline (or, in this case, string) on the opposite foundation wall. (Photo by Roe A. Osborn, courtesy *Fine Homebuilding* magazine, © The Taunton Press, Inc.)

chalkline. It doesn't matter if the center was overshot or undershot, because either way, the point halfway between the two marks is the exact center of the wall. Measure between the two points and make a mark on the chalkline to indicate the center of the wall. Cross out the other two marks to avoid confusion.

For the **two-tape method**, two helpers each take the end of a tape measure, and each holds the 2-in. mark on one of the corner pencil marks. Take the business end of the tapes across the opposite foundation wall and cross the two tapes directly over the chalkline on the parallel wall. Move left or right until the two tapes measure the same. This point is the exact center of the wall. As with the one-tape method, make a mark here for reference.

Measuring and marking the second two corners Now you can find the two corners on the parallel wall by measuring off the center mark. First, measure the distance between the two corner marks on the baseline. Divide that number in half. This is the distance from the center mark you made on the opposite wall to the other two corners of the rectangle. Measure from the center point and mark out the corners on the parallel wall. Then measure the overall length between the corners you marked; it should match the length of your baseline.

Measuring the diagonals of the rectangle

Now that you've marked the corners of a rectangle, take diagonal measurements from opposite corners as a way to ensure that the rectangle is perfectly square. *Square* means that the lines that meet at each corner are exactly 90° to each other.

Have your helper hold the 2-in. mark of the tape at a corner mark on the baseline. Measure the distance to the opposite diagonal corner and make a note of it. Repeat the measuring process between the other pair of opposite corners. This measurement should equal the first. Our tolerance for differences in the diagonal measurements is ⅛ in.

If the distances differ by more than ⅛ in., shift the second set of corner marks in tandem to the left or right as needed to fix the discrepancy and recheck. When the diagonal measurements are equal, snap chalklines on the two perpendicular walls to finish the rectangle.

Often one side of the rectangle won't have a continuous wall. It may be only 4 ft. to 10 ft. long, such as with an attached porch wall. That's okay, as long as the corners of a rectangle are created, it can be checked for square and used as a reference to continue from (see the drawing on p. 28).

Finishing the layout

Now that you've established a rectangle, it's easy to locate the rest of the layout by measuring parallel lines off any side of the rectangle. Have a helper hold the tape measure at the 5⅝-in. point across the line you choose to reference. Pull the business end of the tape to the wall you want to mark and measure back 5⅝ in. from the overall plan measurement. This will indicate the edge of the mudsill. Mark a point at each end of the wall and snap a chalkline between them.

Often a reference line from the rectangle needs to be extended to reach a garage or wing of the house. The easiest way to do this is to set up a taut string line on top of the reference line you need to extend and tie it off past the end of the foundation to the leg of a sawhorse. Take the measurements from the string to the foundation. Avoid pushing the end of a tape measure to the string; you may drive it out of alignment. Instead, have someone hold the tape under the string at the 5⅝-in. mark and measure out to the foundation wall. Mark for the mudsill and snap the chalkline. You can now use this chalkline as a reference to measure from.

On large, complicated foundations, you may find it necessary to establish more than one reference rectangle. Always begin with a primary rectangle and measure over to at least one side of a secondary rectangle. This maintains dimensional continuity across the mudsill layout.

Marking mudsills on foundation drops

Very often, the height of a house foundation is not poured to be at the same elevation throughout the structure. There a several reasons for this: The house is located on a sloping piece of ground, the garage is below the level of the main part of the house, or the house plan calls for different

A site-built rig made from 2x stock and outriggers can be easily set up to support string lines over dropped portions of the foundation.

floor levels. The areas where a foundation changes elevation are called "drops." Transferring lines from one level to another makes laying out mudsills more complicated. It's hard to make a straight line when the foundation top is broken into two or more levels. We've found the easiest way to mark accurate mudsill layout lines is to set up strings at the main foundation elevation. We hold the strings up with braces at each corner of the foundation that is dropped. The strings match the inside edge of the mudsill and we plumb down to the lowered sections of the foundation. Setting strings lets us use the same principles we use to lay out and square a flat foundation.

Setting up string lines On a part of the foundation with a drop, select an area on which to establish a rectangle, just as you would on a flat foundation. At each corner of the foundation

Foundation Corner Poles

Even when the foundation level steps down to coincide with the existing grade, we still want to check the layout marks on one plane. To keep our lines at the original foundation elevation over the drops, we set them up on foundation corner poles.

A reusable corner pole can be made with a few simple pieces of stock steel. We use 1½-in. angle iron for the corner section that fastens to the corner of the foundation. A few random holes are drilled on both sides of the angle iron big enough to let the shank of a common masonry nail slip through. Weld or bolt a 4-ft. to 6-ft. length of ¾-in. hollow tubing onto the angle iron. An outrigger section will ride up and down on this tube to make the tool adjustable.

Make the outrigger section by welding two 8-in. pieces of flat steel stock perpendicular about midway along a 1-ft. length of 1-in. heavy-gauge hollow tubing. Drill and tap threads into the 1-in. pipe to accept a small thumb screw that will clamp the outrigger section onto the post at various heights. Slip the 1-in. outrigger section over the ¾-in. tubing, and the unit is complete.

The procedure for use is the same as the site-built unit, except the string outriggers can be moved up and down the pole to the exact position. We have a few different poles with different lengths of the angle iron and hollow tubing to use for different foundation drop heights.

A simple tool for holding layout strings at foundation corners can be made from common steel stock.

that is dropped, set up something to hold string lines. We make simple tools called foundation corner poles for just this purpose (see the sidebar above).

A quick temporary corner pole can be fabricated on site with two 2x4s nailed together to form a corner. That corner is then nailed to the corner of the foundation and extended to the height of the original foundation grade. Nail a couple of 1x2 outriggers at approximately the same level as the top of the foundation. Run a string from each outrigger toward the respective mudsill marks on the upper foundation. The dry lines can slide back and forth along the outriggers until the dimensions and squares are true. Once set, a plumb bob transfers the crossing of the two lines down to the foundation.

Measure from the baseline to the opposite string line parallel to your baseline. Double-check that the measurements are equal at both ends of the line. (Photo by Roe A. Osborn, courtesy *Fine Homebuilding* magazine, © The Taunton Press, Inc.)

Draw two tape measures from the corners of the baseline. Cross them at equal measurements on the parallel string line and mark the point with a piece of string or alligator clip. This point marks the center of the opposite wall. (Photo by Roe A. Osborn, courtesy *Fine Homebuilding* magazine, © The Taunton Press, Inc.)

Starting with a baseline and one parallel string line Starting with the main elevation of the foundation, establish the baseline as described earlier. Measure from the baseline to the parallel string tied between the outriggers on the opposite wall's corner posts. Move the string along the outrigger until it is 5⅝ in. in from the edge of the foundation wall. Adjust the opposite end of the string, too, and recheck your first measurement. Pull the string tight when you have it parallel to the baseline and re-evaluate a second time. The rechecking is to ensure that the corner posts and outriggers didn't move when you made corrections to the string. Remember to account for the 5⅝-in. mudsill at both the baseline and the string when taking your measurements.

Establishing a rectangle The process of establishing a rectangle on the foundation is similar to the one you followed earlier, but you'll have to use alternative methods to make marks on the strings. Measure and mark the two corners at both ends of the baseline as described earlier. Use either the one- or the two-tape method to find the center of the opposite string line. Because you won't be able to draw a pencil mark on the string line when you make the diagonal measurements, tie a short piece of string or use a small alligator clip to mark the center location. Measure back from the center point to mark the second pair of corners of the rectangle. Again, tie pieces of string to mark them. Check the rectangle for square by measuring the corner-to-corner diagonals and make any adjustments.

Move the strings that run from the baseline to the corners, so they line up over the corner marks on the baseline. Slide the strings along the arms of the outriggers until they cross the string at the back of the foundation directly above the pieces of string you tied on to indicate the back two corners. Pull the lines taut and recheck the measurement of the string parallel to the baseline.

Check the diagonal measurements from corner to corner to check for square. Make adjustments just as you did for a regular foundation, except here you'll move the strings left or right to correct. When a foundation wall level drops partway along its length, the string will extend from the baseline corner over the wall to the corner in the air. Don't overlook the fact that you'll have to snap a chalkline along the top portion of the foundation. Make a pencil mark on the foundation beneath the string at the drop. It's best to do this before you mark the lower portions of the foundation, forget about it, and take the strings down.

Plumbing down to mark lower foundation levels Now you've established a reference rectangle with chalklines and strings. To transfer the mudsill lines (the elevated strings) down to the foundation at the dropped areas just use a plumb bob. We plumb down and mark the dropped foundation at two locations from each string and then snap lines through the marks we've made. The lines intersect at the corner. We've found that's easier than trying to plumb and mark right at the corners where the strings meet up in the air. If there are several drops in the foundation level along a wall, you have to plumb down at several points along the string line. Mark one point at each end of the wall section and snap a chalkline through them.

Leave the strings up for the time being and move on to check the foundation for level. We'll return to the special situation of installing mudsills on drops after describing mudsill installation on a single-level foundation, later in this chapter.

After the string lines have been set up to establish a perfect rectangle, drop a plumb bob and mark the corners on the dropped foundation level below. Snap chalklines from these points to guide the mudsill installation. (Photo by Roe A. Osborn, courtesy *Fine Homebuilding* magazine, © The Taunton Press, Inc.)

The strings will come in handy later to measure stud lengths from.

Checking the Foundation for Level

If you have a crew of four or more you can assign a couple of people to check how level and flat the top of the foundation is while others are laying out chalklines for the mudsill. You can use a builder's level to check the foundation, but using a water level might be faster and it certainly is cheaper.

MUDSILLS   33

Our method of checking the foundation level is simple and serves three functions. We make level marks at each corner of the foundation a couple of inches from the top, and then we snap a chalkline around the outside face of the foundation. This level reference line is used to check how flat the foundation top is and as a reference to shim the mudsill level. Later, the level line comes in handy to guide the siding process.

Marking and snapping a level reference line

You can use a laser level, a builder's transit, or even a simple low-tech water level to set marks for the reference line. The marking process and resulting level line will be the same for all three. We prefer a water level for its speed; durability; and, of course, low cost (see the sidebar on the facing page).

Marking inside and outside corners Select one corner of the foundation as the starting point; measure down and make a horizontal pencil mark about 2 in. from the top. Using your leveling device, make marks on all inside and outside corners of the foundation level based on this reference point.

Sometimes it's hard to make a mark on a corner because it's chipped or not formed well, so mark the face of each wall that meets at a corner. Also mark the halfway point of any walls exceeding 30 ft. to make snapping the chalkline easier and more accurate.

Sometimes there's a question about which side of the foundation wall to mark, for example, walls that separate a basement from a garage. Always mark the side that the mudsill will be lined up to.

Marking dropped sections of the foundation
When there's a drop or a step in the foundation, mark the level on the wall just before the drop. Make the mark equal to your first reference mark just as with the corners. Measure the height of the drop and round to the nearest inch. Then measure that distance down from the upper-level

Leveling the foundation begins with a reference point. Mark down from the top of the foundation 2 in. at one corner. Level all other marks to this point. (Photo by Roe A. Osborn, courtesy *Fine Homebuilding* magazine, © The Taunton Press, Inc.)

mark and make a new (lower) mark on the dropped portion of the wall.

Snapping a level chalkline Before snapping a chalkline between marks, it's helpful to scrape and tap off any excess mortar or concrete from the top 3 in. of the foundation with a hammer claw or flatbar. This leaves a smooth surface for an accurate chalkline. Pull the chalkline tight between your marks before snapping to ensure a straight line. We use red chalk for this line; it doesn't wash off in the rain like blue or white. Even though we can level the mudsill in just a few hours, we'll later use the line as a guide for siding.

Once the level perimeter line is complete, walk around the foundation with a tape measure and check how flat the top is. Measure from the top of

Using a Water Level

Here's how to use a water level. Start out with a tube about 100 ft. long and fill it with water. Air bubbles in the hose will give you inaccurate readings so filling it without air bubbles is critical. One way is to hold one end of the tube in an unaerated water faucet and let the force of the water stream fill the tube. Another way is to droop the tube into the foundation hole or down an earth bank. Put one end at the bottom of a gallon jug of water. Suck on the other end until the siphon action begins to draw the water into the tube naturally. Hold the loose end of the tube a little below the bottom of the jug until the water fills the entire length. Make sure that the end inside the gallon bottle always stays below the water line, or it will suck in air and you'll have to begin again.

Hold the two ends of the water-filled tube alongside each other and notice how the level of the water in each end matches. The water in the tube forms a slight U shape, called a meniscus. Before you begin the leveling procedure, it is important to choose one part of the meniscus as the reference point that you'll be using otherwise your marks could be off. We generally use the bottom of the U as our benchmark.

Using a water level is usually a two-person process. One person is the lead and directs the procedure. Beginning at the reference mark you made earlier 2 in. down from the top of the foundation, hold one end of the hose on a corner. Have your partner go to the next corner and hold the hose still against the foundation. It's important that each operator holds a finger over his tube end when moving from corner to corner to prevent water from spilling out. Raise or lower your end of the hose until the meniscus matches the reference mark on the foundation. Wait a few seconds to be sure the water has stopped moving. When you're satisfied, call to your partner to make a mark on his corner at the meniscus line.

Cover the ends of the hose and instruct the advance guy to go to the next corner and start the process again. It's best for one person to stay at the original reference mark as long as the tube reaches. When corners are too far away, you'll have to set up at one of the corners that the advance guy has already marked before you can continue.

When the lead person has to use more than one corner as a reference, make your way back to the original reference corner. By checking back to it, you can see if there's any deviation. If the final check is off by more than $\frac{1}{8}$ in., you know there may have been a marking or reading mistake along the way. It's also a good practice to double-check suspect marks, especially if you discover a bubble in the tube.

During winter, we fill the hose with windshield washer fluid to prevent freeze-ups. It's important when using washer fluid to refill the tube each time you use it. (Just drain the hose into the washer reservoir in your truck.) The consistency of the fluid changes throughout the tube when left in it for a while, and that can result in incorrect—not level—readings.

A water level is quick and easy to use. Raise and lower the hose until the meniscus matches the reference mark, then mark the advancing corner. (Photo by Roe A. Osborn, courtesy *Fine Homebuilding* magazine, © The Taunton Press, Inc.)

the foundation to the chalkline every 4 ft. or so. A deviation of about ¼ in. from the reference is acceptable. A deviation of ½ in. to ¾ in. is workable. Anything greater than that requires a conference with the general contractor, because extra costs are usually involved for the labor that will be needed to correct this problem.

We write deviation measurements on the foundation top with crayon, so we can refer back to them during the next process: setting the mudsill.

Installing the Mudsill

The hardest part of installing the mudsill is actually done—establishing the layout and level lines. From here you simply fasten the mudsill flush with the layout lines and shim it level using the perimeter line as a guide. We'll describe how we go about marking, drilling, and fastening the mudsill. But first, you'll need to decide which system to use.

Choosing a mudsill system

Before you plug in the power cords, you need to decide which mudsill plating method to use. There are regional practices that framers rely on, but it's worth putting some thought into your choice rather than following the pack. The two systems commonly seen are a single-plate and a double-plate mudsill.

Single-plate mudsill A single-plate mudsill is the fastest system and uses half the lumber that a two-plate system does. A single pressure-treated lumber plate is bolted down to the foundation. Sill seal gasket material is sandwiched between the plate and the foundation.

There are a couple drawbacks to the single plate. Unless the top of the foundation is level, the mudsill will have to be shimmed. Shim material inserted between the foundation and the mudsill leaves gaps, and the sill seal won't bridge the space. This leaves uncontrolled entry avenues for air and insects. Plus the shims must be made of rot-resistant material. Furthermore, joints between pieces of mudsill lumber at the corners and on long walls should be reinforced with metal plates.

Double-plate mudsill We prefer the double-plate method because we can maintain straighter edges and more accurate corners. This method uses twice as much material and takes about 30 percent longer to install, but when your goal is a precise framing job, the extra material and labor are worth it.

Rot-resistant, pressure-treated lumber is used for the lower plate, just like the single-plate system, and sill seal is used between it and the foundation. The upper plate can be pressure-treated, but it's not necessary; ordinary dimensional lumber is fine. Using two plates allows the corners to be cross lapped and seams between lumber lengths to be staggered for stability. We can insert the shims to level the mudsill between the plates, thus keeping the shims off the foundation. And any spaces between the layers will be covered by sheathing so air infiltration and insect concerns are eliminated.

Marking and drilling the layers

Mudsills are anchored to the foundation with bolts or steel straps that are embedded into the foundation by the foundation contractor. Most of the foundations we frame on have ½-in.-diameter anchor bolts. We'll describe the process for marking, drilling, and setting mudsills over bolts now and cover the process for using straps later. The first step is to check the material and set pieces on top of the foundation.

Look through the mudsill stock you had delivered. Use the straightest stock for long foundation walls and put the crooked lumber aside to cut up for the shorter pieces.

Start at a corner and align pressure-treated 2x6s along the chalkline toward the inside of the foundation. Slide the stock along the line until the end overhangs the adjacent line at the corner by 5⅜ in. Continue laying down full-length 2x6s until you come close to the end of the wall.

Anchor Bolt–Marking Tool

Rather than measuring, squaring, and marking each foundation anchor bolt with a tape measure, you can speed up the process with an anchor bolt–marking tool made from flat steel stock. It's about 10 in. long with a small hole drilled 5⅝ in. in from one end. Drill or grind a ¼-in. depression at about a ½-in. radius—on one end of the stock—to "wrap" around the foundation bolt. To use, push the tool against the foundation bolt and eyeball it square to the 2x6 you're marking. A pencil mark in the hole indicates your drilling point.

You can also make an anchor bolt marking tool from a piece of 1x3 and a nail. To index the foundation bolt, make a small V notch in one end of a 8-in. to 10-in.-long 1x3. Drive a 6d common nail 5⅝ in. back from the notched end until the point protrudes ¼ in. Push the notch to the bolt; eyeball the tool perpendicular to the 2x6; and tap on the nail to drive the point into the wood, marking the location of the hole to be drilled.

The time it takes you to make a marking tool will be saved marking out its first foundation. If you use mudsill stock that's a different width than a 2x6, you can make the tool to match. Just measure several pieces of the stock you intend to use and take the average. Use that measurement as the distance back you set the nail or drill a hole.

Mark the location of the foundation bolts on the mudsill for drilling. Line the mudsill plate stock on the opposite side of the chalkline and use an anchor bolt–marking tool to mark the bolt location. (Photo by Roe A. Osborn, courtesy *Fine Homebuilding* magazine, © The Taunton Press, Inc.)

Measure and cut the last piece, keeping in mind that it has to extend over the perpendicular line at the corner by 5⅝ in. Next, use a bolt-marking tool to locate the holes to be drilled through the sill (see the sidebar above). Make sure that the plates are lined up precisely to the layout chalkline or your holes will be off.

Without a marking tool, simply measure the distance from the edge of the 2x6 that's on the chalkline to the center of the bolt. Then measure on the 2x6 from the opposite edge toward its center that same distance. This marks the center of the bolt, but it's a slower process than using a marking tool.

After all the 2x6s along a wall of the foundation are marked for bolt holes, drill them out with a ⅝-in. or ¾-in. bit. It's best to lift the stock onto a scrap of lumber to keep the bit from dulling when it punches through the sill and, possibly, into the concrete.

Fastening the mudsill

Brush away any wood chips from drilling and roll out sill seal over the bolts before setting the mudsill in place. Lift and drop the mudsill plate over the bolt without flipping it over. If you flip it over the holes won't line up.

After you set the first layer of the mudsill in place, it's helpful to drive a few concrete nails through it and into the foundation. The nails aren't intended to hold the 2x6s to the foundation but to keep them straight and on the chalkline. Pay special attention at the corners to be sure your cuts were accurate and that the plate from one direction doesn't push the adjacent one off its chalkline. If this happens, trim the long one and refit.

For the second layer of mudsill, mark and drill in the same fashion as the lower one. Remember to crosslap the ends of the upper plate with the lower one to tie the corners together. Stagger the butt joints between the mudsill by about 4 ft. to help keep the system straight.

If the foundation sub left the bolts tall enough to reach through both plates, drill holes the same diameter in the top piece as in the lower one. If

Before laying the drilled-out mudsill plate over the bolts, install sill seal material to reduce air infiltration and pest pathways into the house.

Crosslap the mudsill layers at corners and stagger joints between the layers by at least 4 ft.

Fastening Mudsills with Straps

- **Step 1.** Poke sill seal over strap and bend legs flat.
- **Step 2.** Bend straps up on sides of mudsill.
- **Step 3.** Nail strap to mudsill.
- **Step 4.** Shim upper mudsill level; nail on strap/anchor.

Labeled parts:
- 2x6 upper plate of mudsill
- 2x6 pressure-treated lower plate of mudsill
- Foam sill seal gasket
- Strap anchor embedded in concrete
- Concrete foundation
- Rebar

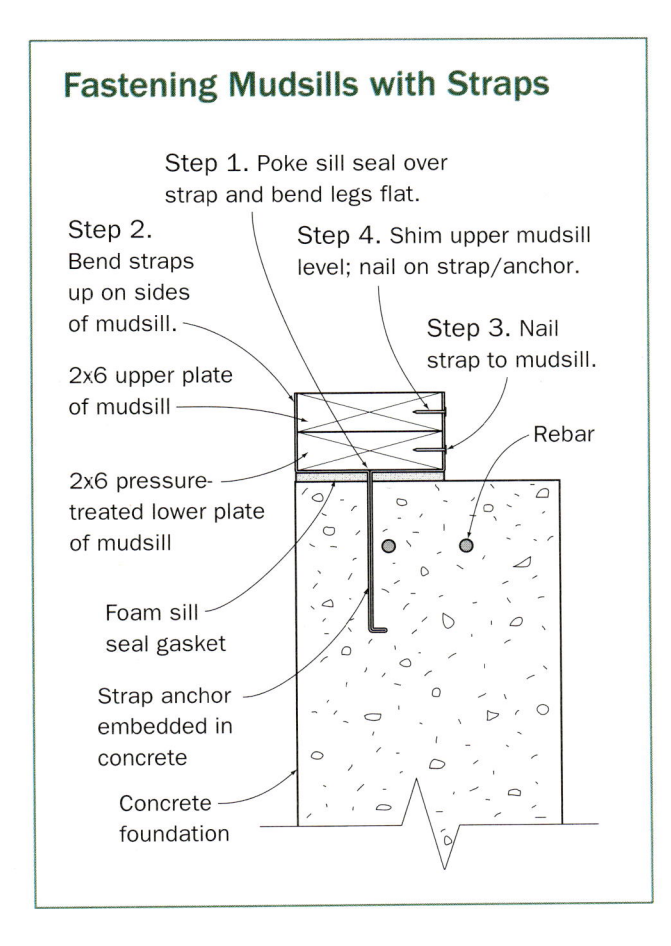

the bolts are too short, install the washers and nuts on the lower sill. Snug the nuts down with a wrench. There's no need to overtighten the nuts and draw them into the wood. Drill the holes in the upper layer large enough to accommodate the diameter of the nut, usually 1⅛ in. or more.

Set the upper sill in place; and, keeping the outside faces flush, nail it to the lower one with only one nail every 4 ft. Using only one nail allows shims to be slipped in between the layers easily if needed. Put washers and nuts on the bolts that extend through both layers of the mudsill. Only hand-tighten them at this point, because you may have to loosen them during the shimming process.

Fastening mudsills with straps On foundations with tie-down straps rather than bolts to hold down the mudsills, you don't have to do any drilling. Just roll the sill seal out and poke the straps through it; then separate and flatten out the straps. This way the straps hold the sill seal in place until you set the wood on top. Align the mudsill with the chalkline. Bend the straps up and nail them into the edges of the lower layer of the mudsill. Now apply the upper 2x6, crosslap the corners, and stagger the joints as noted above. Don't nail the straps to the top yet; wait until you complete any necessary shimming (discussed next), then nail them off.

Using Shims to Level the Mudsill

Now it's time to get back to the level reference line you snapped around the foundation earlier. The mudsill must be leveled so the first-floor deck will be as flat as possible. This is key to keeping walls and subsequent floors level too, without having to make adjustments along the way. The more care you put into leveling the mudsill now the less you'll have to adjust the rest of the framing later on.

Planning the shimming process

Low areas in the foundation are easy to fix with shims, but high spots require a little more work. For instance, you don't want to shim the entire mudsill for a ⅜-in. high bump that's only 2 ft. long. A better solution would be to highlight the area and trim the rim joist and the ends of a few floor joists when you install them later. If I-joists or floor trusses are being used, consider dadoing the top of the mudsill just where the joists or trusses sit. When an entire foundation wall is ⅜ in. high, then shimming up the rest of the mudsill may be more practical.

Determine the average height at which to level the mudsill. Mark the high spots where you'll trim the joists or dado the mudsill. Write the distance that the joists will have to be adjusted on the mudsill so you won't have to check again during the floor framing process. Then mark the low spots the same way. Write how thick the shims need to be right on the top of the mudsill.

Measure from the top layer of the mudsill to the level chalkline snapped around the foundation. Where the foundation is low, insert shim material between the mudsill layers to make the top flat and level.

Inserting shims

Our goal is to level the mudsill to within ⅛ in. We use rips of OSB, plywood, and hardboard of various thickness as shims. If the mudsill has to be raised ¼ in. along a whole wall of the foundation, for example, use ¼-in. hardboard strips. Or a shallow dip may need only ⅛-in.-thick strips. Use increasing thickness of shim stock to blend into deeper (¼ in. or greater) depressions.

Shimming with sidewall shingles is an option some framers use. Although it works fine in the short term, the shingles are soft and may compress under loaded conditions. Plywood, OSB, and hardboard are much denser and unlikely to compress.

Establish the desired measurement for the top of the mudsill off the reference line. Moving along the perimeter, measure the mudsill wherever you've nailed it with a single nail—about every 4 ft.—and pry the two plates apart until the top plate is at the correct height. Because the two plates are only tacked together, it's easy to separate them. Insert the shim stock between the two plates as shown in the photo above and then drive in a few more spikes to draw the plates together. Finish by tightening the nuts on the foundation bolts, unless that's already been done on the lower plate. Make one last double-check for level around the mudsill by measuring from the top to the reference line. Fine-tune any of the shims as necessary.

Nail off the entire mudsill with spikes staggered 12 in. apart along each edge of the mudsill. If you're using tie-down straps, nail them to the top of the mudsill after shimming is complete.

Framing Walls on Drops

The string lines you set up to locate the mudsills on the foundation drops earlier can be readjusted to help you frame the walls needed to create a plane to frame the floor on. You can use the strings to measure the exact length to cut each stud. This eliminates the need to shim the mudsills on drops.

Determining stud height

For the dropped sections of foundation, follow the same process described earlier for installing the mudsills. Locate, bolt, and nail the mudsill down completely. Nail the top layer of the mudsill down and don't worry about shimming: Any variation in the height of the foundation will be taken care of by cutting the studs to custom lengths. Lay out the stud and rough opening

The mudsill blends into and becomes the top plate of knee walls built on the dropped sections of the foundation. Set a string level with the top of the main foundation height to measure stud heights from. Cutting each stud to fit eliminates the need to shim the mudsill below.

locations on the mudsill (see chapter 5). Then set the strings dead level to the average height of the foundation (see "Checking the Foundation for Level," on p. 33) with the water level by adjusting the outriggers up or down. Pull the string taut and measure down to each stud location. Keep in mind that the string will dip in the middle on long runs (over 30 ft. or so). We often add 1/16 in. or 1/8 in. to studs in the middle of long runs to account for the string dip.

Mudsills become top plates

The mudsills at the top elevation of the foundation should carry through into the top plates of the dropped walls. Run the lower pressure-treated sill at least one stud location into the dropped portion of the foundation. Continue the mudsill/top plate from that point with regular dimensional lumber. Toenail studs into the mudsill and through nail the lower top plate into the studs. After all of the dropped walls are framed, check the mudsills/top plates for correct dimensioning and square. When you're satisfied, install the upper mudsill/second top plate; crosslap the plates at the corners and overlap the butt joints of the lower plates by at least 4 ft. (see chapter 5 for more information).

Ready to Move On

From this point, you can install any carrying beams or walls level and straight; and from there, set the first-floor deck to the precise dimensions without any extra effort. There will be some adjusting at each stage of framing to ensure accuracy, but the mudsill requires the most work. We'd rather spend the extra time necessary to correct the flaws in the foundation with the mudsill rather than struggle with out-of-square and unlevel floor decks and walls. All of the time spent dimensioning a mudsill and getting it level and square will be saved 10-fold as the framing progresses.

MUDSILLS 41

Chapter 3

CENTER BEAMS

BEAM BASICS

PLANNING A
BUILT-UP BEAM

INSTALLING THE BEAM

OTHER BEAM
MATERIALS

INSTALLING SUPPORT
COLUMNS

BEAM/JOIST
CONFIGURATIONS

Most of the houses we frame have either a crawl-space or a full-basement foundation. (Few of the houses in our area are framed directly on a concrete slab—a practice that is more common in the South and out West.) And most of the house foundations we frame on require a center beam that spans the foundation. The function of a center beam is to provide a straight, level surface, most often even with the top of the mudsill, which will support the floor joist system between the foundation walls. Variables such as spans, loads, concentrated loads, ceiling height restrictions, column spacing, and cost all contribute to the selection of the type of material used to construct the beams. (The term *girder* is often used interchangeably with *beam* in residential construction. A girder is a type of beam; but for our purposes, we will use the term *beam* throughout the book.)

Regardless of the beam material, the installation principles remain the same: set it straight and level. First we'll follow the process of planning and installing the most commonly used beam, a built-up beam made from several layers of dimensional lumber. Then we'll look at the differences you'll encounter installing beams made of other materials, such as engineered lumber and steel. We'll also cover support columns and look at some beam/joist configurations that enable you to frame a floor system in which the beam is flush with the floor joists.

Center beams provide a level surface, usually even with the top of the mudsill, to support the floor joist system between the foundation walls.

Beam Basics

Most beams used to support floor joists in full-basement and crawl-space foundations are dropped into recesses in the foundation, called beam pockets. In a simple home design, the center beam spans the foundation from pocket to pocket. In large homes, or ones with complex designs, there may be several support beams. Some beams may span only a portion of the basement rather than going from end to end.

Most beams are supported at regular intervals along their length by Lally columns or posts set on footing piers. The top of the beam is usually set flush with the top of the mudsill, and the floor joists set on top of the mudsill and the beam. There are other systems that incorporate the beam within the floor joists; we'll describe those at the end of the chapter.

Planning a Built-Up Beam

You can use your house plans to figure out the cut list for planning a built-up beam. You may find it worthwhile to draft a simple sketch of the beam to help make up the list. The sketch also comes in handy when you assemble the beam on-site to remind you what stock was ordered for which spans or to explain your plan to someone else.

We'll use an example of a three-piece 2x12 beam to illustrate the process (see the drawing on p. 44).

Measuring for materials

To make the drawing, measure the distances from the beam pockets in the foundation to the center of each support column. The locations of the support columns are indicated on the plans, but it is important to verify that the actual pier footings are placed properly. If they aren't, make the adjustments on your sketch to reflect the on-site conditions. Draw a pencil line for each beam layer.

It's unlikely you'll find stock lumber that will reach the entire length of the beam unless the house is very small, so you'll have to plan for butt joints in each layer. By code, joints *can* fall in the span between columns; but the location of those joints is critical. Placed improperly, they leave a weak point and the beam may fail. Unless you have an engineered plan or are skilled at performing the calculations to determine the exact spot for those joints, you'll be safer to locate joints over columns.

Start from the back of the beam pocket and determine the distance to the first butt joint for the first layer of the beam. Let's assume the beam pocket is $5\frac{1}{2}$ in. deep. Plan to leave a $\frac{1}{2}$-in. air space between the end of the beam and the

Planning a Built-Up Beam

Center Beam Plan (3 piece, 2x12)

Layer						
	5" into beam pocket		Stair opening / Trim off excess.			Face of foundation wall
1	13' 9"	6' 1" ± falloff		8' 6" ± falloff	14' 7"	
2	7' 1"	14' uncut (13' 4")		16' uncut (14' 4")	7' 6"	
3	13' 9"	6' 7"		7' 3"	14' 7"	

Spacings: 5" — 6' 8" — 6' 8" — 6' 7" — 4' 8" — 7' 3" — 7' 1" — 7' 1" — 5"

Materials List

2x12 kiln-dried spruce
5/14'
4/16'

3½" concrete/steel columns
6/7' 6" with plates

12 lagbolts, 2" x ¼" with washers

Cut List

	Quantity	Length	From
	1	16' uncut	1/16'
	1	14' uncut	1/14'
Share {	1	6' 7"	Piece of 14' (7' 13")
	1	7' 3"	Piece of 14' (6' 7")
	2	13' 9"	2/14'
Share {	1	7' 1"	Piece of 14' (6' 11")
	1	6' 11" falloff	Piece of 14' (7' 11")
	2	14' 7"	2/16'
Share {	1	7' 6"	Piece of 16' (8' 6")
	1	8' 6" falloff	Piece of 16' (7' 6")

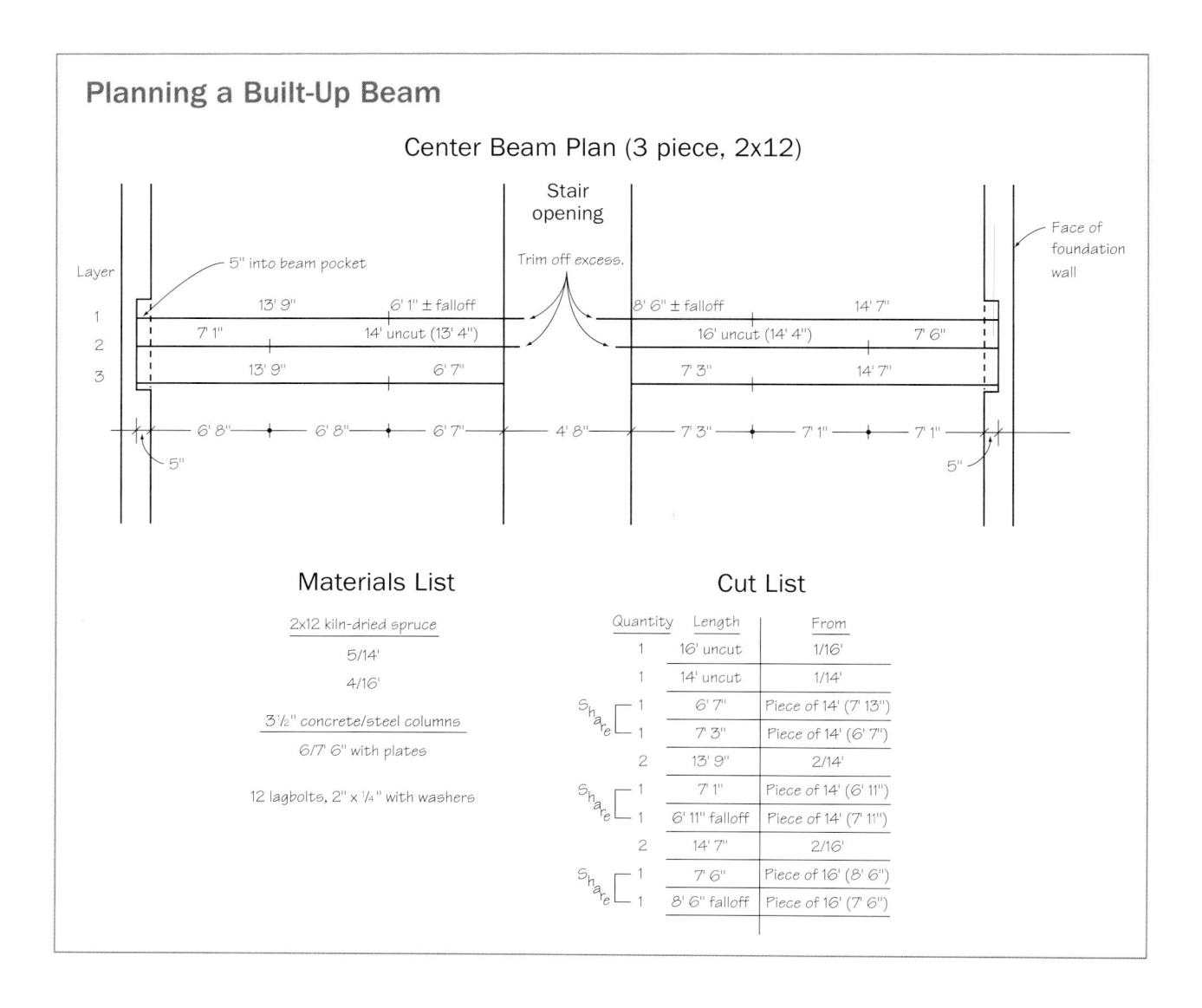

concrete. That leaves 5 in. of beam bearing in the pocket. The center of the first column is 6 ft. 8 in. from the inside face of the foundation wall and the next column, 6 ft. 8 in. beyond that. You can make the first joint fall on the second support with a 14-ft. length of beam stock trimmed to 13 ft. 9 in. (6 ft. 8 in. plus 6 ft. 8 in. plus 5 in.).

It's preferable to stagger the joints over different columns so there's at least one layer to provide continuity across each bearing point. The two outer layers can break over the second column, and the center layer can break over the first and third columns. This makes the length of the first piece of the center layer 7 ft. 1 in. (6 ft. 8 in. plus 5 in.) and the length of the second piece 13 ft. 4 in. (6 ft. 8 in. plus 6 ft. 8 in.).

Continue the process to determine the lengths for all the pieces and label them to keep things organized on the job site later. One easy labeling system is to mark layers by number and the pieces of each layer by letter. So the first piece of the first layer would be 1A; the second piece, 1B; and so on. Then the first piece of the second layer would be 2A.

Plan to use the longest lengths of available lumber when designing the beam layers. If the

Sometimes beams are interrupted by a detail in the floor, like a stair opening or chimney hole. Let the beam run long into the opening space and trim the end later, after the opening size is established. (Photo by Tom O'Brien, courtesy *Fine Homebuilding* magazine, © The Taunton Press, Inc.)

columns are set 5 ft. apart, you can reach across four of them with a 20-ft. length of lumber without any joints. This makes the installation process easier and minimizes joints.

Making a materials list

From the completed beam sketch, make up a materials list and a cut list, with lengths and corresponding labels to speed production. Order a little extra lumber so you can be selective choosing the pieces that make up the beam (see "Selecting Joist Stock," p. 70). The extra material can be used as floor joists, cut into headers, or returned.

You need to choose and order the support columns, too. Take field measurements to determine the rough height you need to order, so the columns will be long enough for trimming.

Sometimes beams are interrupted by a special detail in the floor, like a stair opening or chimney hole. Plan to let the beam run a little long into the opening space rather than trying to trim it exactly. For example, if you determine that the last section of a beam running into an opening should be 13 ft. 2 in., just use a full 14-ft. piece of stock and let it run long. When the floor joists around the special details are laid out, you'll see precisely where the beam needs to be trimmed. Just leave the end of the beam nail-free and fasten it together after the trimming process.

Installing the Beam

We do a few things to ensure a precise beam installation, which include keeping the beam straight during assembly, marking the beam location accurately, and bracing the beam securely while we frame the floor system.

Marking the beam location

Most beam pockets in the foundation are oversize, so you'll need to mark the exact beam position. Measure from a corner of the mudsill and mark the exact center of the beam on the mudsill at each end of the foundation. From the reference mark, square out lines indicating the edge of each beam layer. For example, if there are three members, you would mark $\frac{3}{4}$ in. to the left and right of the center mark to indicate the middle layer of the beam. Then mark $1\frac{1}{2}$ in. beyond each of those marks for the outer layers.

Ideally, the beam pocket is large enough and is in the correct position to accept the beam. If not, you'll have to enlarge the pocket with a cold chisel or rotary hammer, or you'll have to change the beam location to match the pocket. Be cautious, however in moving the beam location.

CENTER BEAMS **45**

Measure and mark the precise location for the center beam within the beam pocket. Make the marks on the mudsill and line up the beam with the marks once it's installed. (Photo by Tom O'Brien, courtesy *Fine Homebuilding* magazine, © The Taunton Press, Inc.)

There are many issues to consider, such as joist span, utility location conflicts, and loads from bearing walls. Consult with the building designer before moving a beam.

Temporary beam support To prepare for assembling and installing a beam you'll need to have ready some temporary supports that can hold the beam in place, and you'll need some staging so you can reach the beam. We accomplish both by using homemade A-frames (see the sidebar on the facing page).

Space the A-frames 12 ft. to 14 ft. apart underneath the beam location. Most beam sections will reach between the A-frames, and those that don't will be supported by those that do. Staging planks set on lower or middle crossbars of the A-frames get you in a good position to assemble and place the beam.

The closer you can get the beam to the proper height when assembling it, the easier it will be to make fine adjustments later. Run a string from one beam pocket to the other as a reference for the A-frames. Determine the difference between the height of the beam and the distance from the bottom of the beam pocket to the top of the mudsill. Insert some blocks and shims to make up this difference, raising the string. The tolerance can be crude at this point; within $\frac{1}{2}$ in. is ade-

Set up staging to support the beam temporarily during assembly and installation. Gauge the height of the supports by running a string between the foundation beam pockets. (Photo by Tom O'Brien, courtesy *Fine Homebuilding* magazine, © The Taunton Press, Inc.)

Making A-Frame Staging

Homemade A-frames have a lot going for them. They are inexpensive, portable, and quick to set up; and they provide multilevel staging. We use 8-ft. studs to make our A-frames—any taller and they get difficult to handle and, possibly, a little dangerous. And we make them about 3 ft. wide. This size gives plenty of stability and still leaves room in a 4-ft.-wide truck bed. The steps are formed from 1x6 or 1x8 ledger board, which helps keep a thin profile without sacrificing strength. We insert 1x2 fill spacers between the ledger steps, not so much for strength but to enable the frames to slide one on top of the other during loading and unloading from the truck.

The frames are easy to make, just copy the photo for the basic structure. Glue and screw the ledger board steps onto the edges of two 2x4 legs. Keep the legs parallel and square, and space the steps 16 in. to 24 in. apart. The spacing isn't important, but it is important to set the steps on all of your A-frames at a consistent height.

Once you've made two sections, lay one ledger face down and set the other half inside and on top with the steps facing up. Drill a $\frac{1}{2}$-in. hole a few inches down through both pieces of the 2x4 legs at one end. Insert a $\frac{1}{2}$-in. bolt with washer and secure the bolt with two $\frac{1}{2}$-in. nuts over another washer. Lock the two nuts tightly together. Done.

If you use the A-frames on a finished concrete floor or you have to open them wide to get a certain height, tack some strapping across the 2x4s near the bottom. It will prevent the frames from opening flat out and dropping down.

A-frames have a multitude of uses on a framing job and are easy to build.

quate. Open or close the bottom of the A-frames until the top crossbars match the string.

Beam support for a crawl space Temporarily supporting a beam in a crawl-space foundation is easier. Make up several H-cradles to support the beam from short lengths of 2x stock. Nail the crossbar at the level of the string you've strung from one beam pocket to the other. If the working level is above waist height, add outriggers to help brace the assembly and keep it from tipping.

Assembling the beam

The first thing to do when assembling the beam is to crown the lumber, or determine the direction in which the lumber curves along its thin dimension. The process is explained in "Selecting Joist Stock" on p. 70.

After crowning your beam stock, select and cut the sections of the beam to the lengths you determined on the sketch. Label the pieces and then spread them out on the basement floor in

CENTER BEAMS   47

Partially assemble the beam on the basement floor before lifting it onto the staging. Tack two or three layers and at least two segments together. Be sure to make the tops of the layers flush, leaving any height deviation in the lumber on the bottom edge. (Photo by Tom O'Brien. courtesy *Fine Homebuilding* magazine, © The Taunton Press, Inc.)

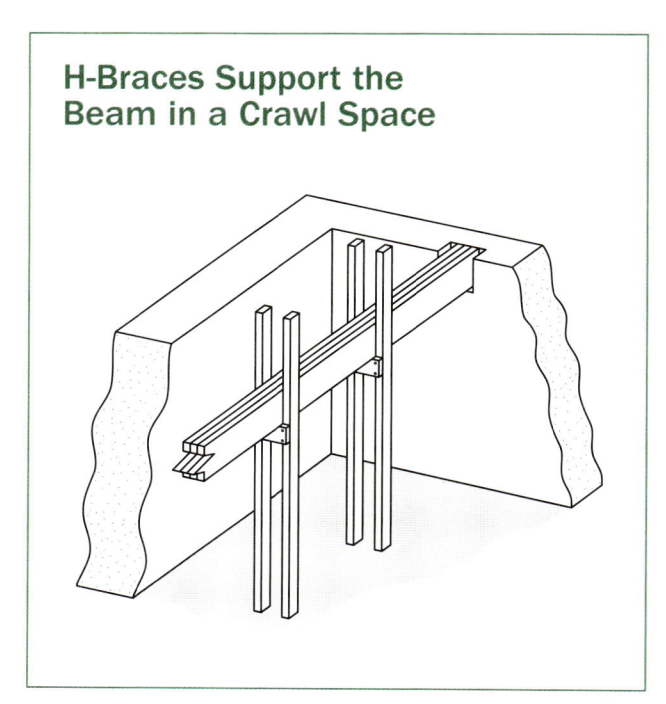

H-Braces Support the Beam in a Crawl Space

the beam is flush with the floor joist system, as described at the end of this chapter).

Starting at one end of the beam, line up the first and second layers. Use the edge of a square to match the crown (top) edges of the boards flush with each other. This process works best with two people. One person works the ends of the beam pieces back and forth, while the other person squares the members flush and tacks them together. Nails staggered every 3 ft. or 4 ft. are sufficient at this point. Build the beam on as flat a surface as possible. Any waves or hooks left in the beam once it is tack nailed together will be hard to get out later.

It's important to make the top of the beam as flat as possible, so the floor joists will be well supported. Leave any height differences between the layers on the underside of the beam. (Not all stock is exactly the same width.) The excess has to be trimmed to flatten the bottom of the beam only at the small areas where the columns support it.

After about three sections of two layers of the beam are assembled and before the beam becomes too heavy or awkward, lift it onto the A-frames. Orient the partially assembled beam with the crown edge up and slide it into the beam pocket. Use a ½-in.-thick block to space the beam from the back of the pocket. Stuff a couple of blocks in

their approximate location. It's much easier to assemble part of the beam on the basement floor and lift it into position on the A-frames than to assemble all the pieces in place. In addition to fastening the beam layers together with nails, we use construction adhesive between the layers. The beam will be stronger, and you'll reduce the likelihood of a squeaky floor later on (particularly if

on one side of the pocket to keep the beam upright.

Continue adding sections to the beam until you reach the opposite beam pocket, making sure the beam ends ½ in. from the end of the pocket.

Keeping the beam straight during assembly

Straighten out the two-layered beam by eye before nailing it off. If it's crooked when you nail it together, you will have a tough time later trying to straighten it out.

Fasten the two layers permanently together with rows of 12d or 16d nails staggered 12 in. to 16 in. apart along the top and bottom edges. Drive the nails in at an angle so they won't protrude out the other side. Bend over any nails that do stick out so they don't snag clothing or hold successive beam layers away. If you use a pneumatic framing nailer to drive the nails, check the beam for air spaces between layers. Voids may occur because of cupped lumber or because the nailer didn't draw the layers together. Drive the nails around air spaces with hammer blows until the gaps close.

Straightening and bracing the beam Until now we have been keeping the beam straight by eye. If you continued to build out a three-layer beam and nail it off completely, you would have a difficult time trying to work out any curves, dips, or bumps. So at this point, while the beam consists of only two layers, it's time to straighten it out.

Orient the ends of the partially assembled beam to the reference marks on the mudsill using the blocks installed earlier to hold the beam upright in the beam pocket. Cut three short (2 in. to 4 in.) blocks from a uniform piece of lumber such as 1x3 furring, 2x4, or plywood scrap. Two pieces will be used as spacer blocks and the third as a gauge block.

Nail a spacer block on one side of the beam, flush with the top edge; nail the other spacer on the same side at the opposite end of the beam. Pull a string line tightly across the blocks about

Set the partially assembled beam on top of the staging and slide one end into the beam pocket. Wedge blocks between the beam and the sides of the beam pocket to keep the beam from rolling until the rest of the layers are added. (Photo by Tom O'Brien, courtesy *Fine Homebuilding* magazine, © The Taunton Press, Inc.)

1 in. from the top of the beam and tie it off to nails set beyond the spacers.

The A-frames supporting the beam may have settled, and the beam may be sagging in the middle. Look down the length of the beam to see if this is the case. Adjust the A-frames to lift the beam into a fairly level position again.

Run 1x or 2x braces from the mudsill across the top of the beam to hold the beam straight. Put one brace where each Lally column will support the beam or every 8 ft., whichever is less. Nail the end of each brace to the mudsill and let the beam end float for now.

CENTER BEAMS 49

Add layers to the beam, one piece at a time. Check that the beam is straight before nailing off each layer, because it will be difficult to straighten the beam later. (Photo by Tom O'Brien, courtesy *Fine Homebuilding* magazine, © The Taunton Press, Inc.)

Slide the gauge block along the length of the beam between the beam and the string. You will be able to tell where and in which direction the beam needs straightening by whether the string touches the gauge block or there is a space between the gauge block and the string. Straighten the beam parallel to the string at each brace location. Nail each brace to the beam once you have it gauged accurately. The braces will keep the beam from rolling over as you proceed with the next step, and it will be easier to add the rest of the layers to the beam if it is straight.

Adding layers to the beam Remove the supporting blocks from the beam pockets, being careful to keep the beam upright (reinsert the blocks once the beam is complete). Install the third layer of the beam and tack it in place, crown up, tops flush. When you have the layer complete end to end, check to see that the beam is still straight to the string. Then nail off the beam completely. You don't have to angle the nails with this layer; drive them straight into the lumber. If your beam has a fourth layer, it can be added the same way. As you add successive layers, be careful to keep the joints staggered as marked on your sketch.

Setting the beam height

The top of the beam must be set flush with the top of the mudsills. Until now we have just set the top of the beam roughly level by eye. Dimensional lumber beams should actually be set slightly higher than the mudsills. A two-plate mudsill is 3 in. thick and can be expected to shrink $1/8$ in. to $1/4$ in. over the course of the first year or two as the house dries out. A dimensional lumber center beam will be $7 1/2$ in. to $11 1/2$ in. tall and shrink $3/8$ in. to $5/8$ in., depending on its moisture content. To compensate for shrinkage, plan on raising the beam $1/4$ in. to $3/8$ in. above the top of the mudsills.

Don't perform the following procedure without first leveling the mudsill. As a reference to level the top of the beam, run a series of strings perpendicular across the top of the beam from one side of the mudsill to the other. Set a string over each column location. It's important to use thin twine that can be pulled tightly to avoid sagging. Use a spacer block under the string at each end, just as when straightening the beam.

Strings that run perpendicular to the beam work better as a reference than ones that run the length of the beam. Usually the length of the beam is greater than the distance across the beam. Longer strings will sag more and be less accurate.

Place an adjustable lift beneath the beam within 6 in. to 12 in. of each column position. We use heavy-duty screw jacks, but a simple lift made from 2x4s or 2x6s works to raise the beam

Replace the temporary beam supports with adjustable jacks or site-built beam-adjusting supports. Run string lines over the top of the beam between the front and rear mudsills and raise them on spacer blocks. The strings act as guides for adjusting the final height of the beam. (Photo by Tom O'Brien, courtesy *Fine Homebuilding* magazine, © The Taunton Press, Inc.)

into place, too (see the sidebar on p. 52). Keep the jacks away from the column locations, so the permanent columns can be installed later without jockeying the jacks around. Now adjust the beam until it's $\frac{1}{4}$ in. to $\frac{3}{8}$ in. higher than the mudsill. Use a gauge stick referenced to the string to check the height. Adjust each jack just a little at a time and bring the beam up to position slowly.

Shimming and strapping the beam

Once the beam is lifted to the correct height along its midsection, it's time to install permanent shims in the beam pockets. Shim blocks should be dimensionally stable and, if the shim is made of more than one piece, the lower piece should be made of rot-resistant material, because it will be in contact with concrete. Steel and pressure-treated wood are two common choices.

The thickness of the space affects your choice of material. Spaces $\frac{1}{2}$ in. or less are best filled with steel plates. Several pieces can be stacked to fill the void. No matter what shim material you use to fill the bulk of the space, it's easiest to use thin steel stock to make the fine adjustments. Pressure-treated plywood is a good choice for the first layer

Adjust the height of the beam using a gauge block that's the same thickness as the spacer blocks raising the strings above the mudsill. Raise the beam about $\frac{1}{4}$ in. higher than the mudsills to account for shrinkage. This precaution isn't necessary for beams made of engineered lumber or steel. (Photo by Tom O'Brien, courtesy *Fine Homebuilding* magazine, © The Taunton Press, Inc.)

CENTER BEAMS

Site-Built Beam-Lifting Jacks

When you don't have adjustable screw jacks to level the center beam, you can make a reasonable facsimile on-site. On the basement floor, set an 8-ft.-long 2x6 to one side of each column location perpendicular to the beam. If the floor is terribly uneven, you might have to do a little shovel work so that each 2x6 has good bear-ing along its whole length. Measure the distance the beam has to be raised and add it to the distance from the bottom of the beam to the 2x6 on the ground. Now add 4 in. to that and cut two 2xs to that length.

For example, if the distance between the beam and the string is 1 in. and the beam is 7 ft. 2 in. above the flat 2x6, you add the measures together for a total of 7 ft. 3 in. To that, add 4 in. to get a length of 7 ft. 7 in.

Nail the two 2xs together at the tip of one end and spread the other ends apart, forming an inverted V. Slide the nailed end under the beam above the 2x6 on the ground and set the loose ends on the 2x6, forming an A. Tack the top of the lifting jack to the bottom of the beam and tap the legs of the A toward the center. Drive each leg equally inward, and the beam will rise. The 2x legs of the A are cut 4 in. longer than necessary so they will have plenty of additional adjustment upward if the 2x6 on the ground sinks down.

Once you have a beam-lifting jack near each column location, adjust each lift, a little at a time, equally along the length of the beam as you raise it. This allows the beam-lifting jacks to share the weight of the beam equally rather than overstraining one. Have a pair of 12-in. or longer 2x blocks, with two spikes started into each, near each lift. When the beam reaches the correct height, nail a block behind each leg to keep it from kicking out.

A site-built beam-lifting jack, made by nailing 2x6s together into an A shape, can be used to raise and support the beam when screw jacks aren't available. (Photo by Tom O'Brien, courtesy *Fine Homebuilding* magazine, © The Taunton Press, Inc.)

After the beam has been leveled and shimmed in the beam pocket, tie the ends to the mudsill with steel straps. Use pieces of lumber-banding straps or tie-down ribbon. Line up the end of the beam with the marks you made earlier. (Photo by Tom O'Brien, courtesy Fine Homebuilding *magazine, © The Taunton Press, Inc.)*

in contact with the concrete when you have to fill more than a ½-in. thickness. Additional layers can be made from scraps of plywood or engineered lumber.

Never use regular lumber in the flat-grain position, even if it is pressure treated. It can shrink and let the beam settle. Instead, cut and install pressure-treated lumber shims upright in the long-grain position. These shims work best to build up spaces of 3 in. or more.

Don't forget to shim the sides of the beam to the beam pocket. Replace the temporary blocks you used, if they weren't made of pressure-treated lumber. It's okay to use blocks in the flat-grain position here, because the blocks aren't in compression.

Tie the top of the beam to the mudsill with steel straps. The straps hold the beam to the marks you made on the mudsill. We use 12-in. to 16-in. pieces cut from the banding straps that the lumber came bundled with. You can also use perforated-steel tie-down ribbon.

Lay the straps in an X pattern over the top of the mudsill and onto the top of the beam. Drive two or three nails into each beam and mudsill.

Other Beam Materials

Once you understand the principles of planning, building, bracing, and leveling a built-up beam, working with any of the other beam materials will be second nature. Each material has advantages and disadvantages. And some of the different beam materials require installation procedures that differ slightly from those used for built-up beams.

Just like a built-up beam, all of the following beam materials need to be designed for the installation. Most suppliers of engineered lumber and steel beams will determine the size beam you'll need for the given application, and they'll specify the location of the support columns as part of the service they offer with the sale.

Solid wood

The shear bulk of solid-wood beams can make them difficult to work with. Long solid-wood beams can require heavy equipment to lift them into place. We've framed houses that used two shorter solid-wood beams that met in line over a support column. Where two pieces meet over a column, we use a large steel plate on the bottom

LVL beams are assembled in layers like traditional built-up beams, but they are more dimensionally stable and stronger than sawn lumber, and they come in longer lengths.

to fasten the pieces together and to fasten them to the top of the column. Steel plates bolted onto the side of the beam will also support a splice. Selecting the beam is actually the most critical aspect of the job and is of great importance when using solid wood. If the beam is warped at all, it is unlikely that it can be straightened out. Use kiln-dried lumber to reduce the likelihood of the beam twisting or warping after it's installed.

Laminated veneer lumber

Laminated veneer lumber (LVL) may be the choice for a beam when you want to reduce the number of support columns; LVL beams can span greater distances than similar-size beams made from solid-wood lumber. Their layout and installation are the same as built-up beams, with a few exceptions.

LVL is heavier and is available in longer lengths than dimensional lumber, so it's a good idea to order section sizes according to the size of the available crew. The material is usually $1\frac{3}{4}$ in. thick and $5\frac{1}{2}$ in. to 18 in. deep, and it is built up in layers just like a dimensional lumber beam. Because LVL is dimensionally stable you don't have to adjust for shrinkage when setting the height of the beam, so set it level with the mudsill.

LVL material is much denser than regular lumber, which makes nailing layers together more difficult. Pneumatic nailers won't always drive nails in completely. It might help to use C-clamps to draw the LVL boards together before pneumatic nailing. Or drive the nails home with a hammer.

Parallel strand lumber

As with LVL beams, the length of parallel strand lumber (PSL) beams is limited only by freight restrictions; most can be ordered and installed in a house as a single unit. They usually aren't built up in layers but come the width needed for the span and load requirements. In our area, common sizes range from $3\frac{1}{2}$ in. to 8 in. thick and 7 in. to 18 in. deep. They can be special ordered to just about any length. In other parts of the country, dimensions may vary.

The beams are very dense and heavy, so a crane is the best method for placement. While the crane eases the beam in, you can safely install the temporary adjustable supports. And as with the LVLs, there's no need to adjust for shrinkage with PSL beams, so set them level with the mudsill. The main reason to choose a PSL beam over an LVL beam is the finish appearance. When the beam is intended to be left exposed in a finished room, PSL is the preferred choice.

PSL beams have the same benefits as LVL material but usually come in single-width pieces (3$\frac{1}{2}$ in. or 5$\frac{1}{2}$ in.). This makes them heavier to handle but eliminates the need to assemble layers. (Photo courtesy Truss Joist MacMillan.)

Steel

We always use a crane to place steel I-beams. Measure the actual pocket-to-pocket distance before ordering a steel beam, otherwise you'll need a torch to cut it if it's too long. Deducting 1 in. from the overall length is a good idea if you're bearing into deep beam pockets. This way you'll be sure the beam isn't too long.

The bottom of the beam pocket will need to be at least an extra 1$\frac{1}{2}$ in. deeper from the top of the mudsill than the beam is tall. This allows for a 2x6 plate to be bolted to the top of the beam. The 2x6 makes the transition between steel and lumber framing. The top of the 2x6 needs to be flush with the top of the mudsill. When you order the steel, have the supplier drill staggered holes every

Steel beams can span great distances in a single bound without intermediate supports. This can make for a column-free basement. Order them predrilled for attaching a wood plate that makes the transition from steel to wood framing.

2 ft. along the top of the beam so you can use lag bolts to attach the wood plate to it.

Columns for steel beams are usually specified larger than those used for other beam materials because of the additional loading. Steel beams can span greater distances than other beam materials, so fewer support columns are needed. The fewer the columns, the more weight each one supports. If they are the concrete-filled Lally type, cut and install them as described later.

When square hollow steel columns are used, they need to be fabricated to the exact height required, so you'll have to plan ahead. With either type of column, you will need to through bolt or weld the top cap to the beam.

Installing Support Columns

The specifications for most residential projects call for the standard 3$\frac{1}{2}$-in. concrete-filled steel Lally columns as permanent supports. The columns can be installed at this point, but because there is no weight on the beam yet, we sometimes wait until the floor system is complete. This reduces the chance of a permanent column being knocked out of place. When they're loaded with the weight of all the house's framing, they're less

CENTER BEAMS   55

Concrete-filled, tubular-steel columns are the most common support posts for basement beams. They are easily cut to length with a pipe cutter but can also be trimmed with a circular or reciprocating saw outfitted with a metal-cutting blade. (Photo by Tom O'Brien, courtesy *Fine Homebuilding* magazine, © The Taunton Press, Inc.)

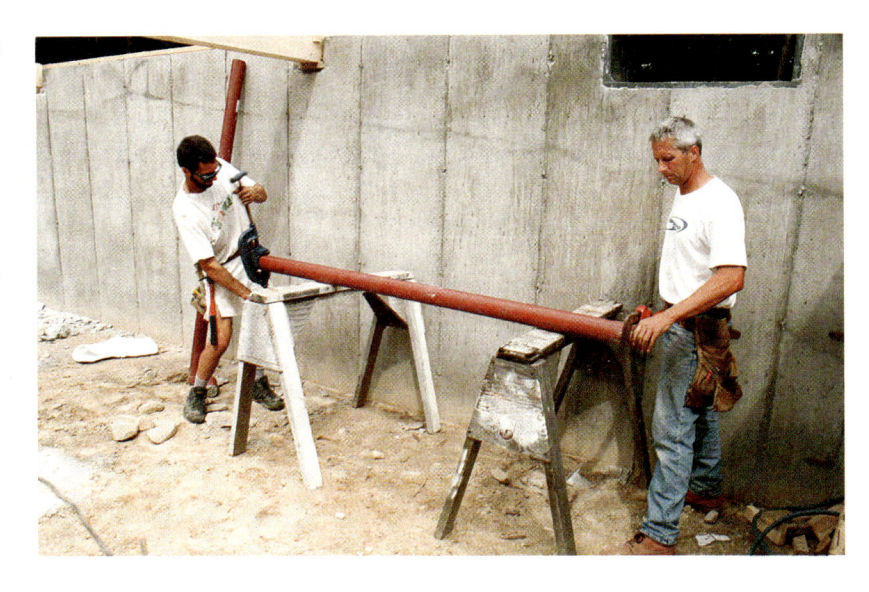

likely to move. Don't wait too long to install the columns though. Once the load-bearing walls and second floor are framed, it may not be possible to lift the beam up without powerful building jacks. Whether it's done now or after the joists are installed, the process is the same.

Rechecking beam level

Recheck the top of the beam to the strings. If the strings have been stretched for more than a day, tighten them to get rid of any sagging. Mark out each post location on the bottom of the beam and measure the distance from the concrete pier to the bottom of the beam at each point. If the bottom of the built-up beam layers varies, you'll have to chisel off the excess to create a flat spot to set the column plate to and from which to measure. Sometimes it's difficult to get an accurate measurement because the top of the concrete pier is rough. Hammer or scrape off the high spots; or if the surface is just too rough, you can pour on a thin layer of mortar to smooth the surface before measuring. Write the measurement on the beam and make a list in descending length order. Plan on cutting the longest posts first. That way if one of the cuts drifts short you can substitute it for one of the shorter columns and recut the longer one.

Cutting columns

Subtract the thickness of the top and bottom plates, if they aren't welded to the column, and mark the column to length. A large pipe cutter is the fastest and easiest way to cut a column, but it's an expensive tool. You can call around to see if any of the tool rental stores have a large pipe cutter.

An alternative is to cut the column with a metal-cutting blade mounted in either a reciprocating saw or a circular saw. With this option, you'll need an accurate line around the circumference of the column.

An easy way to get an accurate cut line is to wrap a large piece of paper around the column several times. A sheet of newspaper or a large blueprint drawing works well.

Keep one edge of the paper lined up with the mark and match the edge of the paper to itself as you wrap it around. Draw a pencil line at the edge of the paper.

Gently cut through the metal skin of the column. Once you're most of the way through the steel, a light tap will break off the unwanted piece. Sometimes the concrete core of the column extends beyond the cut-steel casing. Tap on the concrete with a hammer, and the excess will chip off.

Nail the column cap plate to the bottom of the beam and tap the base until the column is plumb. (Photo by Tom O'Brien, courtesy *Fine Homebuilding* magazine, © The Taunton Press, Inc.)

Installing the column

Fasten the column cap to the underside of the beam. To make it easier to install the column, raise the beam up about 1/8 in. with the temporary support. Slide the column into place and set it on the baseplate. Plumb the column by eye and lower the jack until the column bears some of the weight of the beam. Check the column with a level and tap the bottom with hammer blows, cushioned by a wooden block, until it's plumb. Draw a mark around the baseplate of the column as a reference in case it's bumped out of adjustment.

The base of the column can be secured in place with just a couple of concrete nails if a concrete slab will be poured around it. If the finish slab is already poured, you'll have to install a lag shield into the concrete. This process will require you to set the column temporarily in place, plumb it, mark the location of the lag shields and then remove the column so you can drill holes for the shields. Once the shields are in place, you can set the column again and bolt the baseplate down to the floor.

At some point, the column will have to be welded to the top and bottom plates. The small embossed centering tabs on the plates won't keep the column from being knocked out of place, so welding is important.

Other beams in the house Beams in the basement are common, but you may also encounter them in between floors or to support ceiling joists. If the beams are long, like basement beams, then the same processes for layout, assembling, straightening, and bracing will apply.

Often the beams in other parts of the house are short. They can easily be assembled and lifted in one piece. Just be sure to assemble them on a flat surface, so the beam will be straight when you install it.

Beam/Joist Configurations

All of the beams we have discussed so far are part of a floor system in which the floor joists sit on top of the beam. Some house plans call for beams built into the floor joist system, whereby the top of the joists is either flush with the top of the beam or slightly below it. This may be to meet local building codes for basement ceiling headroom or when the owners plan to finish the basement space as living area. Building and setting beam heights for this type of system are done in the same way as just discussed. Depending on the height of the beam, it will either sit on top of the mudsill or be held in shallow foundation pockets. Because this type of integral beam/joist system involves a discussion of floor joisting, the topic will be covered at length in the next chapter.

Chapter 4

FLOOR FRAMING

JOIST LAYOUT FOR CONVENTIONAL FLOOR DECKS

FRAMING JOISTS FOR CONVENTIONAL FLOOR DECKS

INSTALLING SUBFLOOR SHEATHING FOR CONVENTIONAL FLOOR DECKS

FRAMING FLOORS WITH I-JOISTS

FRAMING FLOORS WITH TRUSSES

The mudsills and beams take a lot of effort to install accurately but don't look like much once they're finished. When you're framing a house it's not until the joists and subfloor are finished that there's something more to look at than a hole in the ground with a few sticks.

The floor deck provides a work platform on which to build the walls and then either the next floor or the roof. Whether working on the first, second, or even third floor of a house, the joist layout and framing procedures are the same. Throughout this chapter, we will refer to joists and their relationship to the mudsill. For second- and third-floor framing, the joist would sit atop a wall plate rather than a mudsill. Just as we took extra care to dimension and square the mudsill correctly, we need to maintain those standards to create a precise frame and to make the wall framing faster and more accurate.

We'll begin this chapter with a discussion of conventional (dimensional, solid-wood) lumber joist framing with standard 2x8, 2x10, and 2x12 material. Later, we'll cover engineered I-joists and floor trusses. While most of the layout and installation processes are the same for I-joists and trusses, there are specific differences from conventional floor framing that warrant discussion.

It takes a lot of work to install the mudsills, beams, and support walls to get the foundation ready to install the floor deck. Double-check everything one last time before laying out and installing the floor joists. (Photo by Roe A. Osborn, courtesy *Fine Homebuilding* magazine, © The Taunton Press, Inc.)

The process of framing floor decks can be broken into three stages: layout, joist framing, and sheathing. At each step, the concerns should be about maintaining the dimensional accuracy established with the mudsills, maintaining the quality of the materials installed, and maintaining some degree of production speed.

There are faster ways of laying out and framing floor decks for production homes. But the way we look at it, each correctly dimensioned, square, and straight floor deck will serve as the work platform on which to build the walls for the next floor. The extra time you spend ensuring the accuracy of the floor speeds up production time when framing walls and the next floor or roof.

Joist Layout for Conventional Floor Decks

A well-planned and clearly marked floor-joist layout prevents mistakes and speeds production. Most house plans do not come with a framing layout for the floors. But creating your own is easy and makes the joist system more apparent. Working through the details on paper will also help you prepare a lumber list and a cut list, which will be useful for ordering materials and organizing the work on site.

Planning the layout

Joist spacing is a function of the joist span, joist size, joist material, and live load of the floor. Architects and building designers generally specify joist size, material, and spacing on the plans. We follow these directions but when the specifications are omitted from the plans, we are sometimes forced to consult the span charts in our building code book for dimensional lumber or an I-joist manufacturer's guide. Common joist spacing is based on divisible increments of an 8-ft. (96-in.) standard. Joist spacings of 12 in., 16 in., 19.2 in., and 24 in. are all used, with 16 in. being used most frequently.

Start with an extra set of floor plans. Choose a starting point for joist layout that minimizes subfloor waste. A good place to start is a 90° corner of the largest section of the floor, where the two longest perpendicular walls meet. The smaller floor sections will blend into the larger layout. Measure the layout on the plans to match the joist spacing specified by the designer or the span tables so joist location will be as accurate as possible on a small scale.

Draw a line for each joist, header, and in-floor beam. Different colored pencils work well to differentiate each joist length and make it easy to use the plan for accurately ordering material later.

FLOOR FRAMING

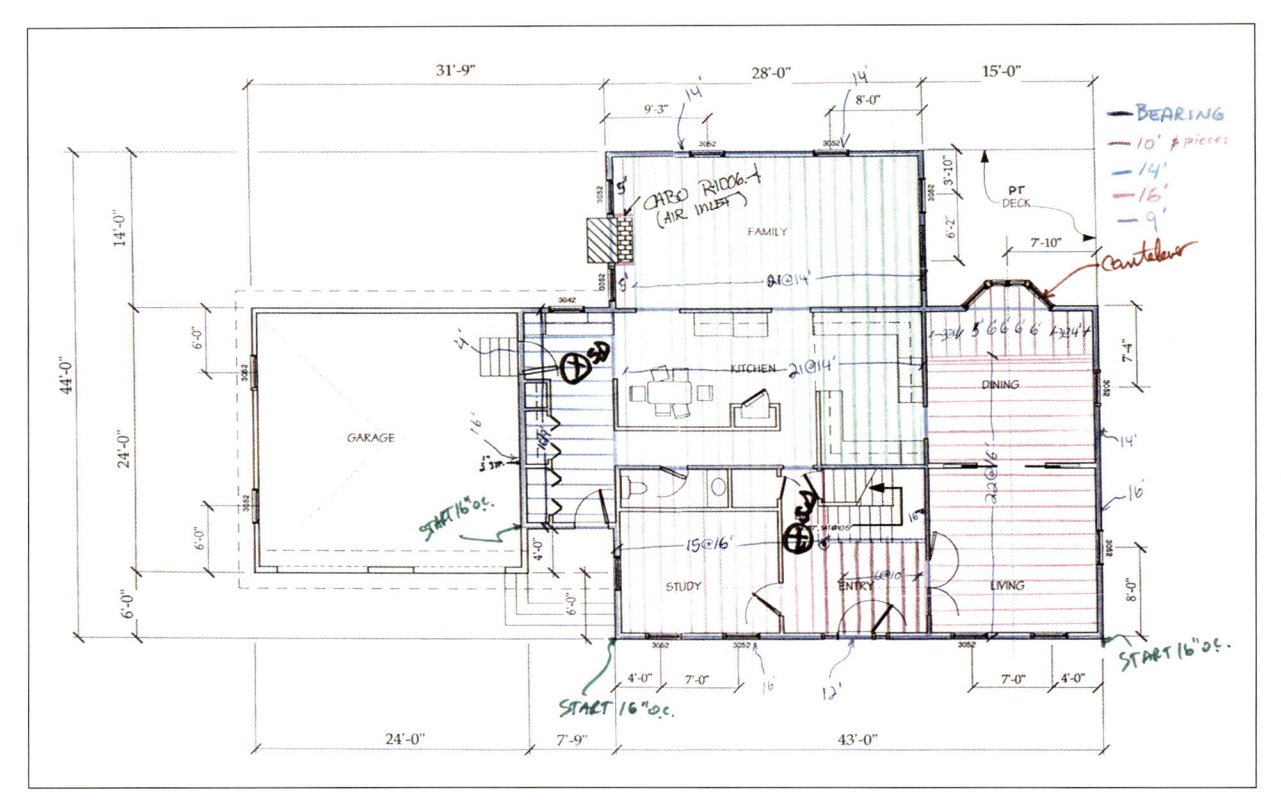

Before any lumber is ordered, a detailed framing plan should be drafted. The plan exposes potential problem areas—such as bearing walls, plumbing routes, and floor openings—that require special attention. Joist lengths are color coded for ordering and then for pre-cutting on site. (Photo by Roe A. Osborn, courtesy *Fine Homebuilding* magazine, © The Taunton Press, Inc.)

Other colors for headers and tail joists make them stand out too. Highlight details like stair openings, HVAC chases, and load-bearing joists.

Consider everything that can interfere with common joist layout and indicate them on your detailed floor-framing plan. The list includes HVAC risers and duct pathways, plumbing drains and vents, chimney chases, masonry chimneys, radon vent pipes, stairway openings, laundry chutes, elevator or dumbwaiter shafts, large electrical conduits, bathroom or kitchen exhaust vent ducts, and floor safes (see the sidebar on p. 62.)

Also write down the precise rough opening dimensions needed by the trade contractor plus any clearance air space required by building code. When in doubt, make the opening a bit larger than needed. Later on, it's easier to decrease the opening size than it is to rip it all apart to enlarge it.

Most openings have a similar configuration, as shown in the drawing on the facing page. Common joists that are interrupted by an opening will need to be supported by a header, which is a short, usually perpendicular section of joist material that is connected to one or more joists at right angles. Generally building codes permit a single header on openings less than 4 ft. and double headers on wider spans. We like to double all headers that will carry more than one cripple or tail joist, which is the short joist that remains when a common joist is interrupted by an opening. There is a limit to the span of a double header. To be on the safe side, it's best to consult your lumber tables or call an engineer before using a header that exceeds 8 ft.

Example of Floor Joist Opening (top view)

Labels: Rim joist, Mudsill, Tail joists (a.k.a. cripple joists), Double trimmers, Double headers, Center beam, Tail joists, Common joists

Lumber and Cut List

Lumber take-off lists are helpful for making up joist orders, and cut lists help designate on-site tasks.

Framing Materials	Qty.	Length
1x3 furring	10	16'
Sill seal	2 rolls	
Center Beam		
2x10	9	16'
	3	14'
Lally columns	6	7' 6"
Sill Plates		
2x6 PT*	16	16'
2x6 studs	14	16'
Walk-Out/Half Walls		
2x6 plates		
2x6 studs		
Header stock		
First-Floor Deck		
Floor Joists		
2x10	10	20'
	54	18'
	14	16'
	42	14'
Rim Joist Stock		
2x10	Included	
Joist Hangers		
2x10 single	24	
2x10 double	11	
Steel bridging	1 box	
Construction glue	12 large tubes	
Subfloor Sheathing		
3/4" T&G OSB*	52	
3/4" T&G fir		

*PT, pressure treated; T&G, tongue and groove; OSB, oriented strand board.

The header is flanked by trimmer joists. Trimmers are common joists located to the sides of the opening. We double up the trimmer joists, unless the header is carrying only one tail joist that is less than 4 ft. long. Our rule of thumb errs on the conservative side. Building codes permit lighter framed openings, but we've found that floor bounce and deflection increase when we exceed our minimum standard.

Draft lumber and cut lists From the marked-up set of plans, draft a materials list for your lumber order. Because the joists are color coded by length on the plans, you can just count off the quantity of each length to order.

Add to that, stock for rim joists, headers, and tail joists. Determine from the rough opening locations and dimensions the precise length of each cut member. Write these lengths on the plans for reference during installation. Include extra pieces (5 to 10 percent of the total count) of each joist length so you can be selective of the ones you use. Crooked, cracked, or otherwise unsuitable joists can be cut up for short pieces or returned to the supplier.

FLOOR FRAMING

Avoid Problems: Check the Details

Have a preliminary meeting (or exchange a few faxes) with the plumber and HVAC contractor to identify any joists (and other framing members) that will pose a problem with their systems. They need to understand the joist layout to plan their work. They also need to see how their work will affect other trade contractors.

Show them your joist layout plan. It's important to determine where competition for space between joists may be so you can untangle a problem now during the planning stage. Sometimes all it takes is shifting a joist sideways a couple of inches to accommodate a duct. (Because of the floor sheathing—you'll learn more about this later in this chapter—some joists cannot be moved.) Other times, joists will have to be "headered" off to make space for plumbing.

Avoid positioning joists directly beneath parallel nonbearing walls even when they're specified by an architect. This is especially important with walls that will contain vents, drains, or ductwork, because the joists beneath the wall will inevitably be cut. When building designers specify joists beneath parallel nonbearing walls for "structural purposes," a joist positioned just $1/2$ in. to the side of the wall will serve to support the wall. This helps the joist evade damage from another sub's reciprocating saw.

When a load-bearing wall runs parallel to the floor joists, designers usually place double or triple joists beneath it to carry the burden. When the plumber or HVAC sub plans to use that same wall for drains or ducts you need to make adjustments.

Identify the exact location of the wall, and space the joists $1/2$ in. beyond its outside edges. Then use solid blocking between the joists every 2 ft. or so beneath the wall (see the drawing below).

It's also good practice to double-up the joists beneath large bathtubs and whirlpools, if the fixture will sit mid-span of the joists. The doubled joists support the extra load imposed by a water-filled tub.

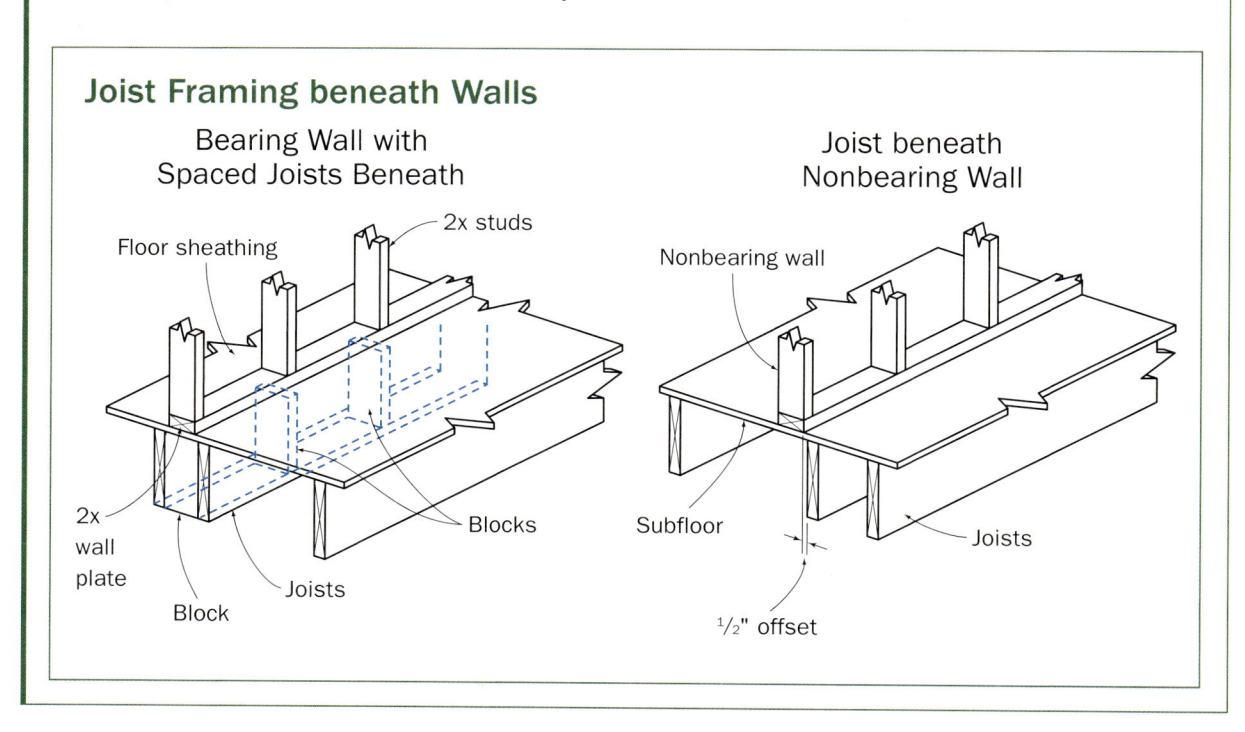

Joist Framing beneath Walls

Bearing Wall with Spaced Joists Beneath

- 2x studs
- Floor sheathing
- 2x wall plate
- Block
- Joists
- Blocks

Joist beneath Nonbearing Wall

- Nonbearing wall
- Subfloor
- Joists
- $1/2$" offset

Mark all the joist layout details first, such as stair openings, HVAC chases, and in-floor beams. Highlight them in crayon to be sure the rest of the crew doing the joist installation takes notice.

Now draft a separate cut list for the lengths of all headers, tail joists, blocking, joists that butt one another over the center beam, joists that fit between two rim joists, and other joist parts. The list will be useful on site to delegate work.

Save the marked-up floor plan for use on the job site to direct the different length joists to the appropriate area with just a glance. Follow your sketched layout to mark out the joist and detail locations onto the mudsill, plates, and beams. The plans will also be useful for laying out rough openings and other distinct parts of the floor system.

Marking the joist layout

We take great care installing and adjusting mudsills, center beams, and load-bearing walls to match the dimensions on the plans. Everything is set level and square so the floor deck will be precise. If a floor deck is supposed to be 48 ft. long don't settle for 47 ft. 11¾ in. on one end and 48 ft. ⅝ in. on the other. The closer the floor deck is built to the dimensions on the plans, the easier the rest of the framing process will be; and the results will be better, too.

Marking the rough openings of special details Before beginning the joist layout on the mudsills and beams, brace and string the carrying beams if you didn't already during the beam installation. Leave the lines up after the beams are straightened to check again after the joists go on (see "Straightening and Bracing the Beam" and "Setting the Beam Height" in chapter 3).

Mark out the special details before you lay out the common joists. Frequently, the details will include specific joists, headers, double joists, or tail joists that fall on or very close to a common joist. By knowing the location of all the details before you mark the common joists, you won't have to cross out parts of your layout and leave confusing lines. The details indicate locations of things such as chimney and stair openings, cantilevers, plumbing fixtures of concern, HVAC chases, and in-floor beams. Lumber crayons are useful to mark these details. Crew members are alerted by the bold crayon that something is different.

One person should do the layout for the joists to ensure consistency. Layout errors due to simple miscommunication can slow the joist-setting process. Clearly mark, directly on the mudsill or beam, the lengths of any headers or tail joists that need to be cut to length for an opening. If everything is marked out on the mudsills and beams, it doesn't matter which member of your crew follows behind the layout person to install the

FLOOR FRAMING 63

Mark rough openings that cross a carrying beam precisely. Make equal marks on the opposite mudsills and snap chalklines across the beam. This is more accurate than measuring a third time along the beam.

The blue string was stretched between the common joist layout marks on the opposite mudsills. This gives a precise starting point to mark the joist layout on the center beam.

joists, because the layout is obvious and easy to understand. The lengths of the parts should correspond to those marked on the detailed plans and the lumber cut list.

To mark rough openings that cross a center beam, such as a stair opening, make equal marks on the opposite mudsills and snap chalklines across the beam. This is more accurate than measuring a third time along the beam.

Make notes where tub and toilet drain outlets will be located. Later, if you find one falls on a common joist center, mark the joist location to one side of the drain or the other. Allow an extra 1 in. for clearance beyond the width of the drain. Be sure to measure and mark the joist location on the opposite wall or beam, so the off-center joist position won't be overlooked on that side.

Marking the layout for common joists There are three steps to marking the layout for common joists: Making marks for the joist layout, drawing a square line across the mudsill or plate to highlight the mark, and making an X on the side of the line to indicate the joist location.

Starting from the end of the building that you determined on the layout plan to be the best starting point, make marks ¾ in. shy of each 16-in. symbol on the measuring tape, presuming a 16-in. on-center layout (see "Marking Layout Spacing" on p. 66). Do the same thing on the opposite mudsill or wall, starting from the same end of the building.

Any joists that fall on or within 1 in. or 2 in. of special features, such as a double joist at the stair or chimney opening, are redundant and can be omitted unless there's a special reason to include them, such as their falling at either a 4-ft. or 8-ft. increment, which corresponds to sheathing layout. The on-center joist layout continues through areas where tail joists rest to indicate their position.

Snap a chalkline at the first layout marks on the front and back mudsills across any intermediate bearing walls or beams. The chalk marks left on the intermediate supports give you a reference to continue the layout. This helps keep a uniform starting point for the layout at the internal bearing points so the joists will line up straight from front to back and make subflooring installation easier. Measure and mark the rest of the beam 16 in. on center (o.c.) from that starting point.

Next, draw a square line across the mudsill, plate, or beam at each common joist layout mark and make an X on the side of the line that you want the joist to line up to. The lines and X's make it clear to other workers where to place each joist.

When you encounter stair, chimney, HVAC, or other openings that have headered-off tail joists (also known as cripple joists) use a different symbol than an X to indicate which side of the line the tail joist goes. Use a T or C, so the joist installers will understand they won't be installing full-length joists. Write the measurement of the piece right on the mudsill or plate to communicate clearly with the people doing the assembly.

The joists in the first section (or front section) of the house will be set ahead of the square mark. *Ahead* means on the side of the layout line in the direction you pulled the tape measure when you made the marks. So when you install the subfloor sheathing, one end of the first 8-ft. sheet of floor sheathing will line up with the outside edge of the rim joist and the other end will fall on the center of the sixth floor joist in. Mark the X ahead of the layout lines for this section.

The second section (or back section) of joists is on the opposite side of the center beam. The X marks for the joists here will be set behind the layout lines (commonly referred to as "X back"). The joist layout is set back 1½ in. to adjust for the overlap between the joists where they meet

When marking the layout for floor openings that will have headered-off tail joists (also known as cripple joists), use a different symbol than an X to indicate which side of the line it goes. The T or C tells the joist installers they won't be installing full-length joists.

FLOOR FRAMING 65

Marking Layout Spacing

To mark an "on-center" (o.c.) layout you need to know two things: the thickness of the joist stock and the spacing between joists. For the purposes of this description, we'll consider standard 2x stock to be 1½ in. thick and the spacing to be 16 in. on center. By setting one edge of the joists ¾ in. (half the thickness of the 1½-in. stock) shy of each 16-in. mark, the center of each joist will be set on center. Subfloor sheathing panels are 8 ft. long, and the panels' edges will fall on the center of a joist without the need for trimming the first sheet in a row.

An easy way to mark a layout for on-center spacing is to measure from a starting point (the end of mudsill or end of wall plate, for instance) and make a mark at 15¼ in. Draw a square line across the plate at the mark and make an X forward of the line to indicate on which side of the square line the joist will rest. Drive a small nail on the line and hook the end of a tape measure onto it. Stretch the tape out along the mudsill or plate. Now make a mark at each 16-in. symbol on the tape, making your way down the sill. Square off the marks and make Xs drawn in the same manner as the first.

The layout process is the same for other on-center spacings. Measure and mark the first layout point ¾ in. shy of the first spacing point, be it 12 in., 19.2 in., or 24 in. Drive a nail and continue from there.

When you use lumber other than standard 2x stock, you'll have to adjust for the width of the material before you start your layout. Engineered I-joists are a good example of this. I-joists commonly come 1¾ in. and wider. Mark the first layout point back half the thickness of the joist. If the joist is 2¼ in. thick your first mark would be 1⅛ in. back from the on-center point. Then drive a nail, hook the end of your tape on the nail, and continue from that point.

Stretch a tape measure from the corner of the mudsill or top plate where the joist layout begins. Make marks for the side of each common joist. (Photo by Roe A. Osborn, courtesy *Fine Homebuilding* magazine, © The Taunton Press, Inc.)

You may find it faster to just hook the tape to the end of the plate and mark the layout without driving a nail into the first line and re-indexing the tape. To do this, just mark each on-center point half the joist thickness back. This especially saves time when laying out short plates.

You'll need to make one modification to this process on most projects when marking out the second, or opposite, section of floor joists to the first section you laid out. If you marked the joists

over the center beam or wall (see the drawing on p. 68).

You could keep all the joists on the same side of the layout lines, if you took the time to trim each one so they matched butt to butt over the beam. But this is a lot of extra work and usually not worth the effort. We'll examine how setting the second series of joists back 1½ in. affects the placement of subfloor panels later in this chapter, when we get to subflooring.

Some buildings are extra deep and have three sections of joists with two center beams. In this case, the third section of joists would be set ahead (X ahead) of the mark, matching the first section.

The two outside mudsill plates need only one square line and an X to indicate on which side of

Draw a square line to indicate the side of each of the common joists marked out, and scribe an X on the side of the line where the joist will rest. (Photo by Roe A. Osborn, courtesy *Fine Homebuilding* magazine, © The Taunton Press, Inc.)

Clearly mark out the joists that will lap over the center beam with multiple lines. A single line will be obscured when joists are placed. Also indicate precisely where each joist will sit with Xs made toward the front or rear of a beam. F and R symbols can also be used to avoid confusion. (Photo by Roe A. Osborn, courtesy *Fine Homebuilding* magazine, © The Taunton Press, Inc.)

out the same way with the X ahead of the on-center lines, there would be a conflict on the center beam or wall where opposite joists meet. To avoid this problem, mark the X on the opposite side of the line. You will have to trim the first sheet of subfloor sheathing 1½ in. shorter, but it's easier than cutting all the floor joists to butt one another over the beam or wall.

The same process used to lay out floor joists is used to lay out wall plates for stud locations and to lay out roof rafters and trusses.

FLOOR FRAMING 67

the line the joist rests. Internal beams and walls, where joists from adjoining sections overlap, need additional lines to indicate the outside edges of the joists. A single line would be obscured beneath the lapped joists.

Draw a minimum of two or, better yet, three lines to indicate the sides of both joists lapping at the beam. Mark Xs toward the front and the back edges of the beam or wall between these lines to avoid confusion of where to set the joists coming from front or back. Sometimes, instead of Xs, we write an F for "front" and an R for "rear." Whatever delineation you use, it's important to make it clear to all crew members which side of the lines you are using for joist placement.

No matter whether you're marking out a simple joist system without cumbersome details or a complicated floor system, it's important to be as clear and accurate as possible. Don't leave anything to question regarding location of the special details or the length of pieces. Workers that

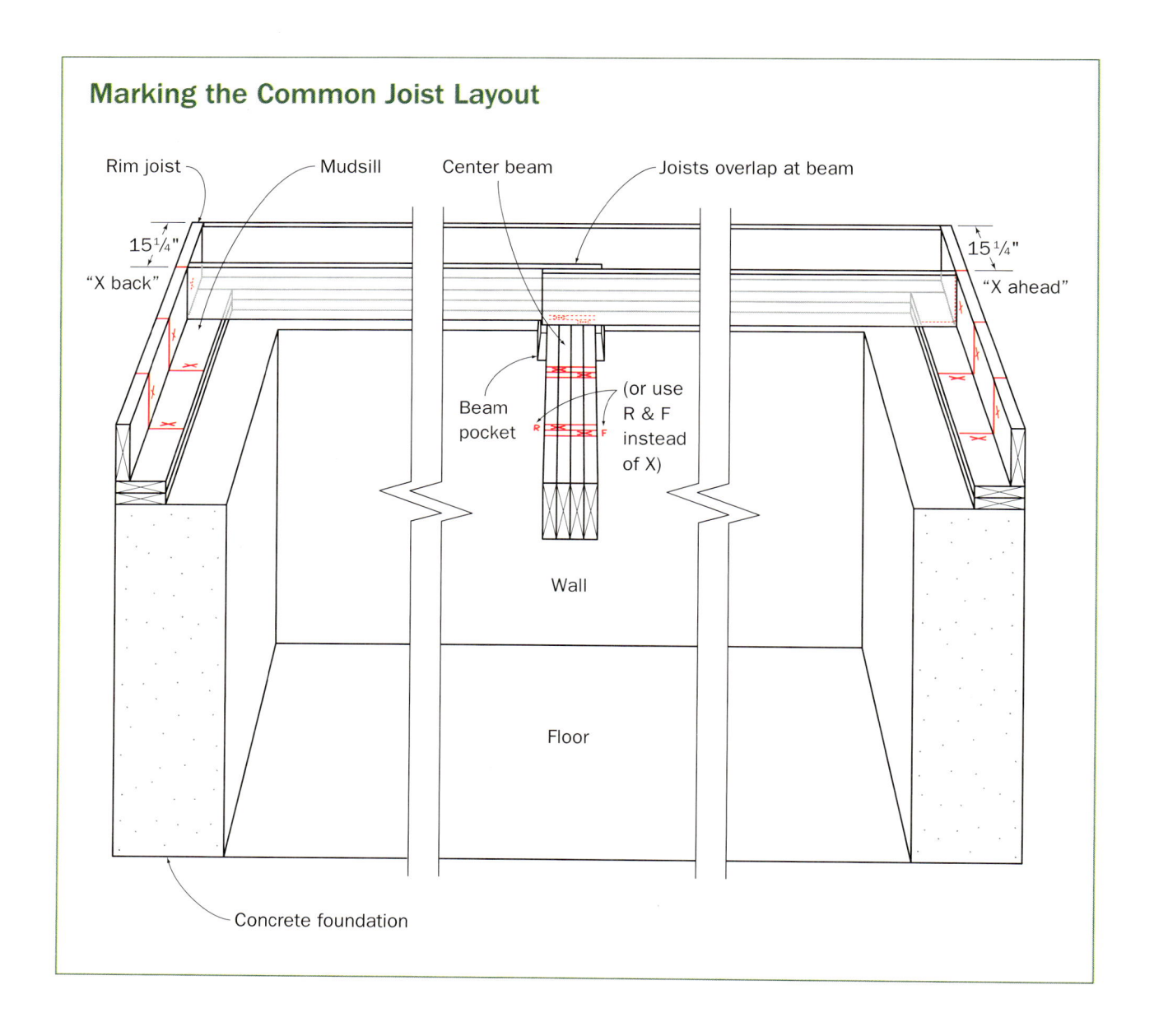

Marking the Common Joist Layout

- Rim joist
- Mudsill
- Center beam
- Joists overlap at beam
- 15 1/4"
- "X back"
- 15 1/4"
- "X ahead"
- Beam pocket
- (or use R & F instead of X)
- Wall
- Floor
- Concrete foundation

68 CHAPTER FOUR

follow behind you may have only the benefit of your markings to instruct them how to assemble the floor.

Framing Joists for Conventional Floor Decks

Installing joists is actually a rapid task, especially if you made up lumber orders and cut lists. You can keep several workers going on different tasks all at once and out of each other's way. The first step is to wrap the perimeter of the building with the rim joist, then transfer square marks up onto the rim joist to orient the ends of the joists to plumb. While the rim's going on, others can cut headers and tail joists for the basic details like stair openings and HVAC chases. Then the joists can be installed and sheathed to form the floor deck. But the first thing to do is look through the lumber pile and decide what each piece can be used for based on its quality (see the sidebar on p. 70). Once you've culled through the lumber you can start installing the rim joists.

Installing rim joists

Rim joists are known by many different names: ribbon, box band, box closure, band joist, and header joist. Rim joists go around the outer perimeter of the mudsill (or the top plates of exterior walls), and they serve several purposes. Nailing through the rim joist into the perpendicular floor joists keeps the floor joists from rotating. The rim joist serves a structural purpose, too; it transfers loads from the wall or roof above to the wall or mudsill below. It also closes the floor area along the outside edge parallel to the floor joists.

Rim joists are sometimes used at the transition point where joists change direction within the floor system; again, to prevent joist rotation, to transfer loads, and to serve as a break point for the subfloor edges.

Select straight stock for the rim joists, so that a crown in the lumber doesn't leave a space between the rim and the plate or mudsill. If a crowned piece is used, it may eventually settle under the weight of the house, causing problems later. When straight stock is scarce, you can make a saw cut in the middle of the rim joist about two thirds the way across the board and push the joist

The rim joist is nailed flush with the outside edge of the mudsill and/or top plate of walls. It closes the perimeter of the floor joist system and prevents the ends of the joists from rolling until the subfloor is installed. (Photo by Roe A. Osborn, courtesy *Fine Homebuilding* magazine, © The Taunton Press, Inc.)

FLOOR FRAMING **69**

Selecting Joist Stock

Every piece of sawn dimensional lumber has a crown. It's the natural curve each piece takes on after being cut from a log. To determine the crown of a joist, hold the joist on edge and look down it to determine which way the crown goes. On some joists, the crown is difficult to determine. You have to flip the joist over to confirm the crown's direction and severity. Once you determine the direction of the crown, make an arrow mark or a V on the side of the joist with crayon so it's clear. The arrow or V should point to the convex edge of the joists. Stack crowned joists with the crowns facing the same way. Set aside joists with excessive crowns, more than $1/4$ in. over 10 ft., and cut them for headers and tail joists later.

Sometimes we encounter a unit of lumber with so many pieces that exceed our $1/4$-in. maximum standard crown that we're forced to make adjustments. In these situations we grade each joist with an A, B, or C designation and group them together during installation. If we didn't make this extra effort, we could end up with a straight A joist next to a $3/8$-in. crown—a C joist—then back to an A, leaving a washboard effect in the floor and making the installation of the tongue-and-groove subflooring next to impossible.

A joists work well for rim joists and beneath tile areas like kitchens and baths. B's go beneath hardwoods, and C's can be used under areas getting carpet, where larger-than-average crowns won't be noticeable.

We only use kiln-dried (KD) lumber for floor joists. KD lumber is less likely to move or change shape over time than green lumber. And because it's preshrunk, the drywall won't settle much, tiles won't tend to crack, and doors and windows won't bind, unlike in new homes framed with green stock. You may find the extra cost for the KD lumber worth it.

We use the same crowning and lumber-grading methods to select wall studs, ceiling joists, and roof rafters.

Each piece of dimensional lumber usually has a slight warp in the height, called a crown. Prepare the joists for installation by eyeing and marking the crown on each one. Install joists with the crowns facing upward. (Photo by Roe A. Osborn, courtesy *Fine Homebuilding* magazine, © The Taunton Press, Inc.)

Dimensional lumber can be purchased as either green (GRN) or kiln dried (KD). Grade stamps printed on each piece of lumber designate the species and grade of the wood and note whether it is green or dried.

Rim joists that run parallel with the floor joist direction can function as in-floor headers over window and door openings. Provided the rim doesn't break over the opening, a single rim joist can carry the wall weight above narrow openings. For wider spans, double-up the rim. (Photo by Roe A. Osborn, courtesy *Fine Homebuilding* magazine, © The Taunton Press, Inc.)

Select and install straight rim joists so the bottom edge makes full contact with the plate or mudsill. When straight stock is scarce, make a saw cut in the middle of the rim joist about two thirds the way across the board and push the joist down to the plate. (Photo by Roe A. Osborn, courtesy *Fine Homebuilding* magazine, © The Taunton Press, Inc.)

down to the plate. Because the rim joist is supported along its whole length by the mudsill, cutting partway through it doesn't jeopardize its integrity.

Rim joists can function as in-floor headers over window and door openings. In-floor headers allow you to skip the traditional header and jack studs for openings in exterior walls running parallel to the joist direction. Provided the rim doesn't break over the opening, a single rim joist can carry the wall weight above short openings. For a wider span, such as a sliding glass door, double-up the rim over the opening. This method uses a little less lumber when framing openings, but the primary goal is to increase the thermal efficiency of the wall (see also chapter 5).

Check the end of every rim joist and, if needed, cut it square. Square ends are especially critical at the corners for maintaining the floor's dimensions (see the photo on p. 69). We will go back later to adjust the corners, but having the rim joists meet square from the outset makes the job easier.

ADVICE

Cutting the Rim Joist Stock

We used to take extra care to cut the rim joist stock to break on the center of a joist layout. Because the structural panels that sheathe the wall extend down to cover and secure the joints completely there isn't any real benefit to breaking rim seams on joists. However, on projects that won't be receiving structural panel sheathing, we recommend cutting the rim stock to break at the end of a joist or blocking the joint.

FLOOR FRAMING

Installing the rim joists is simply a matter of toenailing them into the mudsill with 12d nails. Make sure that the edge of the rim joists is absolutely flush with the mudsill. Once all of the rims are in place, square up all the layout lines from the mudsills or plates onto the inside of the rim joists.

Preparing joists for installation

While some of the crew installs the rim joists, others can continue crowning the joists and checking the ends that will butt the rims for square. If needed, trim one end square so it won't push or pull the rim joist out of plumb when it's installed.

At the same time, framing members for special rough opening details in the floor can be cut and grouped into "kits." For the short lengths, cut up joist stock with excessive crowns. When a kit is finished and clearly marked, place it near the location of the rough opening, ready for installation.

Some jobs have joists that must be cut to length to fit between two rim joists or between a rim and an in-floor beam. Cut these joists $1/16$ in. short to prevent bowing the rim joists out and make sure both ends are trimmed square. Once cut, stack them outside the foundation close to where they'll be installed.

Installing the joists involves both detail and production work. Designate one or two people to take on the slower task of installing all of the special rough opening details and leave the rest of the crew to the production work of installing the common joists.

Detail work Most of the details you'll encounter will be to create openings in the floor for chimneys, stairs, etc. and will follow the same configuration as shown in the drawing on the facing page.

To minimize floor squeaks, which are common at joist/header connections, we follow a nailing sequence to connect the members of a floor rough opening. Steel joist hangers add to the

Metal joist hangers connect joists to beams and headers. Select hangers sized for the joists being installed.

strength of the connections but may not be required by your building code.

First position the inner trimmers and locate the header. If the header is a double, first install the one that will connect to the tail joists. Drive five 12d or 16d spikes through the trimmers and into the ends of the first header layer. Next, mark the location of the tail joists on the header and connect them in the same fashion. Nail the second piece of the header through to the first piece and then butt-nail through from the trimmers. Finally, add the second trimmers to the assembly and nail them securely to the first along the top and bottom edge 12 in. to 16 in. apart.

Often there will be flush in-floor beams set along a center load-bearing wall. This allows the ceiling beneath the joists to carry flush through without being interrupted by a dropped beam. Set the beams in place at the same time as the rim joists and transfer the joist layout onto them. The joists that fit between in-floor beams and rim joists will have to be cut to length, because they can't overlap the beam. After the beams have been straightened, take the measurements for the joists and mark them clearly on the plate or beam. Deduct an extra $1/16$ in. from the measurements to allow the joists to slip into place without pushing the rim out of place.

Framing Sequence for Floor Joist Opening

Layout marks
First (inner) trimmer
First header piece
Tail joist
Tail joist
First trimmer

Step 1. Nail through inner layer of trimmer into outer layer of header.
Step 2. Nail through outer layer of header into tail joists.

Step 3. Nail through inner layer of trimmer into inner layer of header.
Step 4. Nail through inner layer of header into outer layer of header.

Step 5. Nail outer layer of trimmer to inner layer.
Step 6. Nail hangers onto header/trimmer connections and tail joist/header connections.

Note: Each part should be flush at the top as you assemble.

FLOOR FRAMING

Set the joists inside the rim joists, flat on the plates and across the center beam or wall. Face all the crowns in the same direction, so the joists can be easily rolled up and nailed to the rim. (Photo by Roe A. Osborn, courtesy *Fine Homebuilding* magazine, © The Taunton Press, Inc.)

Joists that lap across the center beam or wall are nailed together with four to five spikes driven through the wood diagonally. Align the joists on top before nailing. Toenail the joists to the beam or plate with three or four spikes on the layout lines. Install shims under any joists that need to be raised. (Photo by Roe A. Osborn, courtesy *Fine Homebuilding* magazine, © The Taunton Press, Inc.)

Production work Once the common joists are crowned, carry them to the area where they'll be installed. Set the joists inside the rim joists on top of the mudsill and across the center beams. Lay the joists flat on the mudsill with all the crowns pointing in the same direction. If the crowns are all facing the same direction, it is easy to walk along the mudsill and tip them upright and into position. Place and install only one section (front or back) of joists reaching over a beam or wall at a time; otherwise the joists will clutter the beam and make rolling them in place difficult.

Work the joists on the rim end, rolling each one upright with the crown up. Nail each joist through the rim with three to four 16d nails. Then drive three toenails through each into the mudsill. If a joist is shorter in height than the rim, lift it up flush with the top of the rim and through nail it only. Shim beneath it before toenailing it down to the plate.

When we encounter a joist that's $1/4$ in. or more taller than the rim, we prop it up on top of the rim and trim the excess off the bottom. The cut should run about 2 ft. or so along the length, gradually tapering down to nothing.

After the first section of joists is fastened, you can move onto the opposite section and fasten them in the same manner. Don't yet nail any of the joists to the beam or to one another where they lap over a beam.

When all the joists are nailed to the perimeter rim joists, recheck the strings set up earlier to straighten all the interior center beams and walls

> ## ADVICE: Large Overlaps Can Result in Floor Squeaks
>
> *We limit how far floor joists overlap where they meet over a beam. There's no code limiting the overlap. You can overlap joists as far as you like, but there's a downside when you do. The bigger the overlap between opposite joists, the more likely squeaks will develop. When you walk across the middle of a room, the joists beneath you deflect downward. The end that cantilevers the beam or wall rises a little. The slight motion and friction at the lap joint can cause squeaks. To avoid this problem, we trim all joists so none overhangs the bearing point by more than 4 in. This leaves the lap between joists about 1 ft. long, depending on the width of the beam. There's no benefit to making a perfect cut when trimming the overlap, so we just eyeball the cut and zip through the joist with our circular saws.*

as well as any exterior frame walls. The beams and walls may have been bumped out of adjustment during the joist installation. Be sure to restraighten them now.

When you're satisfied that everything is straight, walk the beams and nail the overlapping joists to each other. If one joist is not as tall as its mate, lift it so they're flush on top before nailing. Slip a shim under the short joist. Fasten the overlapping joists together with four to five spikes driven diagonally so that the nail points don't protrude from the other side.

Toenail the lapped joists down to the beam or plate with three or four spikes on the layout lines. Here you can see the benefit of drawing multiple lines for these joists during layout; with only one line, you'd have difficulty orienting the joists to position.

Each joist must bear a minimum of 1½ in. at each end, and there must be a positive connection between opposing joists where they meet over a wall or beam. There are three basic ways to make a connection between joists at these points. The most common is to lap the opposing joists by a minimum of 3 in. Another method is to make a splice with either a wood block or steel connector plate to bridge across the joint. Finally, the subfloor sheathing can span across the joist joint by a minimum of 3 in.

Recessed beams in a floor system

A recessed beam can be designed to accept the floor joists in several configurations but there are two underlying support systems. The joists can rest on a ledger nailed to the bottom edge of the beam or they can be supported in joist hangers nailed to the beam. Before the advent of joist hangers, the ledger system was more common than it is today.

Ledger system The ledger system is probably the faster of the two systems to install, but a little planning is needed first. The floor joists must have a continuous positive connection across the beam. There are three ways to link joists across an in-floor beam. The subfloor sheathing can span across the beam and catch the opposite joist by at least 3 in. Second, you can drop the beam enough to allow the minimum of a 2x2 scab block to link the joists together. Or you can nail a steel strap across the top of the opposite joists.

Determine the height of the top of your beam based on your choice for the joist link (subfloor, scab block or steel strap). Add an additional minimum of ⅛ in. of space between the bottom of the joist link and the top of the beam to adjust for differential shrinkage. This will prevent the beam from forcing a hump in the floor. Leave a minimum of ¼ in. of space if you use an engineered-lumber beam, because it is unlikely to shrink.

Sometimes your joists and beam will be made of the same height stock. If you choose to use the subfloor or steel options to link your joists, then you'll actually have to drop the beam to allow for the ledger to be fastened. This is okay but the

Connecting Joists across a Beam

Floor Sheathing Method

- 3" minimum
- Sheathing bridges beam.
- 1/8" space
- Joist
- Ledger
- Beam

2x2 Block Method

- 2x2 scab block
- 1/8" space

Metal Strap Method

- Metal strap
- 1/8" space

Joist Hanger System

- Floor sheathing
- 1/8" space

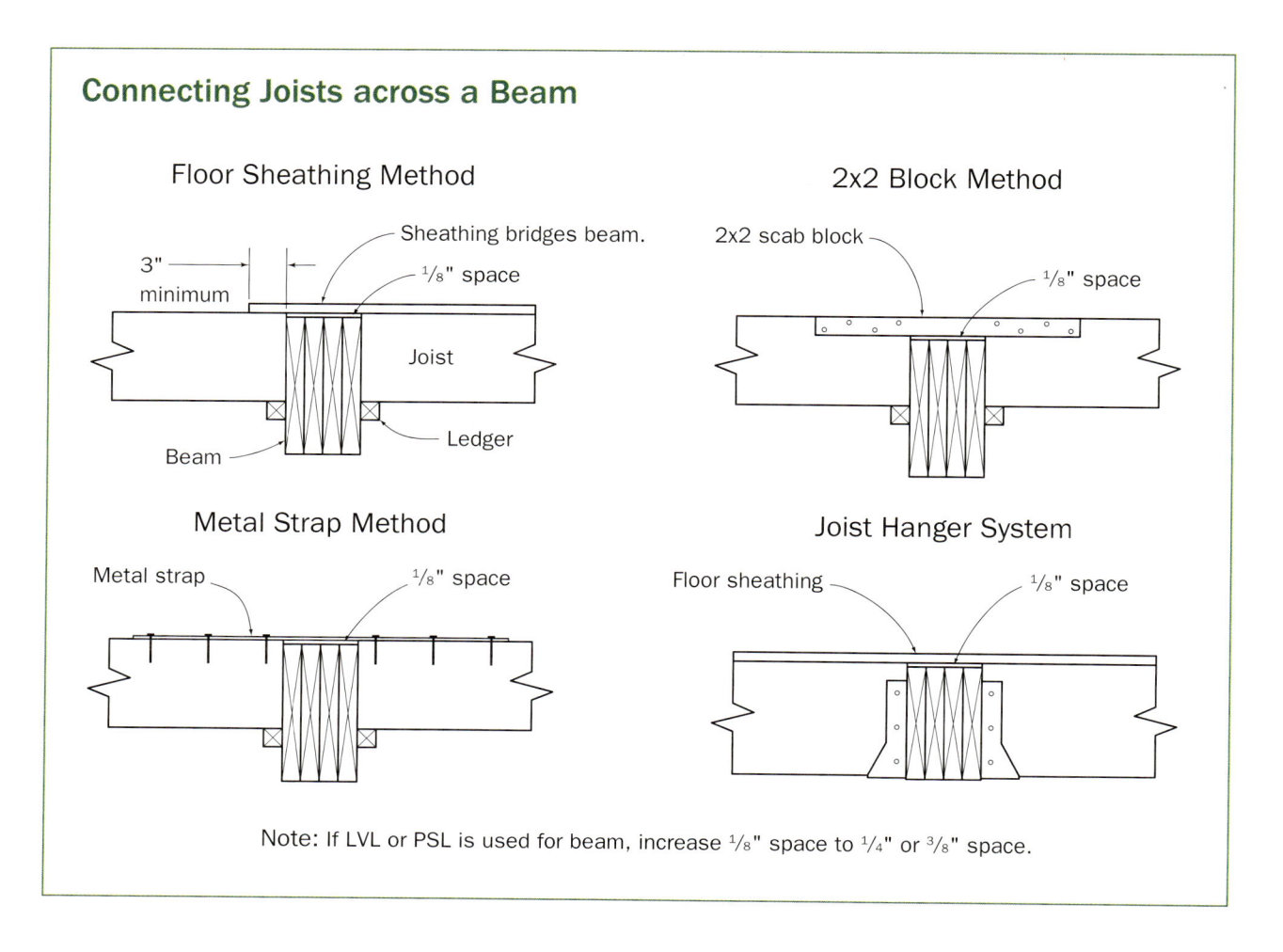

Note: If LVL or PSL is used for beam, increase 1/8" space to 1/4" or 3/8" space.

2x2 scab block may be a better option, because it will reduce the chance that the top edge of the joists will twist.

Set the beam in place then level and straighten it with temporary posts and braces. Mark the joist layout onto both sides of the beam and snap a chalkline to mark the top edge of the ledger. To do this, pull the line tight across the top of the mudsill from one end to the other. If the beam is longer than 30 ft., raise the middle of the chalkline 1/8 in. to compensate for the natural sag in the string.

Nail at least a 2x2 size ledger on both sides of the beam beneath the chalkline. Drive a minimum of three 16d spikes roughly beneath each joist location. You may have to predrill for these nails; otherwise, they may split the ledger because they are so close together.

Measure and cut the floor joists between the rim joist and the beam. Err on the side of short rather than forcing joists into position and pushing the rim joist out. Set the floor joists on the ledger but don't nail them in place yet.

The floor joist height may vary, so you'll have to adjust them to match one another. An easy way to do this is to use the top of the beam as a reference. Measure the distance that the top of several joists extends above the beam and take an average. Cut a gauge block to the average and use it to compare each joist. Some joists will have to be trimmed and some shimmed.

If a joist is higher than the average, remove the excess from the bottom edge of the joist, not the top edge. Taper the cut about 12 in. from the end. If a joist is lower than the average, use shims

To maximize head room in a basement, the beam can be raised into the floor joist system. The joists rest in joist hangers (shown here) or on wooden ledgers fastened to the bottom edge of the beam.

between the bottom of the joist and the ledger. The shims should be dense material like hardboard or plywood rather than shingles, for the same reasons we noted when discussing mudsill shimming.

Now you can toenail the joists to the beam and install 2x2 blocks or steel straps to link the joists that oppose one another across the beam. Don't nail the joists to the ledger. Toenails could split the ledger and weaken it.

Joist hanger system The second method to connect joists to an in-floor beam is with metal joist hangers. This system takes longer to install than the ledger system because of the 12 to 16 nails you'll have to drive into each joist hanger. Joist hangers make a positive connection between the floor joists and the beam so there's no need to install scab blocks or steel straps to link the joists. The joists will thus match the top of the beam.

If your beam is made from the same height stock as the joists then set the bottom of the beam at the same level as the top of the mudsill. If the beam is taller than the joists then drop it down so the top of the beam will equal the top of the joists. Straighten and level the beam; then mark the joist layout onto each side of it.

Measure between the rim joist and the beam and deduct $1/8$ in. The $1/8$-in. space is left at the joist/beam connection to prevent squeaks if there's any joist movement within the hanger. Cut the joists to length and nail a joist hanger to one end of each. To speed installation on beams that are taller than the joists, we nail a temporary cleat, much like the ledger described above but with fewer nails and a little lower than a standard ledger would be.

Set the hanger end of the joists on the cleat where they belong on the layout. Raise the joist $1/16$ in. above a built-up beam and nail the joist hanger into the beam (see the photo at left). The extra $1/16$ in. will allow for a little settling as the joist seats into the hanger. For engineered-lumber beams, raise the joists $1/8$ in. to $3/16$ in. to account for joist shrinkage.

Remove the cleat after all the joist hangers are nailed off. Because the joists are referenced to the top of the beam, it doesn't matter if their heights vary, as it did in the ledger system.

We presumed dimensional lumber joists in our discussion so far. Incorporating beams into engineered I-joists is done exclusively with the hanger system, and the hangers are specially designed for use with I-joists.

Cantilevering conventional floor joists

It is common to encounter floor projections beyond the face of the foundation or exterior wall. These overhangs are known as cantilevers. The floor joists in cantilever situations overhang the mudsill or top plate of a wall. They may or may not bear additional loads from above. When not specified on the house plans we use the "two-thirds in, one-third out" rule of thumb for non-bearing cantilevers when determining how much the cantilevered joist must extend back into the body of the house. On cantilevers that extend out in the same direction that the floor joists run, maintaining the "two-thirds in" is usually not an issue, because the joists extend back to a wall or beam in the middle of the building.

Parallel Cantilevered Joist

(Labels: Common joist, Rim joist, Cantilevered joists, Mudsill, Foundation)

Perpendicular Cantilevered Joists

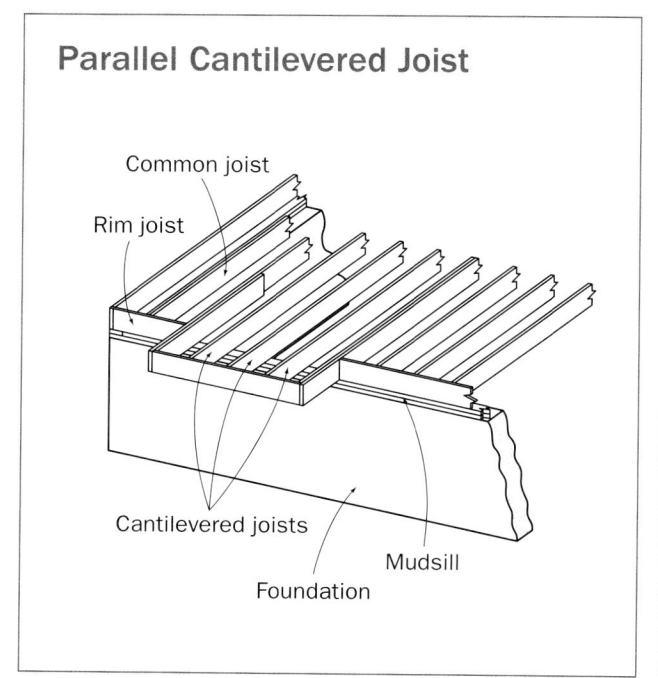

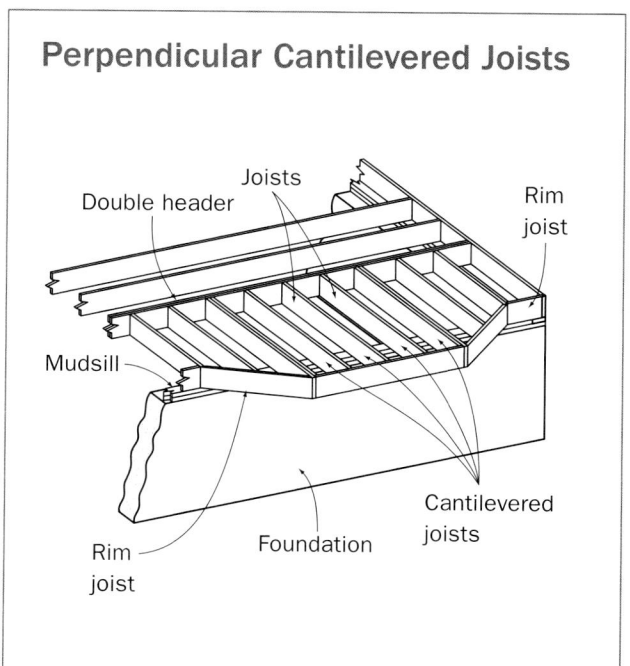

(Labels: Double header, Joists, Rim joist, Mudsill, Rim joist, Foundation, Cantilevered joists)

Simple cantilever—parallel to common joists
As an example of a common cantilever let's look at the 1-ft. overhang typically found on the second floor of a Garrison colonial-style house. On each side of the house where the joists will cantilever, extend the rim joist 10½ in. beyond the outside edge of the mudsill. (Capping the extended joists with a perpendicular rim joist that is 1½ in. thick will bring the total cantilever to 12 in.) Then run a string set on ¾-in. spacer blocks nailed to the ends of the extended rim joists. (We used a similar method with spacer blocks and a string to straighten beams.) Now with the joist layout already marked on the plates, slide each joist out and gauge it to the string with a spacer gauge stick. Next, toenail the joist to the wall plate with three spikes and continue on.

When all the joists are placed and nailed, take a furring strip marked out at the same on-center spacing as the joists and nail it at the outside top edge of the cantilevered joists. The furring indexes the joist spacing so you can handle and nail the rim joist in place without struggling to space the joists too.

Now you can easily nail the rim joist on to the ends of the cantilevered joists. Make sure any joint between rim joists falls on a joist, otherwise install blocks of scrap joist material between the joists and behind the joint for support. Flush the top of the rim with each joist before you nail them together. It may take two people to do this—one to lift or lower the rim and the other to nail. Let the rim run a little beyond the end rim joists. Square and measure to determine the exact corner points and cut off the excess with your circular saw.

Cantilevers perpendicular to the common joists When a cantilever extends out in the opposite direction of the joists, you have to set an in-floor header back two-thirds the distance of the overhang into the floor joist system. The in-floor header is usually made by doubling or tripling one of the common joists and hanging perpendicular joists from the header. (The exact number of layers will need to be determined using tables or your building code book for each situation.) We'll use an example of a 2-ft.-deep by 8-ft.-wide angled cantilever to illustrate the

Nail through one layer of the in-floor header to support one end of the cantilevered joists. Later, nail on the additional layers of the header and install joist hangers to secure the connection permanently. (Photo by Roe A. Osborn, courtesy *Fine Homebuilding* magazine, © The Taunton Press, Inc.)

method. This type of cantilever is common for bay windows.

Lay out marks for 16-in. on-center spacing on the mudsill or top plate to be crossed and on the face joist of the header to match. Before precisely locating the bump-out, cut and lay out the top and bottom plates for the walls. While it may sound a little premature, you want to be certain that the window sizes planned for the sides and the face walls will fit and leave enough room inside and outside for trimming off with the specified casing. Although everything looks okay on paper at a $\frac{1}{8}$-in. scale, get full-scale reassurance before ordering the glass.

Now install the rim joist of the uncantilevered sections of the floor system right up to the edges of the first cantilevered joist. While this step is not necessary, we find this detail helpful for securing and plumbing the rim at the inside corner of the bump-out.

Begin by installing the 4-ft.-long, noncantilevering tail joists between the header and rim joist. We prefer to fasten the joists to the header by nailing through the leading layer of the header into the butt ends of the joists. Later, gang up the other pieces of the header and save the joist hanger installation for last. This method of through nailing to connect the header to the joists reduces the chance of squeaks and is similar to the sequence used for floor openings. Next, move onto the cantilevered joists.

The joists in the 4-ft.-long middle section of the cantilever extend exactly $22\frac{1}{2}$ in. (a total of 24 in. with the $1\frac{1}{2}$-in. rim joist) beyond the mudsill. The joists in the angled flanks should be left a little longer than the anticipated final length. To rough gauge the length of these joists, set the bottom plates of the side walls in position and measure. Once all joists are installed, run a string line to straighten the rim joist on top of the mudsill.

Square up the lines you made earlier, indicating the outside of the 8-ft. bump-out onto the face of the rim joist. Install a rim joist on the outer face of the cantilevered joists and let it run long for cutting in place.

Set all the wall plates in position over the cantilevered joists and rim. Beneath the outside corners of the wall plates, square down a cut line that indicates where to miter the rim joist. Draw a line along the wall plates onto the tops of the

FLOOR FRAMING

Lay the wall plates that will sit atop the cantilevered joists into position. Mark the ends of the joists for trimming. (Photo by Roe A. Osborn, courtesy *Fine Homebuilding* magazine, © The Taunton Press, Inc.)

Once the rim joist is installed to close the ends of the cantilevered joists, sheathe the area along with the rest of the floor. (Photo by Roe A. Osborn, courtesy *Fine Homebuilding* magazine, © The Taunton Press, Inc.)

joists beneath. This line marks the perimeter of the bump-out, so remember to draw the cut lines back 1½ in. to allow for the rim joist. A 2x block held on the inside of the line acts as an accurate guide. Draw the cut lines, then square them down. Trim the joists off at 45° bevels; then cut, fit, and nail the angled rim joists.

Now install the rest of the pieces of the built-up header to support the cantilevered joists.

We install two joist hangers on each of the cantilevered joists. One installed right side up and the other, upside down. The theory is that the upside-down hanger prevents the joist from lifting due to the weight of the cantilever. It's a practice we began at the request of a local building inspector and it's one we continue.

For some framing crews, it's routine to block between the cantilevered joists at the mudsill/wall plate. We haven't found the practice useful. We prefer to leave the space open for sliding in insulation later in the construction process.

Squash blocks transfer loads

The loads imposed by the walls, successive floors, and roof have to be transferred through the floor deck to the foundation beneath. We try to construct all of our framing so the studs are aligned over joists allowing the loads to pass directly through. This process is known as stack framing. But sometimes the loads are concentrated so you have to beef up the load path.

For example, the loads from a wall and roof could be concentrated on a jack stud at the end of a wide header for a sliding glass door. If there is

Install squash blocks to transfer concentrated loads through the floor joist system. The grain of the blocks is oriented vertically. The blocks can be installed when framing the floor deck or from beneath after the subfloor is installed. (Photo by Roe A. Osborn, courtesy *Fine Homebuilding* magazine, © The Taunton Press, Inc.)

Before installing the subfloor, nail blocking on the inside edge of the wall plates that run parallel with the joists to carry drywall or ceiling furring below. The blocking can be 2x or 1x stock. Use leftover scraps or material too warped or knotty to frame with.

not a joist directly below the jack stud, the weight could cause the floor sheathing to deflect. Squash blocks transfer the concentrated load from the jack through the floor joist system and to the mudsill, beam, or wall plate below. Squash blocks are 2x blocks cut the same length as the height of the floor joists. They are installed on end alongside the joists with a load point above and midspace when the load doesn't fall on a joist. Using these blocks is a technique we borrowed from our engineered I-joist experience. Since we began using squash blocks in conventional floor decks, we've virtually eliminated drywall cracks around door and window openings.

Install squash blocking after the rims and joists are installed, before sheathing the floor deck. Using the plans you can pinpoint the bearing points of concentrated loads and mark them for blocking. If it's difficult to locate the points now, you can go back later and install them; it just takes a little longer.

Drywall ceiling blocking

Before covering the floor with the subflooring, we like to install blocking to screw the ceiling drywall into along the exterior walls that run parallel to the floor joists. This is an operation you can do later, but it's much easier now.

Gather up any 1x or 2x scraps that are at least 3 in. wide and 1 ft. long. Crooked or split lumber

FLOOR FRAMING

and even delivery clubs are fine to use here and a good way to use otherwise undesirable material. Place the blocks down on top of the mudsill or exterior wall top plate. Let at least 1½ in. of the blocks overhang the inner edge of the plate and use a framing nailer to fasten them in place.

Installing Subfloor Sheathing for Conventional Floor Decks

The subfloor sheathing, also called subflooring or sheathing, is an integral part of the floor joist system. The sheathing, which is plywood sheets or oriented strand board (OSB), gets glued and nailed to the joists. It keeps the joists straight and distributes live loads between adjacent joists. Once sheathed, the floor becomes a "system" and is stronger than the sum of its parts. Sheathing provides a base on which to attach flooring or flooring underlayment. And it keeps us, and our belongings, from falling into the basement. Subflooring is fast production work, but there are a few processes that are critical to installing a strong and squeak-free deck. First, there's a little planning and preparation work.

Preparing for the subfloor sheathing

There are two things to do to prep for subfloor sheathing. First, the floor joist system has to be rechecked and the rim joists straightened. Then you'll need layout lines to start the sheathing process off straight.

Before installing the subfloor sheathing and after the joists are nailed in place and all the openings are framed, double-check the floor deck dimensions and take diagonal measurements to make sure the deck is square. Because the rim joists were installed with square ends at the corners, the measurements should be close. If any measurement deviates more than 1/4 in., tweak the rim in or out to make the adjustment. Work off the same rectangle area you used to square the mudsill.

To prepare for the subfloor sheathing, straighten the rim joists that run perpendicular to the floor joists. Run a string from the rim joist corners and either use your eye or use a square to gauge the rim to the string. Tap the rim in or out until straight. (Photo by Roe A. Osborn, courtesy *Fine Homebuilding* magazine, © The Taunton Press, Inc.)

Place reference strings along all the rim joists running perpendicular to the floor joists. Set nails to hold the string straight up off the rim at each end. Tap the top of the rim in or out until it's straight by eye, or check with a straightedge, and shim with shingles, as necessary. Squaring the joist ends early helps keep these adjustments to a minimum. Rims running parallel to the joists will be straightened later, after the subfloor sheathing is installed.

Most plywood or OSB used for subfloors has tongues and grooves cut into the long edges. The tongues and grooves lock into each other and eliminate the up and down movement at the unsupported edges between joists. They also add to the strength of the floor system.

It is important that the first row of sheets be laid down perfectly straight. If the row isn't straight, you'll have a hard time getting the tongues in the second row to fit into the grooves on the sheets in the first row. It's good practice to start laying down the first row of sheets from a perfectly straight chalkline, rather than just lining up the first row of sheets with the edge of the rim joist. All successive courses of sheathing will be referenced to the first course, so you'll want it nice and accurate.

Mark in 4 ft. 1/4 in. at both ends from the starting rim joist and stretch a chalkline across the joists. The starting rim is usually the same edge you began laying out the mudsill from. Have someone hold his finger on the middle of the line on long runs (particularly if it's windy) so the line stays straight while snapping.

Strike additional chalklines every 47 1/2 in. from there as a glue guide for each row of sheathing; this is the effective width of the panels after the tongue is interlocked to the groove. The chalklines indicate where to stop dispensing the adhesive for each row of sheathing. This helps keep the adhesive off tape measures, tools, and shoes and keeps the joists beyond the sheathing safe to step on.

Laying the subfloor

There are a number of operations necessary for installing a precise subfloor, including setting and nailing the first course of panels, adjusting joist spacing, spreading glue, and nailing off the deck. Other steps, such as adding blocking and cutting the sheathing, are still important but tangential. Getting the first row of subfloor down straight and secure is the key to keeping the rest of the sheets even across the whole floor.

Setting the first course Spread glue from the rim joist to the first chalkline on every joist except the rim joist that runs parallel to the common joists. (You'll glue these parallel rim joists later when you straighten them.) Next, position the first row of sheets with the tongues toward the rim joist. You'll have to drive each

Completely nail off the first course of subfloor sheathing before running additional rows. Otherwise, the sheets may drift off the straight chalkline when the next sheets are driven in place to mate the tongues and grooves. (Photo by Roe A. Osborn, courtesy *Fine Homebuilding* magazine, © The Taunton Press, Inc.)

successive course of panels into the previous ones to get the tongue and groove to mate. The groove edge can handle more abuse than the tongues so face them to the leading edge (the first chalkline).

Set the groove edge of the first sheet even to the chalkline and line the end of the sheet even with the outside of the same rim joist you used to begin your layout. Use a couple of 6d or 8d nails to tack the sheet to the edge of the rim joist. Line the joist that the other end of the sheet falls on equally along the panel edge and tack the groove corner down. The exposed edge of the joist should be an equal 3/4 in. There's no need to measure the distance, just site by eye.

Place the end of the next panel over the half-exposed joist and line up the groove edge with

FLOOR FRAMING 83

Gluing the Subfloor

The importance of spreading glue onto the floor joists is often overlooked. Fastening subfloor sheathing with adhesive in addition to nails or screws provides a more secure bond. This helps the subfloor transfer live loads between adjacent joists and makes the floor stiffer. Glue also reduces floor squeaks.

Spread a generous bead of glue about 3/8 in. wide on the top of each joist. Determine which joists will host the joints between panel ends and spread a double bead of glue there: one for the end of each sheet. Fill the grooves of the sheets halfway up with glue before installing the next row of sheets. Tongue-and-groove seams that are glued together are much stiffer and less likely to squeak than unglued seams. Gluing the joints between panels also seals the air leaks so the subfloor can act as an air barrier between the first floor and the basement or crawl space.

Don't run glue out too far ahead of the sheets. The glue can begin to cure and won't make a good bond between the sheathing and the joists. This is especially a problem on hot, dry days. Don't spread glue for more than one sheet at a time under those conditions.

Winter conditions also warrant special care. Check the working temperature range of the adhesive you plan to use. Scrape ice and snow off the top of joists before spreading the glue. And store tubes of glue inside at night to keep them warm; this improves the workability. On a winter workday, it sometimes helps to park your vehicle in the sun and leave the tubes on your dashboard until you're ready to use them.

Spread a generous bead of glue about 3/8 in. wide on the top of each joist and a double bed of glue on the joists that hold the joints between panel ends. Glue the grooves of the sheets just laid before installing the next row of subflooring.

the chalkline. If there isn't any adhesive along the exposed joist edge, spread another bead before installing the sheet. Leave 1/16 in. to 1/8 in. of space between sheets for expansion, as recommended by the sheathing manufacturer. Often adhesive will ooze between panels and gauge a space anyway. Tack down this second sheet with nails at each corner and continue on with the rest of the row until you reach the rim joist at the other end.

After the row of sheathing is complete, and before starting the next one, hook a tape onto any of the secured joists at the joint between sheets and measure across the others along the groove edge of the sheets. You'll still be able to easily move the joists under the sheet. Push or pull the joist so that its edge lines up with the center marks on your tape measure. Then nail through the sheet into the joist. Nail off the first course of subflooring securely with 8d ring-shank nails so it doesn't shift when you drive together the tongues and grooves of the next set of sheets. It's helpful to use a 4-ft. T-square to guide your nailing so you don't miss the joist beneath.

Don't nail the edges along the rim joists running parallel to the joist direction. They haven't been glued or straightened yet and will need to remain loose until they are. You can drive a couple of nails halfway just to hold the edge in the meantime.

Running subfloor courses You already have the starter course on straight and nailed securely. You probably began the first course with a full 8-ft. sheet so start the next course with a 4-ft. panel. This staggers the end seams on different joists and makes the floor system stronger. Sometimes, as you run a course out, the fall-off material from the other end of the building is close to 4 ft. You can use these sheets as starters for another course and pick up the 32-in. or 64-in. joist position for the break. Or you can plan to use the pieces as fill-in around stairway holes or other openings to minimize waste.

As you install the sheets, lay each one down gently onto the preglued floor joists. Line the tongue edge up with the groove on the previous row and hold it standing on edge. Pivot the groove edge down slowly, working the tongue into the groove of the already glued and nailed sheet. One way to control the sheet without standing on the joists is to stand on the previous row of sheathing and use your hammer claw to extend your reach. Lowering the sheets down carefully keeps the glue bead between the joist and the subfloor where it belongs for better bonding. If you drop a sheet down too fast or crooked, the adhesive may be slapped out of the joint or miss its mark all together.

Use a 2x block 4 ft. to 6 ft. long to cushion the groove edge. Rap on the block with a sledgehammer to drive the tongue and groove edges together. The joints usually won't look completely closed because the tongue bottoms out in the groove and the top plies don't touch. This is okay. Nail the two bottom corners and top corner that butts the previous sheet. Line the leading 4 ft. end up with the joist equally along its length by eye and tack the top edge. Remember not to glue or nail the end rim joists, just tack for now. Later we'll straighten and nail them.

OSB floor sheathing lies flat and the tongues slide easily into the grooves. With plywood subfloor sheathing, you often need an extra person to stand on the seam to flatten the sheet until the tongue enters the groove. Some sheets will be tough to drive together, others will go easily. It's a good idea to check the tongues and

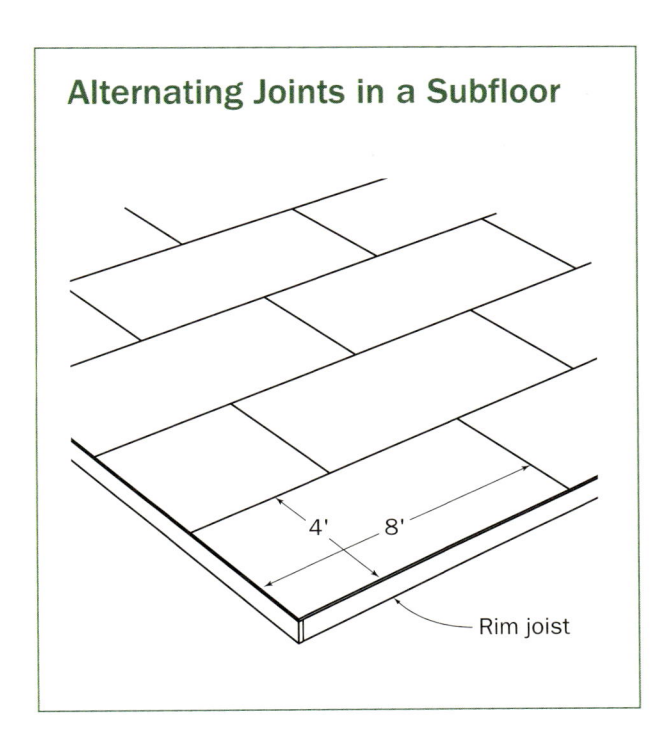

Alternating Joints in a Subfloor

4' 8'

Rim joist

Use a 2x block to cushion the sledgehammer blows that drive the tongues and grooves of the sheets together. Arrows on the joists indicate the direction of the crown. (Photo by Roe A. Osborn, courtesy *Fine Homebuilding* magazine, © The Taunton Press, Inc.)

A 2x block is nailed flush with the top of the joist to support the end of the sheet where the joists overlap. (Photo by Roe A. Osborn, courtesy *Fine Homebuilding* magazine, © The Taunton Press, Inc.)

grooves of each sheet before you set it in the bed of adhesive. Trim off any bad spots in the tongue with a knife and clear out the groove. Waiting too long after filling the groove with glue may make it hard to drive in the next panel, especially on a hot day.

Blocking, floor openings, and other details

When you reach the sheathing course where the joists overlap on a beam or wall, glue and nail a 2x block flush with the top of the joist to support the end of the sheet as needed. You'll have to repeat this every 8 ft. at the end of each sheet in the row. Put a bead of glue on the block before you nail it in place to prevent squeaks.

Before you move on to the next full course beyond the row where the joists lap, make an arrow mark on the pervious sheet of sheathing to indicate the center of each joist. This will make it easier to find the joists and snap chalklines to guide the nailing process.

After laying four or five sheets on a course you may find the leading 4-ft. end of the sheet nearly covers the joist, leaving little room to catch the edge of the next one. This is caused by the space you're leaving between panels. If 95⅞-in.-long subfloor panels are available from your supplier,

Sheets should be spaced 1/16 in. to 1/8 in. apart. Eventually, as the 8-ft.-long sheets are run across the floor joists, the end of a sheet will nearly cover the joist. When this happens, trim about ½ in. off the sheet and continue.

you could try them and avoid the problem. Or, just trim ½ in. off every fifth or sixth sheet as needed.

Whenever sheathing runs by an opening, such as a stair chase or chimney opening, either let the sheathing overhang into the opening or leave a small section out and begin the next sheet beyond the other edge of the opening. Don't glue the trimmer or header joists and only tack the sheathing that covers them initially. These details will be adjusted, glued, and nailed later when the loose rim joists are set.

Because the tongue-and-groove sheets are only 47½-in. wide, there will often be a narrow void at the opposite rim joist; especially on building widths that match full 4-ft. panel increments (24 ft., 28 ft., 32 ft., etc.). Rather than sacrificing several sheets of sheathing for a few inches and their tongues, we cut up scrap pieces of sheathing as fillers. Don't worry about an unsupported edge between sheets; the wall plates will usually cover the joint. If you don't have enough scrap sheathing to use as filler you can use 1x3 furring or 1x6 ledger board to fill the space.

Straighten the rim joists The last step is straightening the rim joists and the trimmers that were left unfastened during the sheathing operation. They were left unnailed and unglued so they could be straightened out later rather than interrupting the momentum of the sheathing production.

Start with a straight reference line to straighten the rim joists. Measure in 1½ in. from the corners at the ends of the rims running parallel to the joist direction and snap a chalkline on top of the sheathing. Move the rim in and out every 4 ft. or so until it measures 1½ in. from the reference line and nail it at that point. Tack the edge and trim any excess sheathing off. Lift the sheathing a little with a flat bar to squirt in adhesive before nailing off the edge every 4 in. to 6 in.

You have to align trimmers at openings in the floor before gluing and nailing, too. Refer back to the plans and measure in from the rim joists to the edges of the openings. Snap a chalkline and trim off any excess subfloor sheathing around the floor openings. Drive nails halfway in on the chalkline, just back from the opening and set up string lines along the inside edge of the trimmers. Pull any of the original tack nails that are holding the sheathing to the trimmers so you can then straighten the edge. Lift the sheathing enough to squirt in some adhesive. Then straighten trimmers to the line and nail the perimeter off. Finally, fill in any missing subfloor around the opening.

Mark the joist centers where they lap one another over the center walls or beams. Later, snap chalklines between the marks and the joist ends to guide the nailing process. (Photo by Roe A. Osborn, courtesy *Fine Homebuilding* magazine, © The Taunton Press, Inc.)

Nailing off sheathing While some crew members are attending to the details, others can nail off the sheathing. After a whole field of sheets is filled in, snap chalklines to indicate joist locations, taking care to shift the lines where the joists overlap or change direction. We use blue chalk, because it's less permanent than the red that we'll use later to mark wall and partition lines; this avoids confusion.

Have only one person do the nailing so he can keep track of what he's nailed off and what's left so there are no skipped rows. Space 6d to 8d nails 6 in. to 12 in. apart in the middle of each sheet and 4 in. to 6 in. along the edges. Check your building code for specific nailing requirements. As

FLOOR FRAMING 87

Successive Floor Decks

On two- or three-story homes, each floor deck is built pretty much the same way as it is for the first floor. The joists are set on top of the wall plates and across a center wall or beam and they're rolled upright and nailed. Then the subfloor goes on. There is one step we take when framing the walls that makes the joist layout easier. Just before lifting the bearing walls that support the next floor we lay out the top plates for the joists. This is quicker than doing the layout from staging. Once the walls are up, you can start in on the process of installing rims. On some occasions, we have tried installing the rims on the walls before lifting them. It hasn't become standard procedure though, because the rims get in the way of the wall-lifting jacks we use. If you have a large enough crew capable of lifting the walls on a project, you may opt to preinstall the rims and save even more time.

you cross the line where the floor joists overlap, draw arrows to indicate the center of each joist.

On hot summer days when the adhesive is curing rapidly, it's a good idea to nail off each row of subfloor rather than waiting until the whole floor is laid down. If you wait, the adhesive may dry before the sheets are nailed and you won't get a good glue bond between the sheathing and the joists (see the sidebar on p. 84).

Framing Floors with I-Joists

I-joists have a number of advantages over dimensional lumber. They are less than half the weight of solid KD lumber. One worker can easily carry a 30-ft.-long, 12-in.-tall joist. We feel lucky when dimensional joists vary less than $1/4$ in. in height; the norm is $3/8$ in. The I-joist height tolerance is within $1/16$ in., so you don't have to worry about trimming or shimming joists to keep your floor flat.

Even KD lumber may shrink or swell after installation, causing floor squeaks, drywall cracks, and nail pops. And as the quality of the trees cut for lumber diminishes so does the conventional

Engineered I-joists are lighter weight, are more dimensionally stable, and are available in longer lengths than common sawn lumber. (Photo by Susan Aitcheson.)

floor joist system. Engineered wood I-joists provide a superior floor system. They are dimensionally stable and won't check, split, warp, or twist. Long pieces (20 ft. or more) of dimensional lumber are usually more costly per linear foot than shorter lengths. I-joists are available 40 ft. or longer at no additional per-foot cost. Another advantage of I-joists is that they have equivalent or greater spanning capacities than solid lumber of the same depth. And I-joists are dead straight, so they don't need to be crowned like solid lumber. Holes for utility runs can be cut through I-joist webs more easily than through solid lumber, and the holes can be larger without sacrificing strength; that makes plumbing and HVAC runs easier.

Wood I-joists do cost more than dimensional lumber. Manufacturers claim that their higher cost is offset by the labor savings realized during comparable installations and the avoidance of "call backs." We haven't found any appreciable labor savings using I-joists on custom houses, but they do make a superior floor deck.

Planning and ordering I-joists

Planning and ordering an I-joist system can be done two ways: by the distributor or by you. Simple floor configurations are easy to do yourself following an I-joist guide and span chart from your supplier. But complicated floors may require engineering calculations that you may not be familiar with. Complex floors may require a combination of I-joists and laminated veneer lumber (LVL) or parallel strand lumber (PSL) joists and beams.

We let the distributor develop a layout on our first few projects until we became familiar with the system. Because they usually provide this service free it makes sense; later, as you become familiar with I-joists, you can do your own planning and ordering.

As with a conventionally framed deck, hangers are unavoidable. Take particular care when ordering and installing hangers for this system. It is easy to get confused because of all of the different types of hangers and the loads they are designed for. You wouldn't want to inadvertently substitute a joist hanger for a beam hanger.

Marking I-joist layouts

Marking layouts for engineered-wood I-joists is nearly the same as for conventional lumber. Flanges are usually wider than solid-wood joists so we make adjustments to keep the joists centered on the layout. Flange widths commonly range from $1\frac{1}{2}$ in. to $3\frac{1}{2}$ in. For example, on $1\frac{3}{4}$-in. I-joists, start out by marking $15\frac{1}{8}$ in. rather than $15\frac{1}{4}$ in. as you would for 2x stock. Drive a nail at the $15\frac{1}{8}$-in. mark, hook the tape on the nail, pull your tape along the mudsill, and mark at every 16-in. center. For an I-joist with a $3\frac{1}{2}$-in. flange, make your first mark at $14\frac{1}{4}$ in., drive a nail, etc. Snap a chalkline from the first joist layout front and rear across the center beam(s) and bearing walls to ensure the layout at the midpoints is straight, just as described for conventional joist layouts (see photo on p. 64). Because I-joists are long enough to reach from one side of the mudsill to the opposite side across a center beam, you won't have to set the layout Xs on the opposite sides of the layout line. Lay out the mudsills the same for the front, back, and middle.

The plan you receive from the manufacturer or distributor will note any special conditions that you'll have to pay attention to. Most notable are squash blocking, web stiffeners, solid blocking, rim joist details, cantilevers, flush beams, hanger locations, and midspan blocking. Make special notes on the plates and beams with a lumber crayon when you do the layout, so the joist installers can complete the details.

Installing I-joist rim joists

Just as with conventional floor joists, install the rim joists first. We prefer to use the I-joist manufacturer's rim joist if it's available. (Because of the shrinkage factors of solid lumber, it is not a good idea to use solid lumber as rim joists for an I-joist floor system.) These rims are dimensionally stable, sized to match the I-joist height,

I-Joist Handling and Precautions

Engineered wood I-joist systems are installed in a manner similar to dimensional lumber systems, but there are differences in how they should be handled on the job site, because they are more prone to damage than solid lumber. Here are some do's and don'ts.

- Don't let the delivery driver dump a load of I-joists without taking precautions. The flanges can be damaged when I-joists are dropped onto a rough or rocky surface, and you'll have to cut around the weakened area. A $\frac{1}{2}$-in. chip out of the top of a regular 2x12 won't affect its performance but may ruin the structural integrity of an I-joist. We've seen flanges pop off the webs when a load of I-joists are dropped off a lumber truck. Don't try to glue a flange back on. The repaired joist will eventually fail.

- Stack I-joists on a flat surface. When left in a twisted position on the ground for too long, they'll take on an undesirable shape. The integrity probably won't be affected, but they will be very hard to handle and set in place. Whenever possible, stack I-joists upright, or blocked level every 10 ft. if stacked flat. And it's important to keep I-joists reasonably dry until they are installed.

- I-joists lock into each other when stacked side by side. This is nice, because piles of joists are smaller than an equal quantity of conventional lumber joists. But be careful to consider the flanges of the I-joist beneath before plunging a saw through that top joist.

- Use the recommended size and number of nails to fasten the I-joists to plates, sills, and to one another. I-joist flanges are prone to splitting if the shank of the nail is too big or if you drive in too many nails. A split in a flange may grow and cause the joist to fail.

- Use the required hangers when the design calls for them. An ordinary joist hanger nailed through an I-joist's web won't hold for long. And don't hang any loads off of the bottom flange; it may separate from the web.

- I-joists are extremely wobbly until braced. Don't try walking on top of them until they're laterally braced or sheathed. Also don't stack up any stock on unbraced I-joists. The whole load may fall when the joists shimmy under the weight.

- Finally, I-joists make terrible staging planks.

Damaged flanges can cause I-joists to fail. Carefully check the joists before installation and handle with care on site. (Photo by Roe A. Osborn, courtesy *Fine Homebuilding* magazine, © The Taunton Press, Inc.)

Whenever possible stack I-joists in the upright position or block them level every 10 ft., if stacked flat as above. (Photo by Roe A. Osborn, courtesy *Fine Homebuilding* magazine, © The Taunton Press, Inc.)

Rim-joist stock is available sized to match the I-joist heights. They have high load-bearing capacity, minimizing the need for squash blocks. They are commonly 1 in. to 1¼ in. thick and are made of laminated strand lumber or plywood laminated veneer lumber (LVL).

and have high load-bearing capacity, eliminating the need for squash blocks around the perimeter in most instances. They are commonly 1 in. to 1¼ in. thick and are made of laminated strand lumber or plywood.

Before these rim joists were available, we ripped rim stock out of ¾-in. plywood or OSB or used I-joist material. Often squash blocks were necessary along side each I-joist because the ¾-in. rims and I-joists weren't strong enough. Manufactured rim stock comes in lengths up to 20 ft.—much better than being limited to 8-ft. rips of sheathing.

Before laying out joists and setting rims, pay attention to the minimum bearing surface on the mudsill required by any wide flange I-joists in the joist plan. They may need more bearing surface than is left once the rims are set. If this is the case, skip the rim joist for the time being and run the joists to the outside edge of the wall plate or beam. Later, block between the joists with rim material.

Use the same care installing rims for engineered I-joist systems as described for conventional joists. Square off the factory ends, especially the ones that meet at corners. And check to make sure you maintain the deck dimensions.

Cutting and installing I-joists

After the rims are installed, carefully measure and cut the joists to length. Don't trust the factory ends of I-joists. They rarely have square ends. Because I-joists come in long lengths, you won't have to lap or splice joists over center beams or walls. The joists can be ordered in lengths that will span from the front to back of most residential applications.

The I shape of the joists make accurate crosscuts difficult. We make up a simple jig for easy and accurate cutting. Measure the length between the rim joists for each series of joists and write the measurement on the mudsill or wall plate in crayon. Cut the joists about 1/16 in. short to keep from pushing out the rim joists. Keep the cut I-joists in order, so that they can be dropped in place without confusion.

Long lengths of I-joists may require two to three people to carry them because of their floppiness. It is critical to position the joists over beams and bearing walls directly on the layout before nailing at either end. Long I-joists can drift off an intermediate layout point while being handled. If this happens and you nail the ends down, the joist will push the walls out when you straighten the middle. To prevent this problem, drive 6d nails halfway in beside the flange into

The I shape of the joists make accurate crosscuts difficult. Make a simple jig for easy and accurate cutting. A square piece of sheathing that fits between the flanges supports the saw, which rides along a guide screwed to one side of the sheathing. (Photo by Roe A. Osborn, courtesy *Fine Homebuilding* magazine, © The Taunton Press, Inc.)

Web stiffeners add strength to the I-joist web. Clinch-nail sheathing the same thickness as the flange overhang to both sides of the web. (Photo by Roe A. Osborn, courtesy *Fine Homebuilding* magazine, © The Taunton Press, Inc.)

the beam on both sides of each joist to keep it positioned until the ends are nailed.

Nail two 8d or 10d nails (whichever is specified) through the bottom flange into the mudsill, plate or beam to fasten the joist down, one on either side of the web. To hold the top, drive one or two nails through the rim joist into the top flange of the I-joist. Be careful not to over nail or use large-diameter spikes (unless called for by the I-joist manufacturer), or you may split the flanges.

Handling special I-joist details

Concentrated load areas and points acting on I-joist floor decks require special details not commonly found in conventional framing. The webs of I-joists can't support the same crushing force as conventional joists, so they need extra support, which is what most of the special details address. The joist areas that need special treatment are indicated on the I-joist plans designed by the I-joist manufacturer or distributor and sent with the joists. Also, every I-joist package comes with a floor-framing-detail guide that depicts just about every detail you may encounter and how to complete each one. Here are several details that are worth commenting on.

Squash blocking Almost every I-joist floor requires some squash blocking. As described earlier for conventional floor framing, squash blocks transfer loads from above that would otherwise crush I-joists. They are 2x blocks cut $1/16$ in. longer than the height of the I-joists. Install the blocks flat against the top and bottom flanges of the I-joist, or flat against the rim board when the load isn't directly above a joist location (see the photo on p. 81).

Likely locations for squash blocks are beneath jack studs carrying large headers for French doors and beneath beam-carrying posts. Sometimes they're necessary alongside I-joists between a center bearing wall and the center beam or

I-joist headers are made by sandwiching lumber between the webs of two I-joists. Size the stock to fill the space between the webs. Nail through the webs only, not through the flanges.

sistered to the ends of I-joists when nonload-bearing stock like ¾-in. plywood has been used as a rim joist.

Web stiffeners Among other details specific to I-joists are web stiffeners, which are pieces of OSB or plywood stock thick enough to match the width of the flange beyond the web. Web stiffeners are called for in areas of concentrated load to strengthen the web. This may occur when a bearing wall sits above the middle of a joist span. Another case for web stiffeners is when an I-joist sits in a hanger that doesn't support the top flange of the joist. The stiffeners are added to keep the joist stabilized in the hanger. Cantilevered I-joists also require web stiffeners.

Cut the stock about ⅛ in. shorter than the distance between the top and bottom flanges and 4 in. to 6 in. wide. Install a stiffener to each side of the I-joist between the flanges. Your nails should be long enough to go through all three layers—stiffener, web, and stiffener. Pound the points of the nails flat against the outside surface of the third layer, a process called clinch nailing.

I-joist headers I-joist headers at floor openings and doubled I-joists that carry headers are built up a little differently than those made with solid lumber. I-joist headers need a filler block between the webs of the mated joists running the length of the header. The blocking is intended to stiffen the webs.

Select filler block stock sized to closely match the height between the top and bottom flanges of the I-joists and the space between the webs when the joists are sistered together. You don't need to rip the blocks, just use stock with the closest nominal width and height.

Drive nails through the web and block, and extend through the second I-joist's web; then clinch over the part that protrudes. Never nail the I-joists together through the flanges. Nails can split the LVL (or solid-lumber) layers, causing the I-joists to fail.

FLOOR FRAMING

Backer blocks Backer blocks are made of OSB or plywood and look like web stiffeners. They're used to stiffen the web or as filler material to even up the surface of the web to the edges of the flanges. This is sometimes necessary to provide good nailing for drywall along a header. Use backer blocks to back up joist hanger locations or to back up the web where the I-joist has to be nailed to a framing member like a stud passing through the floor system.

Measure the distance from the face of the web to the outside edge of the flange. This dimension is the thickness of the stock you need for your backer material. Rip backer material to be within ½ in. of the height of the space between flanges. The length of the backer depends on how you are using it. To back up 2x4 nailing, you'll need pieces only 3 in. long. To back up drywall, you'll have to fill all along the exposed I-joist.

I-joist hangers When hangers are called for, use only specially designed I-joist hangers. Most I-joist hangers are top-flange hangers; they have horizontal tabs bent at 90° to the back of the hanger. The tabs reach over and attach to the top flange of the I-joist header or a beam. Occasionally, face-mount hangers without the top flanges are specified. These are usually found when I-joists meet a solid LVL beam, as in the case of a sunken floor.

Regardless of the type, back up all hangers with backer blocks extending 6 in. to 12 in. on each side of the joist.

We've found that if these so-called squeak-proof floor systems are going to squeak, they're most likely to do it at joist hanger locations. To help ward off these annoying noises, we make sure all hangers are nailed properly. Then for added insurance, we squirt a little construction adhesive into the hanger seat before dropping the joists into place.

Wall plate backers We developed one detail of our own that makes it easy to attach the top plates of walls running parallel to the I-joists overhead. Before installing the floor sheathing,

I-joists use special hangers with horizontal tabs that wrap over the flanges of adjoining I-joists or LVL beams. Squirting a little glue in the seat of the hanger minimizes the potential of a squeaky floor. (Photos by Roe A. Osborn, courtesy *Fine Homebuilding* magazine, © The Taunton Press, Inc.)

Subflooring on I-joists

Engineered wood I-joists are designed as a system that integrates the subfloor sheathing to produce a stiff floor deck. We use a $3/4$-in. tongue-and-groove APA Sturd-I-Floor subfloor system nailed to the joists and glued both to the joists and in between the tongues and grooves, just like we described for conventional floor subflooring.

The span charts provided by most I-joist manufacturers presume that a glued subfloor will be installed and so reduce the span rating of the joists by 4 in. to 6 in. when subfloor panels are fastened with nails only.

Use the same procedures for installing subfloor sheathing as described for conventional solid-lumber joists. Take extra care when cutting the sheathing and avoid cutting sheets directly on top of I-joists. If the saw blade protrudes through the subfloor and cuts just $1/4$ in. into the top flange of a joist, you should replace the joist.

There are some details you'll encounter when framing with engineered-wood I-joists that may not be covered in the manufacturer's guide. When you encounter odd details that you aren't familiar with, contact your I-joist manufacturer's or distributor's staff before trying to solve the problem yourself. We once encountered a framing detail that we could describe only as an "outside loaded flying cantilever." We sketched the problem. After a phone conversation and a couple faxes back and forth with the I-joist distributor's engineering staff, we invented a detail to deal with the problem.

Framing Floors with Trusses

Another common engineered floor system uses open-web trusses to span across mudsills or wall plates. Usually floor trusses are designed and manufactured for each project, unlike dimensional lumber and I-joists, which are selected from stock sizes and cut to fit the project's floor.

Pieces of sheathing nailed to the bottom edges of I-joist flanges provide blocking to nail the top plate of interior partitions that run parallel to the joists. (Photo by Roe A. Osborn, courtesy *Fine Homebuilding* magazine, © The Taunton Press, Inc.)

locate joist bays that will have parallel non-bearing interior walls beneath. Rip scrap pieces of sheathing or cut blocks of 1x or 2x lumber to fit between the webs of adjacent joists and nail them to the top of the bottom flanges at 16 in. to 24 in. on center with 6d nails. Use pneumatic nailers to drive the nails; don't pound them in with a hammer. Hammering may loosen the flange/web connection. You can also nail through the webs of the I-joists and into the edge of the blocks to secure them in place. Later you can attach 2x6 or 2x8 lumber to the underside of the sheathing blocks centered on the wall location. This gives a nailing base for wall plates and the drywall at the ceiling/wall intersection.

FLOOR FRAMING 95

Top and bottom cords of a floor truss, comparable to flanges on I-joists, are made of 2x stock and the webs that crisscross the center of the truss are made of wood or steel. No part of the cords or webs can be cut unless directed by the fabricator/designer.

There are a few features of floor trusses that make them desirable. They can be designed to span the entire distance between the exterior walls. This eliminates the need for a center bearing wall or beam that is necessary with conventional joists and most I-joist floors. And the space between the webs of the joist permits easier plumbing and HVAC installations. One drawback though: Trusses tend to be taller than other joist systems, which can complicate interior and exterior design issues.

Floor trusses usually need to be ordered well in advance to compensate for the fabricator's lead time. This makes maintaining correct plan dimensions when setting mudsills and framing walls critical. Their custom nature requires that they be ordered accurately. Floor openings and plumbing fixture locations need to be communicated accurately via the house plans when the trusses are ordered. The last thing you want is to be laying out a bathroom only to find out the tub drain lands right on a truss.

You can save a lot of labor installing floor trusses. They are usually set on 24-in. centers so there are less members to deal with. The center beam and bearing-wall construction labor can be eliminated. And there's no rim joist to set.

Laying out and installing trusses

Layout for the trusses is based on the truss plan supplied by the manufacturer. When marking the layout, adjust for the width of the truss cord, so the trusses land on center positions. The most common top and bottom cords are 2x4, so the layout offset will be 1¾ in., which is half the width of a 2x4 truss chord.

It usually takes two guys to handle the longer trusses and set them in place. Handle floor trusses

Bottom cord-bearing open-web floor trusses are designed and custom built for each project. A 2x4 brace nail is nailed into an open area at the top end of the trusses to space the trusses and distribute loads from above. (Photo by Steve Culpepper, courtesy *Fine Homebuilding* magazine, © The Taunton Press, Inc.)

in their upright position. Carrying them on their sides can put stress on the truss plates, causing them to loosen or pop and the truss to fail.

Set the trusses in place on the mudsill and nail them down with three or four 16d spikes through the bottom cord. When setting floor trusses on wall plates, make sure the walls are straightened with a string line and braced. Nail the trusses down to one wall plate and let the other end float. Recheck the string line after all the trusses are up and straighten both walls before nailing off the loose side. Also, it's a good idea to brace trusses so that a whole line of them can't fall over like dominos before they are braced.

Floor trusses usually have a notch built into the top ends to accommodate a 2x brace. The brace serves two purposes. First, it ties all the tops of the trusses together to maintain equal on-center spacing and, second, it transfers loads that fall between trusses from a wall above onto the adjacent trusses and through the frame. Mark a 2x brace for the 24-in. on-center spacing before installing it. Don't nail the brace to the end truss but start with the second one in. Nail the brace to each truss until you reach the other end. Again, don't nail the last truss. Run the 2x truss braces on both sides of the building, then return to the loose end trusses.

Plumb up from the plate below at each corner and tack each end truss to its brace in position. After all four corners are tacked, recheck the dimensions and diagonals to make sure you're on target with the plans.

Other floor truss details

Just like I-joists, there are several details unique to floor trusses you may encounter. A couple common ones are web braces and fire stopping, but you may confront others on the engineered truss plans that come with a truss package.

Web bracing Sometimes floor truss systems require web bracing. Look for special notes on the truss engineering documents that are supplied with the trusses. You may have to install extra 2x braces within the web space tying the trusses together. These braces usually help the trusses share a load and are important to install.

Horizontal fire stopping Because floor trusses are open, you should check your local building code regarding concealed spaces. When trusses will be covered on both the top with sheathing and the bottom with drywall, you create a concealed space. Many building codes limit the square footage area of concealed opened spaces.

When you exceed the limit you will have to install draft stopping or fire stopping along the side of a truss to comply with the code. This usually only amounts to $1/2$-in. gypsum drywall or structural sheathing.

Complete the truss installation, bracing, and squaring process. When you're satisfied that the system is square, install the draft stopping. It's easier to add draft stopping before you install the subfloor. Sheathe the floor deck using the procedure described for conventional floor joists.

Stock floor trusses

There are stock floor trusses available that incorporate a short section of wood I-joist at the end. The I-joist ends are trimmable. You order the trusses to the nearest longer stock size to the length you need and trim to fit. You can install rim stock compatible with I-joists rather than the 2x brace used with custom floor trusses. Follow the manufacturer's guidelines for spans and sizing.

Chapter 5

WALL FRAMING

PLANNING EXTERIOR
BEARING WALLS

LAYING OUT BEARING
WALL PLATES

ASSEMBLING THE WALLS

FRAMING OTHER
BEARING AND
EXTERIOR WALLS

The completed floor deck provides the work platform for framing the exterior and interior walls. Even on custom homes, most walls lend themselves to efficient production assembly and a square, flat floor makes the process easy. The sequence for framing walls is similar to framing floors: layout, lumber selection, framing, and sheathing. And there are similar details for framing openings and blocking. There's also some advance planning that's useful to simplify material orders and accelerate on-site production.

Wall framing can be divided into two distinctly different types. Bearing walls, which support weight from above, and nonbearing interior partition walls, which simply divide an area into rooms. Depending on the type of wall being constructed, some details are framed a little differently.

In this chapter, we'll start with the bearing-wall planning you should do before you get on site; then we'll discuss the layout process you do on-site. And we'll examine wall framing and the details of wall components and openings. (We'll cover the layout and construction of nonbearing interior wall framing in chapter 7, along with ceiling furring and blocking.)

Structural wall bracing is an important issue in regions subject to seismic activity and destructive weather, so we'll look at typical details to make walls resist racking forces.

Exterior walls are framed on top of the recently finished floor deck and will be tilted upright after they are sheathed.

Because they are numerous, we won't be able to cover all of the alternative framing details (such as insulated single ply headers or box beam headers) in this chapter. Most of the alternatives can be incorporated into the processes we describe for layout and assembly. Check out Joe Lstiburek's *Builder's Guide to Cold Climates* and *Builder's Guide to Mixed Climates* (The Taunton Press), Rob Thallon's *Graphic Guide to Frame Construction* (The Taunton Press), or the NAHB Research Center's *Cost-Effective Home Building: A Design and Construction Handbook* for more options and alternate details.

Planning Exterior Bearing Walls

Before you snap any chalklines and lay out any plates, gather all the basic wall information from the house plans. You need to determine the wall height as well as stud size and spacing. You may have to garner some of the detail data, like window and door opening sizes, from other sources, such as a manufacturer's product guide. Determine what exterior walls will bear joists or roof rafters and what exterior walls will be nonbearing and run parallel to rafters or floor joists. This affects how you plan and frame openings in the walls.

As with the floor joists, you'll use the information collected to order materials, write lumber cut lists, and plan the wall layout. These all help speed production on site.

Formulate lumber and cut lists

To get a close count for the studs and plates that you'll need to order, use an engineer's triangular scale and a floor plan. Start by highlighting which walls will be exterior and which will support floors or roofs. This will help you see which walls to concentrate on.

Most house plans are drawn to a ¼-in. scale. Use the engineer's rule to make counting easier: the 30 scale on the rule corresponds to 16-in. on-center (o.c.) stud spacing, and the 20 scale indicates 24-in. on-center spacing. Lay the scale along a wall on the plan, placing the number 1 of the scale on the beginning of the wall, and read the count at the end of the wall. Add two extra studs for each window and door opening, and add two studs for each exterior wall corner.

The plate stock is easy to determine once you know the linear footage of the walls. Add up the total length of the walls and multiply by 3 (for one bottom and two top plates). Then divide by the length of stock that makes best sense to use.

(continued on p. 103)

WALL FRAMING

Brief Description of Stud-Framed Wall

Wall Plates
A wall is a collection of studs (usually sized 2x4 or 2x6) equally spaced (usually 16 in. or 24 in. on center) and sandwiched between top and bottom plates. The top plate can be either single or double. Double plating is most common on load-bearing walls unless the roof rafters or trusses and floor joists stack directly over the studs in the wall, then a single top plate can be used.

Headers
Large openings in the wall are made for windows and doors. When the opening is greater in width than the stud spacing—and most windows are wider than 24 in.— then a header must be inserted to carry the load of the interrupted stud(s). A header is a simple beam sized to support the load above the opening it spans.

Jack Studs and King Studs
The header is supported by a jack stud at each end. Jacks, sometimes called trimmers, fit under each end of a header, and they transfer the load that the header carries down to the bottom plate and the framing beneath. Nailed to the jacks are full-height studs called king studs; they support the assembly between the plates. Sometimes jacks must be doubled on wide openings so

Description of a Stud-Framed Wall

Load-Bearing Wall

Labels: Double top plate, Cripple, 41 1/8" header, King stud, Jack, 92 5/8", 38 1/8", 80" jack, 65 1/4", 81 1/2", 13 1/4", 24" o.c., Door RO, Bottom or sole plate, Cripple, Saddle or sill

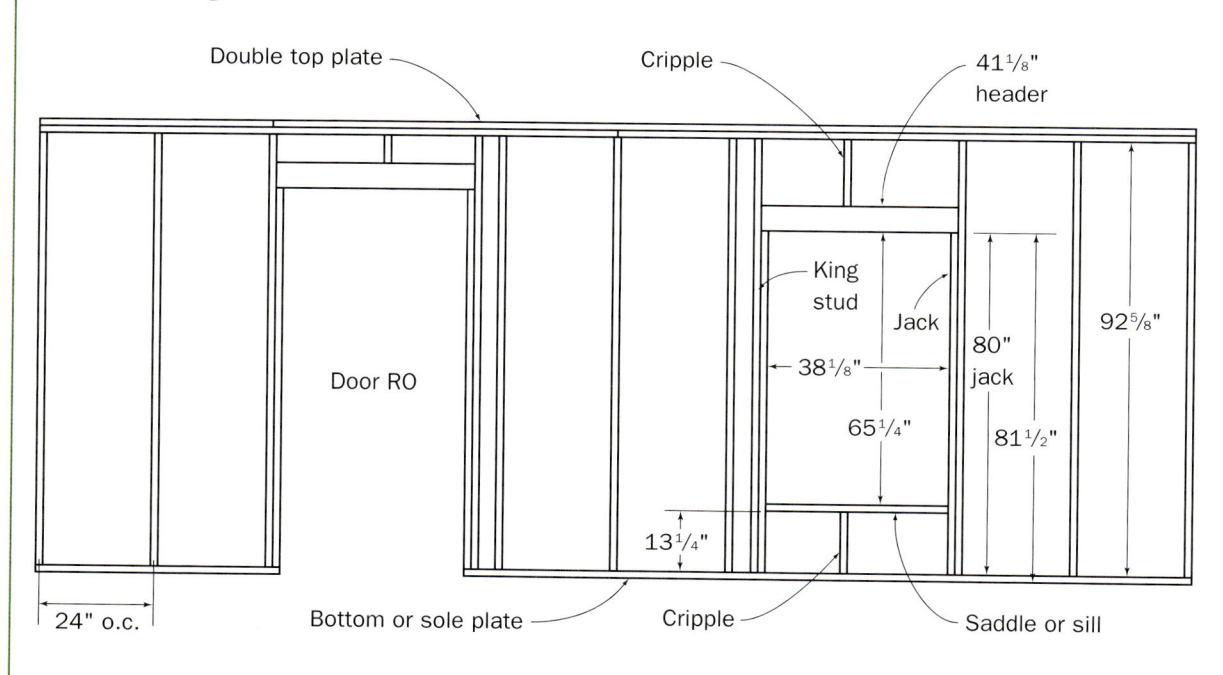

CHAPTER FIVE

there's enough supporting surface for the header to bear on. Jacks can be replaced with a steel header hanger attached to the king stud.

Saddles and Cripples

A saddle (also called a sill) forms the bottom of a window opening. It's a piece of 2x stock laid flat and nailed between the jacks. Cripples are short pieces of 2x stock that run underneath the saddle. And, depending on a header's height, cripples can run from the header to the plate. Cripples are located at the points where a common stud would have been located had it not been interrupted by the opening.

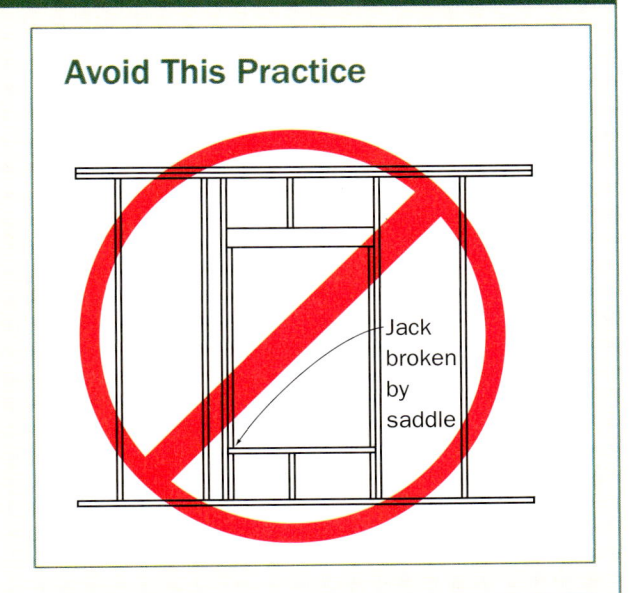

Avoid This Practice

Jack broken by saddle

Nonbearing Wall

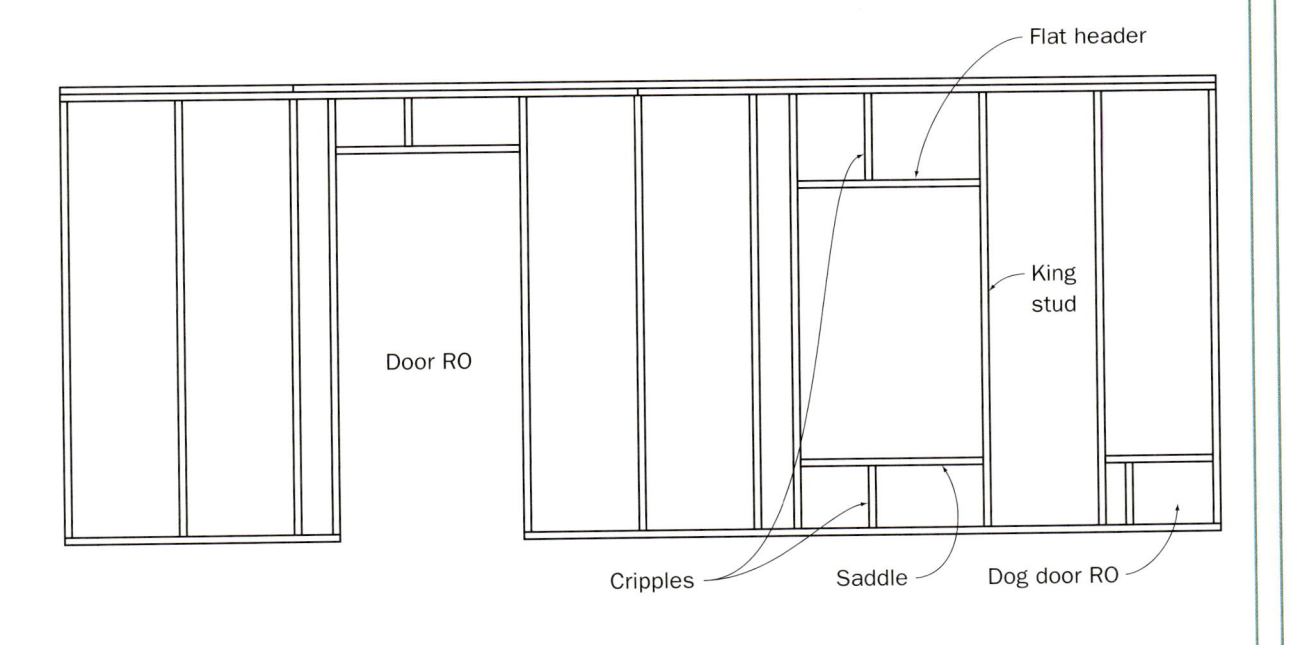

Flat header

King stud

Door RO

Cripples

Saddle

Dog door RO

Determining the Lengths of Rough-Opening Parts

We'll use an example of a rough window opening to illustrate the process we use to determine the cut list for an opening in both a load-bearing wall and a nonbearing wall. Refer to the drawings on pp. 100–101 for a description of the parts of wall openings and their functions. We'll describe them further during the installation section. First, the load-bearing-wall example.

Wall Height
The projected finish ceiling height is 8 ft. so we'll use studs precut at 92⅝ in. and plan for a single bottom (sole) plate and a double top plate. In this example, the window rough opening has a height of 5 ft. 5¼ in. (65¼ in.) and a width of 3 ft. 2⅛ in. (38⅛ in.). The standard height for the top of the windows is 6 ft. 8 in. (80 in.). This may vary, depending on wall height, window height, or client choice.

Jack Height
Window frame thicknesses vary and you should always check the manufacturer's specs; but for our example, let's assume that the thickness of the head jamb of the window plus the space to the rough opening is 1½ in. Thus the rough opening at the top of the window will be 81½ in. from the floor (80 in. for standard top of window height plus 1½ in.). The top of the rough opening is also the bottom of the window header. This means the jack length is 80 in. (81½ in. minus the 1½ in. for the thickness of the bottom plate of the wall).

It was common practice at one time to have the saddle interrupt the jacks and pass through to the adjacent king studs (see the top drawing on p. 101). Though still practiced by some framers and shown in drawings found in many framing books, this method is no longer considered good building practice and may not comply with your local building code.

Cripple Height
The cripples beneath the saddle will be equal to the jack length (80 in.) minus the rough opening height of the window (65¼ in.) minus the thickness of the saddle (1½ in.). The remainder equals 13¼ in. (80 in. – 65¼ in. – 1½ in. = 13¼ in.). Don't calculate or precut the cripples that go above a structural header made of dimensional lumber, because the height of the stock may vary more than ⅜ in. Measure and cut the upper cripples to fit when you're assembling the wall.

Saddle and Header Lengths
The length of the saddle is easy to figure: It's equal to the width of the rough opening (38⅛ in.) because it fits between the jacks. The header has to be wide enough to span the rough opening width plus the two supporting jack studs so add 3 in. to the rough opening width (38⅛ in. + 3 in. = 41⅛ in.). For openings 6 ft. and wider, such as those for sliding doors, we use double jacks under the header for extra support. For those situations, add 6 in. to the rough opening.

Header Stock
The stock you use for a header is determined by the load that header will carry. In our example, the opening is less than 4 ft. Our building code says we'll need a double 2x6, if there is a floor and roof

above the opening and a double 2x4 if there is only a roof above. If there is a concentrated load from above acting on the header, then the header has to be large enough to handle the additional weight (see the drawings on pp. 100–101). Check your local code when determining header thickness and height. For concentrated loads, consult an engineer.

Openings in Nonbearing Exterior Walls

The other type of wall opening to look at is one in a nonbearing exterior wall. Because the floor joists or roof system run parallel to these outside walls, there isn't a significant load bearing on them, only the dead load of the lumber above. The rim joist above will distribute the light load to surrounding studs. This allows you to eliminate the structural header and jack studs, leaving more wall space to fill with insulation.

Plan these wall openings with single king studs located on either side of the rough opening spaced to match the rough opening width. The saddle will be the same size as the rough opening width and so will the nonstructural header at the top of the opening. Determine the lower cripple length in the same way as given in the previous example.

The upper header is set flat like the saddle, and the bottom edge will be located 80 in. from the bottom of the king stud, which is the same level as the bottom of the header in the previous example. The upper cripple length will be the difference between the top of the header ($81\frac{1}{2}$ in.) and the stud height ($92\frac{5}{8}$ in.) or $11\frac{1}{8}$ in. ($92\frac{5}{8}$ in. − $81\frac{1}{2}$ in. = $11\frac{1}{8}$ in.).

Working from a set of plans, make a lumber take-off list for materials to be delivered.

We tend to frame large homes so we opt for 16-ft. or even 20-ft. stock if it's available. On smaller homes, 12-ft. lumber may make more sense. Total your stud and plate counts on the list.

A common ceiling height is 8 ft., but heights of 7 ft. 6 in. and 9 ft. are becoming more popular. Many lumberyards stock precut studs: $92\frac{1}{4}$-in. to $92\frac{5}{8}$-in. studs that correspond to a finished ceiling height of about 8 ft.; 88-in. studs for ceilings about 7 ft. 6 in., and 104-in. studs for ceilings around 9 ft. (The actual height of any finished ceiling depends on details, such as whether you choose to strap your ceilings—see chapter 7— and the choice of the finished floor.) We plan on using precuts whenever possible, because they save labor. Otherwise you can choose a stud length to custom cut from 8-ft. or 10-ft. stock.

Marking rough openings and writing a cut list The cut list can be determined by marking up a set of floor plans with the rough opening (RO) dimensions for each window and door. Indicate any framing details you don't want to overlook, like fireplace openings and pet doors. Draft cut lists for headers, jack studs, window saddles, and cripples beneath the windows from the information you gather. We'll describe how to determine those lengths in a minute.

WALL FRAMING

After you calculate the measurements, write the size and lengths of all the parts for each opening right on the plans. That will make it convenient to refer to as you lay out the wall plates.

When you write up the cut list for headers, jacks, cripples, and saddles, make a quantity list of the lumber to be ordered and add it to the stud and plate count (see the sidebar on p. 102). Because the quality of lumber has been decreasing for years, make sure to order extra for stock you deem unsuitable. A good round number to increase the order by is 10 percent. Stock you put aside can be used as wall backer blocking, truss bracing, and other parts for which warped and too-knotty wood won't matter.

We use a standard form when going through the lumber take-off process so we don't overlook anything. Make several copies of your completed cut list so you can assign cutting tasks to on-site crew members.

Full-height headers Many builders use built-up 2x headers that will completely fill the space between the bottom of the rough opening and the top plates. (This can save time on site, because using this kind of header eliminates the need to cut and install cripples above the header.) In our example, that would be $11\frac{1}{8}$ in. or nominally a 2x12. When you use this method of headering, estimate the height of the header stock at the greater size of an average piece ($11\frac{1}{2}$ in. for a 2x12) and work in reverse to determine the cripple heights. Wait to measure and cut the jacks until the header is installed during wall assembly, since the header height may vary.

Predetermining the header height on the tall side may result in a taller window rough opening if the header is shorter than planned. But that's

Cut List

Determine all the wall parts that need to be cut: studs, jacks, headers, saddles, and cripples, etc. Use the list to help organize on-site tasks.

First-Floor Two-Ply 2x6 Headers

Use	Window Stock No.	Qty.	Header Size	Saddle Size	Qty.	Crip. Size
1/2 14'	2852		$37\frac{1}{8}$"	$34\frac{1}{8}$"	2	$16\frac{3}{4}$"
1/2 14'	2846		$37\frac{1}{8}$"	$34\frac{1}{8}$"	2	$24\frac{3}{4}$"
1/2 14'	2832		$37\frac{1}{8}$"	$34\frac{1}{8}$"	2	$40\frac{3}{4}$"
8'	CN235		$44\frac{1}{4}$" (pad $\frac{3}{8}$")	$41\frac{1}{4}$"	2	$40\frac{1}{4}$"

First-Floor Two-Ply 2x12 Headers

Use	Location	Qty.	Header Size	Pad Down	Qty.	Spec. Jacks
1/14'	Center French	1	81"			4
1/14'	Front door	1	75"			4
1/14'	Rear slider (PS510)	1	$76\frac{1}{2}$"		2/2x4	4
pc. 2/8'	Center dining	1	$33\frac{1}{2}$"			2
pc. 2/8'	Center hall	1	$50\frac{3}{4}$"			
2/10'	Side porch	1	$99\frac{1}{2}$"			
1/12'	Fireplace	1	61"	Crip. down	2	66"

First-Floor Two-Ply 2x6 Header

Use	Window Stock No.	Qty.	Header Size	Saddle Size	Qty.	Crip. Size
2/10'	2052-3452-2052	1	$100\frac{1}{2}$"	2/$26\frac{1}{8}$" 1/$42\frac{1}{8}$"	5	$14\frac{3}{4}$"

rarely a problem. Trouble arises if the rough opening is too short, so err on the side of big.

Door openings Rough openings for doors are planned the same way as a window opening except that you skip the saddle and lower cripples. We add ½ in. to ¾ in. to the rough opening height of a door with the intention of padding the bottom of the rough opening the extra amount to accommodate the finish flooring. This leaves enough space for an area rug between the bottom of the open door and the finished floor.

Interior bearing-wall stud size Interior bearing walls may use different size (2x4 rather than 2x6) studs than the exterior walls, so account for them separately on your list.

Other openings Other openings for fireplaces, pet doors, air-conditioning sleeves, and so on are framed much the same way as either a door or window. Often these openings are narrower than the on-center stud spacing. You can frame off the opening to the correct size by blocking between the studs. Or if the opening is wider, treat it like you would a conventional door or window opening.

Laying Out Bearing Wall Plates

The layout is done in two steps. First mark and snap chalklines on the subfloor to orient the bottom plate of the wall. Then transfer the layout you predetermined on the house plans onto the plate stock set along the lines. The plates give the workers complete directions how to build the wall. This frees you up to prepare the next framing procedure.

Marking exterior and interior bearing walls

The first on-site step for preparing the floor deck for wall framing is to snap a series of chalklines to mark the inside edge of the exterior walls. The lines serve two purposes. They give a straight edge on which to line up the bottom plate during the

Mark the corners of the floor deck for the wall's bottom plate location, here a 2x6 wall. Measure from the edge of the rim joist, not the edge of the deck sheathing, in case the sheathing is trimmed inaccurately.

assembly process so the wall is framed straight. And once a wall is lifted, you'll match the bottom plate up with the line so its placement is straight.

Measure a few samples of the plate stock, because the actual width may vary from one load of lumber to the next. We'll use a measurement of 5½ in. (2x6) for discussion purposes; adjust the measurement for the stock you use.

At each corner of the floor deck, make accurate marks between which to snap chalklines by running a straightedge up the rim joist and measuring 5½ in. from it. The process is continued at every inside and outside corner. Don't trust the edge of the subfloor sheathing which may be trimmed back short from the edge of the rim joist.

After we installed the floor joists earlier, we adjusted the rim joists so the measurements of the floor deck matched the plans. If you weren't able to make any of the corrections then, you can make them now with the wall plates. Adjust the mark in or out to correct any error in a deck dimension, but don't exceed ⅛ in. If the correction needed is greater than ⅛ in. you can adjust the balance in the wall or next floor deck.

WALL FRAMING **105**

After you mark each side of every inside and outside corner in the same fashion, snap chalklines to connect them. For lines over 40 ft., have someone finger the middle of the line to keep it straight. This is especially a concern on windy days. A gust of wind could give you a 1/4 in. or more belly in a string and throw off your reference line.

Next, check the plans and mark any interior load-bearing walls by holding out the measuring tape on one of the fresh perimeter chalklines at the tape's 5 1/2-in. mark. If you have time, continue measuring and marking out for all the interior partition walls. We snap chalklines for both sides of an interior wall to eliminate any chance of positioning the wall on the wrong side of a single chalkline. When we're concerned about rain washing away the chalk before building the walls we snap the lines in indelible red chalk. The advantage of snapping lines now is that you have an open clean floor deck to work on. The disadvantage is you may be rushed to get the bearing walls done to keep ahead of workers.

Planning a wall assembly sequence

Before you spread out and mark up the wall plates, it's a good idea to formulate a wall-building sequence to speed production and

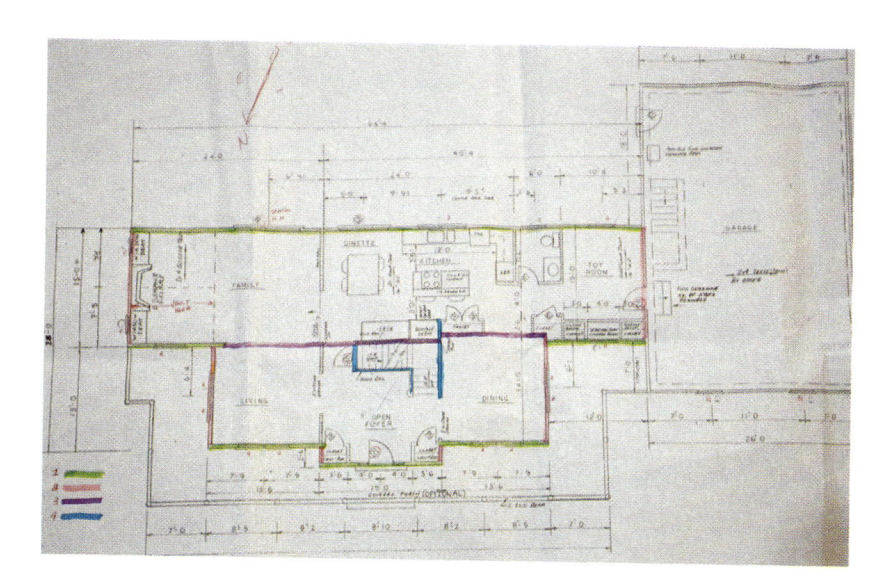

Lines snapped on the deck will be used to align the bottom plate of the wall once it has been lifted.

Use the floor plans to work out a sequence for building and lifting the walls. The floor deck can get overcrowded if too many walls are assembled at once.

minimize competition for floor space during assembly.

We highlight the walls on our house plans to layout, build, and lift in sequence. Usually the first walls are the long bearing walls at the front and rear of the house. The second group of highlighted walls are those that meet the first set at exterior corners. The last walls to build are the interior bearing walls. Sometimes there are a few miscellaneous walls to frame, like those on a bump-out or recessed doorway that fall out of sequence, but those are minor.

Choosing and laying out plates

The plate stock will vary in quality. Use only straight stock for top plates. Starting with straight lumber makes straightening the walls much easier and faster. So the time spent looking through the stock pile is actually time saved and you have the benefit of better quality.

We eyeball each plate the same way we looked through floor joists and mark it for the straightness and best use. The best lumber is marked with a T1 if it's dead straight and T2 if it has less than a $1/8$-in. crown in 16 ft.—suitable for a top plate but not perfect. We also mark the crown on the T2 pieces so we can oppose them when mating the second top plate. T2's also get cut up for short top plate sections.

ADVICE: Storing Lumber

While it may sound like a lot of extra effort, we inspect, mark, and stack our stock neatly on a flat spot or on blocks. We cover piles with leftover lumber tarps to protect them from direct sun and rain. It's not that we're trying to pamper our lumber but to keep it straight, dry, and clean. All of which make for a more accurate and neater job.

Lower-quality material gets marked B1 if it has a $1/4$-in. crown or so on a 16-ft. length. We can use them for bottom plates, because they'll be adjusted to and nailed down at the chalkline on the subfloor. B2's are slightly worse and used as bottom plates in a pinch or cut up for short sections.

Twisted stock or lumber with bad crowns get stacked aside for bracing or blocking or will be returned to the lumberyard.

Preparing plate stock The wide surface of dimensional lumber—the $5\frac{1}{2}$-in.-wide surface on a 2x6—is called the face. The narrow surface—the $1\frac{1}{2}$-in.-wide surface on a 2x6—is called the edge.

Be choosy when you crown and grade your plate stock. Straight lumber can be marked and used as top plates. Pieces with crowns can be used as bottom plates. It is easier to straighten a bottom plate when it is nailed to the deck than it is to try to straighten a top plate once a wall has been lifted.

Set out plate stock along the chalkline on the floor deck. Cut the plates so that the joints between pieces fall at stud locations. Stagger joints between the top and bottom plates by about 4 ft.

Lay a bottom plate on the deck, even with the chalkline, so that the face is up. Lay a top plate next to the bottom plate, toward the center of the house, so that their edges touch. Flush the end of each plate with the outside face of the perpendicular rim joist at the end of the building.

Tack nail the end of the bottom plate to keep it from drifting. Measure and cut the top plate so that it will end in the middle of a stud location. This is a good practice for bottom plates, too; but because the bottom will be fastened to the subfloor, it isn't a critical concern.

Once you have the first pieces of top and bottom plates on the deck, work your way down the chalkline, lining up lengths of top and bottom plates, end to end, until you reach the other end of the building. Alternate the lengths of the top and bottom plates so the joints between the pieces don't land on the same stud. The mill lengths of lumber often run long. A 16-ft. length of stock may actually measure 16 ft. 1 in., so check each piece you use for plates to ensure the breaks will continue to fall on stud centers. When you reach the other end of the building, mark the plates flush with the rim joist but don't cut them yet.

Measure the overall length of the plates from the starting end to the mark you just made at the other end to verify that it matches the dimension on the house plans. If it doesn't, adjust the mark before cutting, so the wall will be the correct length. Provided you verified and adjusted the floor deck measurements earlier, the difference you encounter now should be no more than $1/8$ in.

Plate layout The next step in laying out the plates is to mark the plates themselves. There are several details that contribute to an understanding of wall layout and construction. The first set of details we'll treat are window and door openings which we've already introduced with examples above. The other details revolve around wall intersections.

Marking the plates for rough openings and details Once the plates for a given wall are cut to length and set on the deck, it's time to transcribe the information from the house plans to the plates for correct stud and opening layout (see the sidebar on the facing page). Plan to make two passes across the plates rather than trying to get everything down once. On the first pass, mark out all the rough openings, wall backers, and other details and mark the stud locations on the second pass. This two-pass procedure keeps you organized and focused on one thing at a time in order of importance.

Layout Edge Options

You can mark the wall layout on the face or the edge of the plates. Habit and preference play the biggest roles in which one you choose. There are some differences though.

Marking the layout on the edges (1½ in.) will permit you only to eyeball studs and other wall parts square to the plate as you install them. And once the wall is sheathed, the marks are covered, leaving you no second check that your crew installed all the parts in the right place once a wall is lifted. This method is preferred by production framers, because the layout can be marked a little faster (especially if you frame 2x6 walls); you don't have to flip your square around to mark both plates.

We prefer to lay the plates flat on their faces (see the top photo on pp. 110). The square lines give us a guide to match the studs to. This helps with twisted lumber, because you can nail one end square and rotate the other end in place. The wider faces have more room on which to write framing details, such as the lengths of rough opening parts and other special directions for a custom home. And after the walls are lifted, you can see if something was overlooked, such as a partition backer. The text follows this method, but the procedures are the same whether you make your layout marks on the faces or the edges of the plates.

Plates can be marked out either on the edges (shown here) or on the face (shown in the top photo on p. 110) of the stock.

The marks and symbols you make on the plates communicate the framing details to the crew members building the wall, so you won't have to stop and explain every aspect during the assembly process. There are two common details to mark out: rough openings for windows and doors and partition backers (which are the points, other than exterior corners, where walls intersect). You can mark out rough openings and backers on your first layout pass, but we'll describe them separately just to keep things clear.

The center of all of the window and door openings are indicated on the plans outside the perimeter lines of the house. The measurements are usually taken from the outside edge of the house at the nearest corner (see the photo on p. 106).

WALL FRAMING   109

ADVICE: Rough-Opening Layout Stick

Usually, most of the windows in a home will be the same size. To speed the marking process you can make up a quick layout stick from a length of 1x3 and avoid stretching your tape measure out at each opening. Cut a 1x3, or any strip of wood, 6 in. longer than the rough opening width (ROW). From our example that would be $38\frac{1}{8}$ in. + 6 in. = $44\frac{1}{8}$ in. Draw two square lines in from each end of the stick, each $1\frac{1}{2}$ in. apart. The lines indicate the king stud and jack locations. Measure between the two inside lines; it should equal the rough opening. Square a line in the exact center of the stick and mark across it with a C (for "center"). For this example, the center of the stick is at $22\frac{1}{16}$ in. Write the relevant information on the stick as a reference, including cripple, saddle, and jack lengths.

Now when you approach a window center on the wall plates, all you have to do is line up the center of the stick with the center mark and draw out the stud and jack locations. Because we regularly use the same few sizes and brands of windows from one home to the next, we label the layout sticks with the brand and model of window and save them from project to project.

Most houses have at least several windows of a common size. Make up a simple layout stick to mark out the rough openings of common windows rather than measuring back from the center mark at every RO.

When laying out wall plates, first mark out the details for windows, doors, and other openings. On a second pass, layout the locations of the studs. Mark the center of each rough opening and measure half its width to the left and half to the right of your center mark. These marks indicate the inside edge of the jacks.

Hook your tape measure over the end of the plates and locate the center of the first window or door. Mark a short line with a C over it to indicate that it's a center mark (see the photo above). Continue down the plates, marking the center of each rough opening. Now reverse the tape measure at the opposite end of the plates and back measure to a couple of center locations to make sure they match the plans. Sometimes house designers make errors marking the distances between points and reversing your tape is an easy way to double-check. If you encounter a discrepancy, get clarification on the correct location before continuing. Return to each center mark and sketch out the width of the rough opening as you noted when preparing the plans.

Special framing details are needed at wall intersections. Partition backers are inserted into walls wherever there is a partition. (Perimeter corners of exterior walls are a different type of detail and will be covered later in this chapter.) The backers provide a place to attach the drywall at inside corners of a room. We use a 2x6 flat in the wall or ladder blocking to back up 2x4 partitions. They give full support for the drywall and are easy to insulate around (see the sidebar on p. 112 for alternatives).

Example of Window Layout

Using the example we described earlier of a window with a rough opening width (ROW) of 38⅛ in. and rough opening height (ROH) of 65¼ in. we'll mark out the details. Lay the wall plates out on the floor deck and make the first layout pass to mark the window center locations. Divide the ROW in half (38⅛ in. ÷ 2 = 19 1/16 in.). Then hold your tape so that 19 1/16 in. is on the center mark. Make one mark at the end of the tape measure and another at 38⅛ in. These marks indicate the outside edges of the rough opening. Using your square and a pencil, draw a line at each mark across both the top and bottom plates (see the top photo on the facing page).

From each rough opening line and away from the center, mark two additional lines, one at 1½ in. and one at 3 in. (Using a framing square with the 1½-in.-wide tongue held across the two plates, it's easy to make your marks without having to use a tape measure.) The three lines you've made at each end of the rough opening indicate the locations of the jack stud and the king stud. Put a J to indicate the jack in the first space from the opening and an X to indicate the king stud in the space beside that.

Now write the cut list information within the rough opening space, so the crew member framing the window later will know what parts to use. Write down the saddle length (38⅛ in.), cripple length (13¼ in.), jack length (80 in.), and header size (41⅛ in.; 2x6).

For openings in nonbearing exterior walls there will be only a king stud on each side of the opening. Write down the saddle or nonstructural header length (38⅛ in.) and the two sets of cripple lengths, one below the saddle and one above the flat header (see the drawings on pp. 100–101). Measure out the opening the same as for a headered opening but mark only for the jack locations. Rather than marking the space with a J, mark it with an X to avoid confusion during wall assembly.

We'll look at these details again during the assembly process.

Jack studs and structural headers can be eliminated in most rough openings in nonbearing exterior walls, leaving space for more insulation. Frame the opening with straight studs, instead of a jack and a king stud, and use a flat header. Note that the openings in the foreground are in the process of being framed; a similar, completed one can be seen in the background.

WALL FRAMING   111

Partition Backer Options

There are four basic alternatives for framing interior partition wall backers into exterior wall framing. Strength, amount of lumber, ease of installation, and energy efficiency warrant consideration when choosing among alternatives.

Three-Stud Partition Backer (Channel)
The most traditional and often-used backer uses the most lumber and leaves a cavity that must be filled with insulation before the wall is sheathed. The two studs cause a thermal deficiency by linking the inside drywall with the exterior. Layout this corner as stud-block-stud (X-B-X). The block can be either a solid 2x or several scrap blocks sandwiched between the studs.

Large 2x Backer
Instead of a three-stud backer you can insert the next size wider 2x than the stock used for the interior partition. The most common is a 2x6 backer for 2x4 partitions. Lay out the 2x6 at 1 in. to either side of the interior wall position. Face it flat to the plates on the inside edge. Choose a flat piece of stock so it won't bow or pull the wall stud. We use this detail, because it gives us solid nailing for any trim at the inside corner and leaves the wall cavity open for insulating.

Ladder Blocking
You don't have to mark for the ladder-blocking system when you lay out the wall plates. After the exterior walls are up, cut and install blocks between the two adjacent studs to the partition location. Space the blocks 16 in. to 24 in. apart like a ladder up the wall. Nail them flush with the inside face of the wall and be sure to match one at the horizontal seam between drywall sheets. The drywall can pass through the connection, as shown in the top photo on the facing page, or just butt up to the interior wall stud like other systems. As with 2x6 backer, this alternative leaves plenty of space for insulation. It also uses up scrap blocks of lumber rather than full-length studs.

Drywall Clips
You can skip all the layout and blocking by using drywall clips. After the interior partitions are erected, screw on the clips to hold the drywall.

Three-stud partition backer. (Photo by Scott Phillips, courtesy *Fine Homebuilding* magazine, © The Taunton Press, Inc.)

Large 2x backer. (Photo by Scott Phillips, courtesy *Fine Homebuilding* magazine, © The Taunton Press, Inc.)

This leaves a full stud bay for insulation but no wood blocking for interior wood trim. Be selective when choosing the end stud for the interior partition; a straight one works best.

Ladder blocking nailed between adjacent common studs is easy to install during wall framing or after the walls are lifted. The blocks give fastening points for drywall at 16-in. or 24-in. intervals and space for insulation behind.

Drywall clips. (Photo by Scott Phillips, courtesy *Fine Homebuilding* magazine, © The Taunton Press, Inc.)

The measurements for interior partition walls are generally indicated on the plans within the floor space of the house rather than outside, like the window centers. Some designers write measurements to the center of the partitions and others to the edges. To confound the framer further, sometimes the width of the walls is indicated as 4 in. rather than the actual 3½ in. of a 2x4. Be alert to how your plans are drafted and measured.

Measure from the exterior wall corner to the first partition wall intersection and mark the center. Continue along the plates and mark the centers of all the backers.

From the center marks of the partition locations, measure to the left and right one half the thickness of the partition. For 2x4 walls, the measurement is 1¾ in. Make additional marks 1 in. on either side of the partition marks to indicate the 2x6 backer. Draw lines about 1½ in. on each plate from the edges where the plates touch one another. Marking the lines here ensures that the backer will end up facing the inside of the house, and not the sheathing side, when you lift the completed wall. Make another line connecting the ends of the 1½-in. lines and put an X in the middle to indicate the 2x6 backer.

Indicate ladder blocking by marking the center point of the partition on the plate and write the word *block* nearby. When you stud up the wall during the next phase, insert blocks between the two nearby studs.

Marking stud layout The openings and backers are laid out first so any studs that land where jacks or studs are already located can be omitted and you don't have a lot of erasing to do. Also, studs that would ordinarily land within a window or door opening can be marked as cripple studs or be omitted.

Start the stud layout from the same end of the building as you laid out the floor joists, so the studs will stack above the joists. Even if the studs are spread at a different on-center spacing than the joists (24 in. vs. 16 in.), every third stud should line up with a joist.

Hook your tape measure on the end of the bottom plate and pull it to the first stud location. Mark back ¾ in. from the stud center just as you did laying out the floor joists. For 24-in. on-center spacing, this would be 23¼ in. This leaves the center of the stud at exactly 24 in.

Square a line across both plates and make an X forward of the line to indicate on which side the stud gets placed. Drive a nail halfway in on the line and hook your tape on. Stretch the tape measure along the top of the plates. Mark every stud location, unless it lands within 2 in. of the side of a rough opening. Consider omitting studs that fall this close to king studs rather than duplicating support. Draw square lines for each stud mark and put an X forward of the line.

It's important to continue the same on-center layout you began with the studs through window and door openings and fill in the cripple studs so the joints between sheathing or drywall panels have a break point for nailing. The symbol for the side of the line that the cripples go on needs to different from an X to avoid confusion. Instead, use CR or another mark to denote the side the cripple stud goes on.

For window openings, mark the cripples on the top and bottom plates. Skip the lines and the symbols on the bottom plate of door openings, because there won't be any studs in the space. Mark the top plate on door rough openings, however, when there are cripple studs filling between the top of the header and the top plate.

When we marked out the floor joists, we laid out the "back" of the house (the ones opposite the first set of joists) with the X back from the layout line. This allowed the joists to lap one

Mark for wall backers where interior partition walls meet exterior walls. Mark the center of the wall and measure left and right to mark the sides of the wall. Here a flat 2x6 backer is marked to back up the future interior wall.

After all the stud locations are marked, draw a square line at each mark and indicate on which side of the line the stud will go by drawing an X.

another over the center beam or wall. There's no need to do that for the walls on opposite sides of the house. Even though the studs will stack 1½ in. to the side of the joists beneath some walls, this is still close enough to continue the load path with adequate support.

The last framing detail to decide on occurs at each end of the walls. There are lots of different ways to frame the corners at the end of an exterior wall. For options, see the sidebar on p. 116.

Marking secondary wall plates and layout

The second set of exterior wall plates to lay out are for the perpendicular walls that will fit between the first ones you build. Set out the plates and mark the layout for these walls after the first series of walls are constructed, lifted, and braced. These are usually non-load-bearing walls that run parallel to the floor joists.

To fit the plates between the walls, you have to trim the plate stock to length to fit between the upright walls. Since the on-center stud layout is determined from the *outside* corner of the floor deck, and not the end of these secondary wall plates, be careful when cutting the plates to length. You have to account for the thickness of the walls that are already erected to make sure the top plate you are cutting will fall halfway on a stud location.

To measure plate stock, set a length of stock along the chalkline on the subfloor and against the corner from which you want to begin the stud layout. Hook your tape on the outside of the bottom plate of the already erected wall and stretch the tape out to the other end of the plate. Mark and square across the center of the last on-center stud location before the end of the wall, and trim the plate to the line. Fit the balance of the plates to make up the wall between the upright walls, making sure any break in the rest of the stock falls on a stud center. When you get to the end of the wall, cut the last piece ⅛ in. short. If the plates of the perpendicular walls are too tight, there is a chance they will push the other walls out of plumb when you raise them.

Spread out the rest of the stock for the top and bottom plates of the wall. Although it's important to have joints between pieces of the top plate fall on studs, it's not as critical for the bottom plate.

To lay out the plates, hook your tape over the bottom plate of the upright, already erected wall and make the same two layout passes as you did for the first set of walls. Mark out the windows, doors, and partition backers first and then the stud locations. The second set of walls is likely to

(continued on p. 119)

Stud layout should always be started from the outside of the building, not from the end of the plate of the wall you are marking out. Beginning the layout from the outside of the building ensures that the edges of the wall sheathing will always fall on the center of a stud.

Framing Exterior Corners

There are several options for laying out and framing corners in exterior walls. Four concerns come to bear on the decision about which option to choose.

The amount of lumber needed to frame each corner influences most decisions. Some framers believe that the sign of a high-quality frame is the amount of lumber packed into it. Others believe less is more. Corners that use less lumber usually have more space for insulation.

There's never a concern that the traditional lumber-packed corner can withstand the load imposed on it. But unless there is an unusual load on a corner, even a single stud is structurally sufficient, just like any other stud in the wall. With this in mind, you could consider every corner with more than one stud to be overbuilt. But a light-framed corner may be a realistic concern in seismic areas. There may not be enough lumber to connect tie-down straps or bolts to.

Some corner options don't provide as much nailing for drywall and sheathing. Metal clips, different size studs, or lightweight blocking has to be installed; and this breaks the usual framing rhythm. This may cause you some concern the first time you try a light-framed alternative. But once you get used to working with a different option you'll find it becomes second nature.

Energy efficiency and improved comfort can't be overlooked either. Any solid wood that translates from the inside surface to the exterior will conduct heat more rapidly than an insulated cavity. Many of the following alternative corner details focus on this issue.

Four-Stud 2x4 Corner

The traditional four-stud corner works for 2x4 walls only. Three studs, or two studs filled with scrap blocks, are framed into the first wall you lift and an end stud in the mating wall closes the corner to create an inside edge for hanging drywall. There's plenty of material to nail siding and corner boards to here. But this tends to be the "coldest" corner and uses the most lumber.

Typical four-stud 2x4 corner. (Photo by Scott Phillips, courtesy *Fine Homebuilding* magazine, © The Taunton Press, Inc.)

Four-Stud 2x6 Corner

A similar configuration used when framing with 2x6s, called a boxed corner, forms a hollow cavity that can be filled with insulation. Using a 2x4 filler eliminates the need to frame five or six studs into the corner. Make up a U box with two 2x6s nailed to a 2x4 stud or blocks and fit it at the end of the first wall you lift. Fill the space with insulation before you sheathe the wall. The 2x6 end stud in the mating wall will form the inside corner.

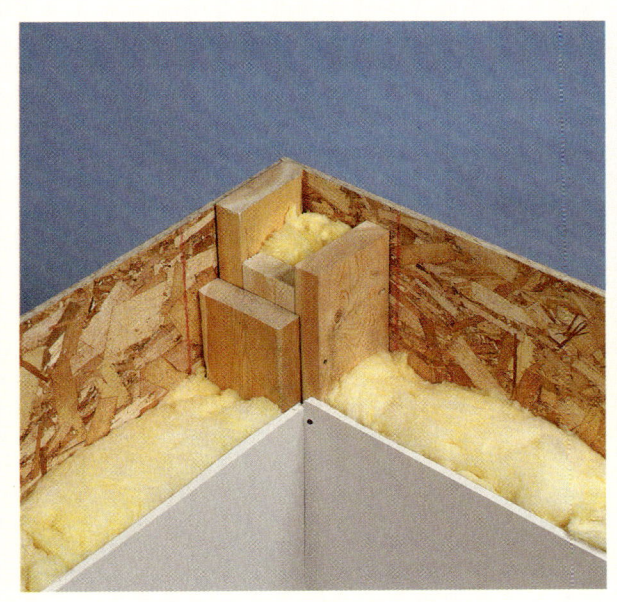

Four-stud 2x6 boxed corner. (Photo by Scott Phillips, courtesy *Fine Homebuilding* magazine, © The Taunton Press, Inc.)

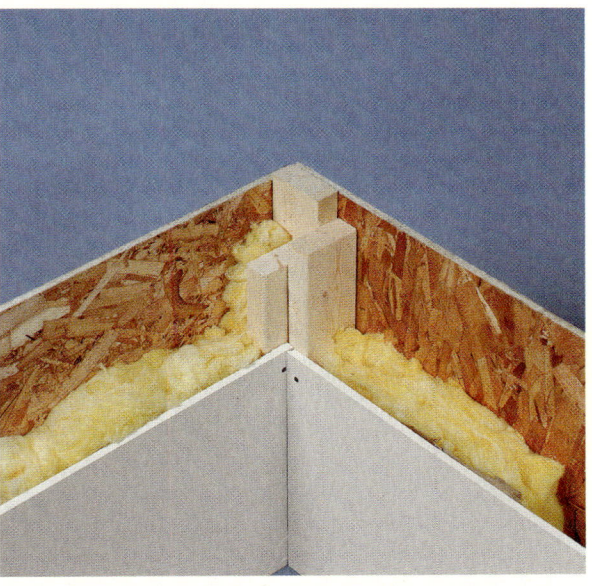

Three-stud corner. (Photo by Scott Phillips, courtesy *Fine Homebuilding* magazine, © The Taunton Press, Inc.)

Three-Stud 2x4 or 2x6 Corner

A three-stud corner, or "California corner," gives good corner support inside and outside. And it leaves a fair amount of space to fill with insulation. This alternative can be framed with 2x4 or 2x6 studs in the same fashion. Nail two studs together in an L configuration and install at the end of the first wall you lift. Face the long part of the L with the inside facing edge of the plates. The end stud on the mating wall supports the inside corner.

Two-Stud 2x4 or 2x6 Corner with Drywall Clips

You'll get a little more insulation inside two-stud corners than you will with three-stud corners. Frame both walls that meet at the corner with a single stud at the end of the plates. After the walls are lifted flush, nail the studs to one another. Before you install the drywall, screw on drywall

(continued on p. 118)

Two-stud corner with drywall clips. (Photo by Scott Phillips, courtesy *Fine Homebuilding* magazine, © The Taunton Press, Inc.)

WALL FRAMING 117

Framing Exterior Corners *(continued)*

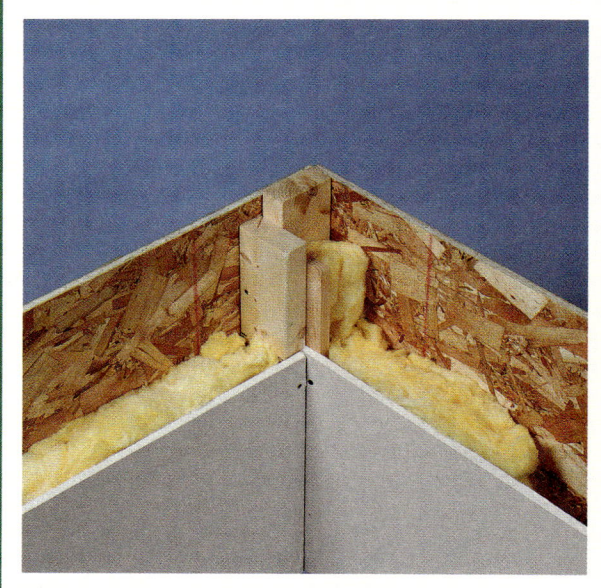

Two-stud corner with nailer. (Photo by Scott Phillips, courtesy *Fine Homebuilding* magazine, © The Taunton Press, Inc.)

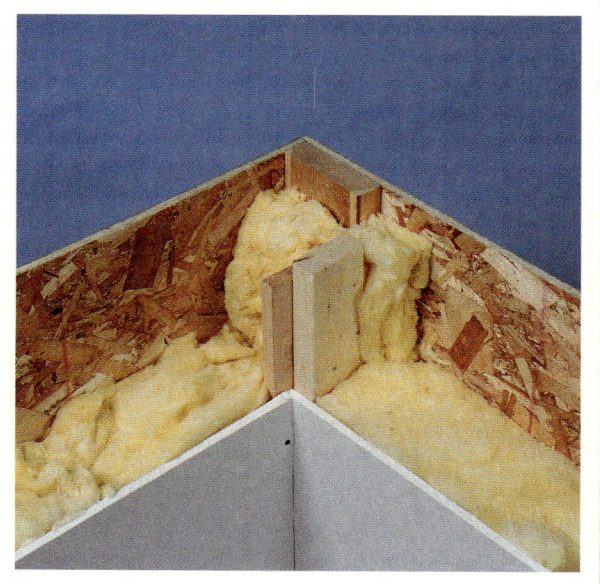

Non-thermal bridging corner. (Photo by Scott Phillips, courtesy *Fine Homebuilding* magazine, © The Taunton Press, Inc.)

clips to hold the sheets at the inside corner. There are several brands of drywall clips made from steel or plastic. Space the clips 16 in. to 24 in. apart and put two at the intersection between sheets.

One drawback with clips is the lack of solid wood for fastening trim, such as baseboard, crown moldings, and chair rail, that meets at the inside corner. You can overcome this problem with a couple of strategically placed scrap blocks of wood in lieu of the clips.

Two-Stud 2x4 or 2x6 Corner with Nailer

Similar to the clip corner, the nailer model uses a 1x3 or scrap strips of plywood or oriented strand board (OSB) to form the inside corner for drywall attachment. Plan how you'll fasten the strip to the 2x4. You can leave the end stud off the second wall you lift and insert it later with the nailer secured onto it. Or you can screw the strip through the stud once it's in place.

Thermal Breaking Corner, 2x6 Wall Only

If you're serious about breaking the thermal bridge at the corner, you can try this configuration. Frame the first wall you lift with one 2x6 at the end. Replace the usual end 2x6 stud of the second wall with a 2x4 stud. There will be a space between the two studs when the walls are mated. The top plates connect the walls, and either drywall clips or the wood strip backer can be used to form the inside corner for the drywall. You can add a couple of short 2x blocks to connect the 2x6 and 2x4 in the middle for added rigidity. This corner offers the best thermal efficiency of the group.

be nonbearing, so the openings can be framed without structural jacks and headers. Check your plans to be sure.

The studs at the end of walls can be laid out to create one of several corner configurations, as discussed in the sidebar on p. 116. Mark both ends of the plates for the configuration you choose.

Laying out interior bearing walls The only interior walls we'll build at this phase of construction are ones necessary to support floor or ceiling joists. Usually this amounts to a wall that divides the house down the middle. (Nonbearing interior walls will be covered in chapter 7.)

Layout the plates for the interior walls after the exterior walls are built and lifted upright. If you framed the exterior walls with 2x6s you may have spaced the studs 24 in. on center. The interior wall is probably only 2x4 and the spacing, 16 in. on center. Like the second set of exterior walls you framed, the plates will start against the inside edge of exterior walls, but the stud layout will begin from the *outside* of the exterior wall so that the studs will stack up over floor joists.

Follow the same layout sequencing as for exterior walls. The partition backers and corners on an interior wall, however, aren't subject to the same insulation concerns as they are on exterior walls. Usually, they are framed in a more traditional fashion.

For corner connections between perpendicular walls use the traditional four-stud corner. And for intersecting wall backers, use the three-stud partition backer. (Both corners are described in the sidebar on p. 116.)

Preparing the stock

While you are laying out the wall plates, other crew members can be preparing the stock needed to frame the walls. All of the stud stock can be crowned and cut to length, if you aren't using precut studs. Though marking the crowns of wall studs isn't commonly done on most crews, we think it is a worthwhile venture. By matching the direction of the crowns, you avoid waves in the walls that can telegraph through drywall or siding. Straight walls are especially desirable during kitchen cabinet and countertop installations.

To minimize handling, plan the stud drop from the lumberyard to be close to where you'll cut and use the stock. Grade each 2x as you pull it from the unit and direct it to one of three stations.

Mark straight or nearly straight studs with a crown mark and an S. Mark the crowns even on dead-straight studs, otherwise someone will think it was neglected and he'll waste time looking at it again. Draw the symbols far enough down the stud so they won't be cut off if you trim the studs to length or cut them for jacks. Use the straight S pieces for corner studs and as studs in walls where cabinetry will be installed, especially built-ins.

Mark all the average-quality studs—ones with a $1/8$-in to $1/4$-in. crown in 8 ft.—with a crown mark and stack for trimming, or place on the deck if precut and ready to use. Less desirable stock can be marked with double crown marks, indicating their lower quality, and be used for double studs nailed together with opposing crowns.

Direct the poorest quality studs to a separate pile to be cut for short cripples, blocking, truss bracing, and nailers or—if there are lots of them—return them to the lumberyard.

Another person can cut all the headers, saddles, cripples, and jacks from your cut list. Label the parts with the lengths and location so there's no question where they'll be installed. Pile rough opening part kits near the section of wall where they'll be installed.

You can also preassemble the headers. For 2x4 walls, use pieces of $3/8$-in. to $1/2$-in. sheathing as spacers to sandwich between the layers of the header so they'll match the thickness of the $3 1/2$-in. wall.

There are a couple of options for matching headers to the thickness of a 2x6 wall. You can nail the two layers together and block the bottom edge out with a 2x3 on edge after the wall is lifted. You can make a sandwich of three layers

Working off the cut list, cut and label all the parts needed to frame the rough openings for windows and doors. Assemble these rough opening "kits" and place them on the deck near where they will be assembled.

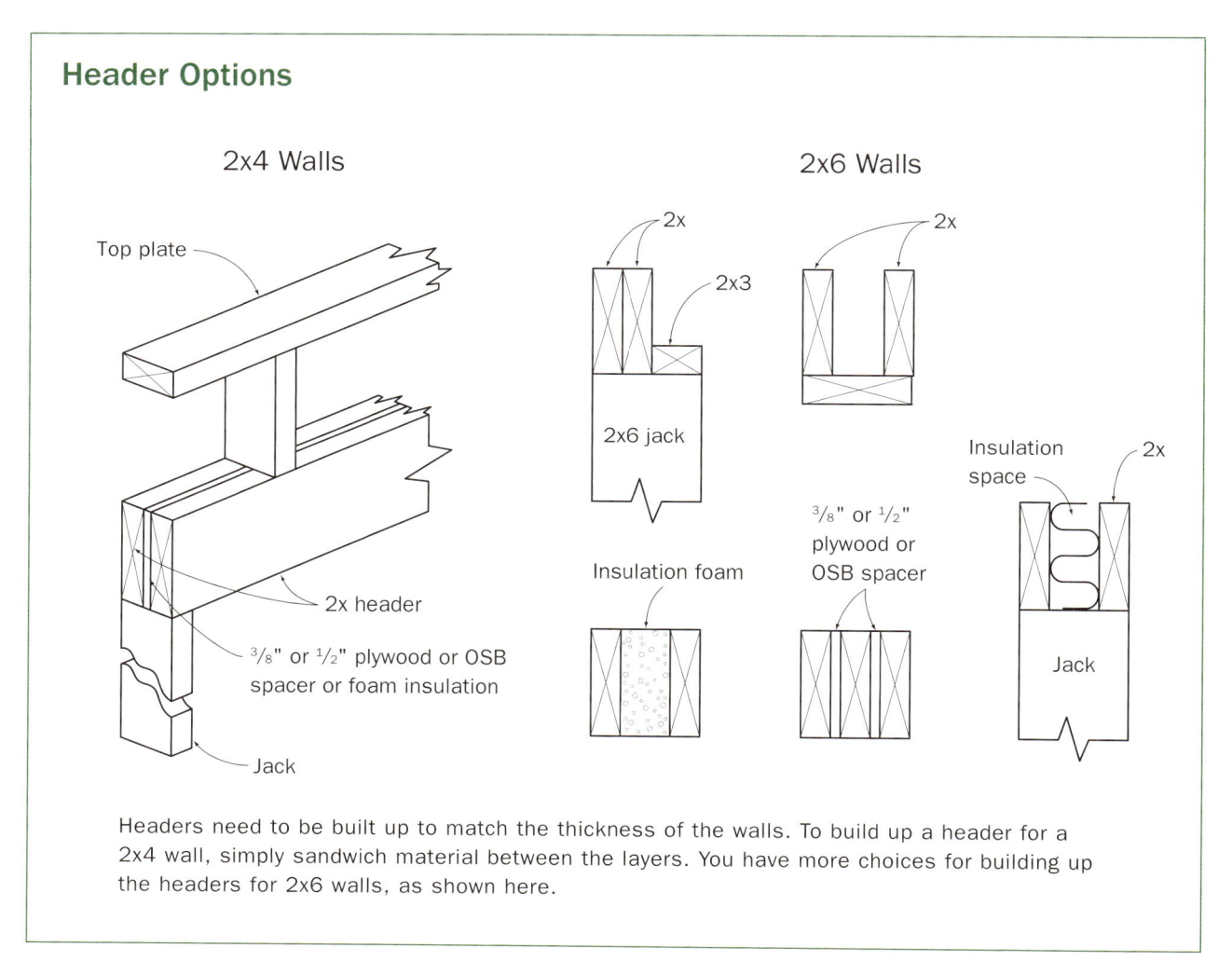

Header Options

2x4 Walls

- Top plate
- 2x header
- 3/8" or 1/2" plywood or OSB spacer or foam insulation
- Jack

2x6 Walls

- 2x
- 2x3
- 2x6 jack
- Insulation foam
- 3/8" or 1/2" plywood or OSB spacer
- 2x
- Insulation space
- 2x
- Jack

Headers need to be built up to match the thickness of the walls. To build up a header for a 2x4 wall, simply sandwich material between the layers. You have more choices for building up the headers for 2x6 walls, as shown here.

with two spacers of ⅜-in. to ½-in. sheathing between each. Or, the one we like for its insulating value, leave the two layers separate and install one flush with each face of the wall. The space can be filled later with foam or loose insulation.

Assembling the Walls

Now the action starts. With an accurate plate layout, square floor deck, and precut parts; the wall assembly will go quickly. In this section, we look at framing the wall, sheathing it, and lifting it upright.

Framing the wall

When you are loading the floor deck with all the studs, jacks, headers, and other materials you've prepared, make sure to put them out of the way of the walls you'll be framing. For an 8-ft. wall, you should stack materials back at least 10 ft. from the edge of the floor deck. You'll need the extra space to swing a hammer or handle a pneumatic framing nailer when you nail along the top plate. For small houses, you may have to leave some of the materials on the ground so you don't crowd yourself.

Tacking down the bottom plate The first step in nailing together a wall is to tack nail the bottom plate on edge to the in-board side of the chalkline. This keeps the wall straight so that when it's sheathed and lifted it will lie flat on the floor and be flat on top. The tack nails also act as a hinge when the wall is lifted so the bottom plate doesn't kick out off the floor. There is usually enough space on floor decks to assemble opposite parallel walls at the same time, so prep both bottom plates.

Move the top plate sections about 8½ ft. away from the foundation edge. Roll the bottom plate up on edge with the layout symbols facing the middle of the floor deck. Align the bottom edge of the plate to the chalkline you snapped earlier to indicate the inside edge of the wall. When you lift the wall, the bottom plate will be lined up with the chalkline.

Flush the end plate up with the rim joist at the end of the deck. Drive a 6d or 8d nail at an angle through the bottom face of the plate into every other joist location; that's about every 32 in. (If the plate is not straight, you'll need to put nails more frequently than every 32 in.) Mix in a 12d or 16d nail every 4 ft. to 6 ft. instead of the shorter nails. The spike will hold better during the wall lift. You can also drive nails through the top face of the plate. If you choose to try this, be sure to use spikes; as the plate pivots up when you lift

Tack nail the bottom plate to the subfloor sheathing with the bottom edge of the plate aligned with the chalkline on the floor deck.

Long walls and tall walls take a lot of force to lift. Give the pivot edge of the bottom plate extra support by nailing some tie-back straps to the floor deck. Pieces of lumber banding strap nailed to the bottom side of the plate and to the subfloor act as a hinge.

the wall, the nail will withdraw from the subfloor. The longer spikes won't withdraw completely.

When you tack down a bottom plate along an edge of the floor deck where the joists run parallel to the wall, you will be nailing only into the subfloor. That's when using pivot straps will be helpful.

Long walls and tall walls take a lot of force to lift. During the first half of the pivot as you lift a wall, the force is pressing against the tack nails and they can tear out, sending the wall off the deck. Give the pivot edge extra support by nailing some tie-back straps to the floor deck. The straps are also useful during the cold months when you're contending with frost, snow, or ice on the floor deck and lumber.

Cut pieces of lumber banding strap or hurricane tie-down ribbon about 12 in. long. Bend them so one leg of the strap is almost as long as the wall plate is wide (5 in. for a 2x6 wall). Slide the long leg between the plate and the subfloor from the bottom side of the plate. Nail the strap to the underside of the bottom plate; then pull the long leg snug and nail it to the floor and into a joist. Make sure the bottom plate matches the chalkline before you nail the strap to the floor.

Nailing the plates to the studs Place a stud tight to the bottom plate at each X mark. Remember to insert straight (S) studs at the ends of the wall and in areas where cabinets or countertops will be installed. Face the crowns of the studs up rather than down. When faced down, the belly will hold the ends of the stud off the floor and make it more difficult to fasten the plates.

Bring the top plate down to the top of the studs. Start nailing the bottom plate and the studs together first. Drive two 16d nails through the bottom of the plate into the butt end of each stud. Space the nails $1/2$ in. to 1 in. in from the edges of the plate.

When using a framing nailer, be careful not to angle the nose of the tool downward. A downward angle may drive the nail through the lumber and into the subfloor.

Make sure that the bottom plate meets flat against the bottom of the stud when driving nails with a nailer. Plates that have a twist to them will touch one edge of the stud but not the other. Drive the plate flat to the base of the stud with a hammer if necessary.

After the bottom plate is fastened, nail the top plate to the studs. Flush up the end of the top plate with the rim joist at one end of the wall. Nail the top plate to the studs the same way as

Nail all studs to the bottom plate first, then nail them to the top plate. Drive two spikes through the plate into the butt end of each stud. Space the nails ½ in. to 1 in. from the edges of the plate.

the bottom plate. Don't nail the tops of any studs that fall within 16 in. of a king stud, however. Leave the tops of the nearby studs loose so you can move them aside to drive nails through the king and into a header without interference.

Assembling rough openings Start assembling the rough openings by installing the king studs between the top and bottom plates and then fasten the jack stud to the bottom plate. This ensures that there won't be a gap between the base of the jack and the plate, which can be the case when the jack is nailed to the king first.

Face the crown of the jack down, opposite that of the king. After the jack is nailed to the bottom plate, flush the top edge of the jack to the king as you nail the two together. Stagger a row of nails spaced every 16 in. or so along the top and bottom edges of the stud pair, working the edges flush as you go. The crown of the jack will balance the crown of the king and result in a straight unit. Take care to angle the nails a little as you drive through the jack to prevent them from extending through the face of the king—the protruding nail tips can shred flesh and clothing.

Install the header tight to the top of the jacks and flush with the face of the wall. Nail through the king stud into the butt ends of each layer with two or three nails. Once the header is nailed in place, reorient any nearby common studs you left loose earlier and nail them through the top plate.

Measure, cut, and install the cripple studs that fit between the top of the header and the top plate. Toenail them to the top of the header and through nail from the top plate.

Draw some guidelines on the jacks to orient the bottom edge of the saddle by using one of the precut bottom cripples as a gauge. Toenail the saddle to the jacks and nail the cripple studs in position. Measure the height of the rough opening just as a final check before moving on. Openings can usually be from ⅛ in. less to ⅜ in. more than called for without a problem.

Door openings follow the same assembly order, except the saddle and lower cripples are omitted. Eventually, the bottom plate in door rough openings will be cut out. One thing you can do now to ease the process later is to make cuts with a circular saw as deep as the blade will go (about 2½ in.) through the bottom plate on the inside edge of the jacks. After the wall is lifted, the cut can be completed with a reciprocating saw.

Full-height header variation When you use tall header stock like 2x10s or 2x12s that fit tight under the top plate, you will have to cut the jacks when you frame the rough opening so that they

WALL FRAMING

When using tall headers, pressed tight against the top plate, cut and install the jacks after the header is installed.

also fit tight between the bottom of the header and the bottom plate. This is because lumber heights vary, making it difficult to predetermine the length of the jacks when you are planning the cut list.

Start assembling a rough opening with a full header by nailing the header tight to the top plate first. Drive the nails through the top plate into the top of the header. You may have to use a few hammer blows to draw the plate and the header together tightly. Nail through the king stud into the butt ends of the header and measure between the bottom of the header and the bottom plate.

Cut the jacks and install them as described for the earlier example. If the jack is a little long, it will push the bottom plate away from the bottom of the king stud. Remove it and trim it; then tap the plate back to the bottom of the king before trying again.

Install the saddle and cripples as before. Check the height of the opening. It will probably be on the tall side, if anything, because we presumed the tallest height for the header when we made the cut list.

Installing partition backers Nail in any wall backers. If you use a 2x6 flat backer, be sure to press it down to the floor deck so it will be flush with the inside face of the wall. It's okay to use

Install the saddle and cripple studs after the jacks are nailed in place.

Nail the second layer of the top plate on after all the studs, backers, and rough openings are fastened between the lower top plate and the bottom plate. Stagger joints between the two top plates by at least 4 in.

2x6s that have a big crown, as long as they aren't twisted or bowed on the flat side.

Preassemble the three-stud backers before you put them between the plates. The filler that spaces the two studs can be another full stud or you can use scrap blocks. Make sure the ends of the studs and blocks are square to the sides before you nail the assembly together. If they aren't, the top and bottom won't sit flat against the plates and will actually cause a hump in the wall. Pay attention to the crowns of the two side studs. Keep them up and the blocks or backer stud flush with the bottom of the crown.

Nailing on the top plate layer Oppose the crowns of the second layer of top plate sections to the crowns of the first so they counteract each other and make for a straight wall. Hold the end of the top layer back from the end of the bottom layer by the width of the wall that will meet it at the corner, for example, $5\frac{1}{2}$ in. for a 2x6 wall. This permits the plates of the perpendicular wall to be overlapped at the corner, similar to the way you overlapped the corners of the top layer of the mudsill.

For extra strength, trim the end of the plates to end over the middle of a stud location. And it's important to overlap the joints between sections of the upper top plate with those of the lower top plate by at least 4 ft. This overlap ties the wall together along its length, makes it easier to straighten the wall, and gives added support when lifting the wall. Nail the upper plate with two 16d nails over each stud location and at the ends. Flush the edges of the two plates as you nail your way along the wall.

> **ADVICE**
>
> ## To Leave a Void or Not
>
> *Some framers leave a void in the upper top plate where interior partition walls tie in. This works when the interior walls are framed with double top plates like the exterior walls and when you can precisely determine the wall location. We've found it easier not to leave the void and to use a steel strap to connect intersecting walls after they are lifted. This gives us more freedom to fine-tune interior wall locations later, and it keeps the continuity of the double top plate with the 4-ft. joint offset that is often broken by the plate voids.*

WALL FRAMING   125

The second set of walls you frame go between the raised primary walls and are built the same way. The only difference is you can't run the upper layer of the top plate all the way out. Omit a 4-ft. to 8-ft. section of upper top plate on each end. Break the joint over a stud like usual and precut the filler plate so it's long enough to crosslap the space left at the end of the upper top plate of the first wall.

Nail the filler plates on when the wall is lifted and joined to the primary wall.

Sheathing the wall

To sheathe or not to sheathe. There are many factors that contribute to the choice: local building practice, building codes, cost, builder's preference, designer's preference, siding, and insulation system.

We use structural sheathing on all the homes we frame. The sheathing gives racking strength to the wall, it laps the rim joist, and it connects the first floor to the second. Also, the sheathing serves as an air barrier, and it gives us a nailing base for siding. It's our personal preference and the regional practice in our area. However there are other ways to brace walls structurally so they resist racking forces; for example, let-in braces and sheer panels, described later in the chapter.

Here we'll illustrate our system of prepping and sheathing a wall to keep it straight and square. Then we'll look at a few things to do before lifting the wall that can save labor later. It's easier to do what you can while things are down low and flat before they become straight and tall.

Squaring the wall Before you can sheathe a framed wall, you have to make sure it's square. If it's sheathed out of square, the ends of the wall and all the rough openings will be out of plumb when the wall is lifted.

Start by checking the bottom plate to see that it's still flush with the chalkline you tacked it to. Often the activity of installing the studs can knock the plate off the line. You may need a few taps of a sledgehammer to move the fully assembled wall back on the line. To bring the bottom plate down to the line, don't tap the bottom plate itself, which could leave a gap between the plate and the butt of the studs. Instead, whack on the top plate to drive the wall down to the line. This is where the sledgehammer comes in handy.

The wall is probably square because you built it to the edges of the square floor deck, but a quick check will confirm this. Measure diagonally between opposite corners of the wall at the plates. If the measurements are within $1/8$ in., consider the wall fine. If they're off more than that, use a

Square up the wall after it's all studded up by measuring diagonally from corner to corner. Adjust the wall if it isn't square with a few whacks from a sledgehammer. Use a wood block to cushion the blows to the top plate.

Prepare to sheath the wall by determining how much to overhang the first course of sheets below the bottom plate. Measure from the top of the floor deck to the bottom of the mudsill to determine the overhang.

sledgehammer to tap the top plate of the long diagonal toward its diagonal mate. When you have the wall satisfactorily square, drive a couple of spikes halfway through the bottom of a header into the subfloor. This will keep the wall square, and the nails will be easy to remove when you trim the sheathing from the opening. If you nail the wall down through the inside edge of the top plate, the nail will be inaccessible after the sheathing goes on.

Laying out for sheathing Sheathing panels have an axis of strength. It's usually the 8-ft. length of the sheet rather than the 4-ft. width. We prefer to run our sheathing with the 8-ft. length running horizontally, with the stronger axis going across the studs. Some carpenters install the sheets vertically, which increases the sheer strength of the wall.

We also run our sheets down past the edge of the bottom plate. Doing this allows the sheathing to overlap the rim joists and the mudsills when the wall is lifted. Though, again, you can sheath just from bottom plate to the top plate and fill in the voids later. It's a matter of preference. We'll describe our process, and you can extrapolate techniques to meet your own preferences and needs.

Mark and snap a chalkline across the wall studs to guide the sheathing installation. Hold the tape measure at the distance from the floor to the mudsill bottom and make a mark at 48 in.

You'll need a chalkline across the studs to keep the panel edges straight and the ends square. Plan to overlap the sheathing below the bottom plate to lap the rim joist and come down to the mudsill or the wall sheathing on the first floor walls.

Measure the distance between the top of the subfloor and the bottom edge of the mudsill at several points around the foundation. For second-floor walls, measure down to the top of the

WALL FRAMING 127

Mark the edges of window and door rough openings while sheathing the wall. Cut the sheathing out of the openings before raising the wall.

sheathing panels on the first-floor walls. Take the shortest measurement you found and subtract it from 48 in., the width of the sheathing. This measurement will be the distance you snap the chalkline up the wall from the bottom of the bottom plate.

Measure from the bottom of the bottom plate at the end studs and make marks for the chalkline. Snap the chalkline across the studs in the wall. Have someone hold the middle of the string on long walls and snap both sides.

Installing the sheathing Start by placing full sheathing panels on the lower half of the wall. Keep the sheets flush with the chalkline. Drive a nail halfway in at the top corner of the end sheets into the end stud. We'll straighten these studs later. Drive one nail by hand into each stud at the top of the panel. (You'll completely nail off the sheets later.)

When panels cross rough openings, make a mark on the inside edge of the jacks. And measure down to the saddle (if it's a window rough opening) and write the measurement on the face of the panel. These marks will guide you when you cut the sheathing out of the rough openings.

Continue to run the sheets of the first row of sheathing to the end of the wall, marking out all the rough openings. Snap a chalkline on the sheathing at the center of the bottom plate and use a T-square to mark lines for each stud and cripple to guide nailing. Draw out the lines on the inside perimeter of the rough openings to use as cutting and nailing guides.

After the first row of sheathing is marked off for nailing, set sheets out for the next row against the first course. Follow the manufacturer's instructions regarding panel spacing.

Offset the sheathing joints of the second row by about 4 ft., just like for floor sheathing. To minimize waste at door openings and tall window openings, slide the next sheet of sheathing down to land on a stud farther down the wall. As long as the edge of the panel catches the jack, you can reduce falloff waste. You can use narrow pieces to fill between window openings that are close together.

Tack the panels of the second row down, and draw the stud and rough opening cut lines. Use framing nailers or hand nail the sheathing down to the studs with 6d or 8d nails spaced 4 in. to 6 in. along the edges and 8 in. to 12 in. at mid-panel. Check your local building code for specific nailing requirements.

Return to the end studs and pull the tack nails out. Run a straightedge or string line from top plate to bottom plate. Straighten the stud, and nail the sheathing to hold it in place.

128   CHAPTER FIVE

Minimize sheathing waste by lining up the factory edge of the sheets with door and window openings and then cutting the sheathing at an adjacent opening. Use excess pieces to sheathe other portions of the wall.

Use a straightedge to straighten the end studs of the wall before nailing the sheathing to them.

The sheathing won't reach to the top of an 8-ft. wall when you overhang the sheets to cover the rim joists and mudsills below. There are several ways to complete the sheathing at this point, depending on if there's another floor or roof going on above or if there is a cantilevered floor.

Sheathing details On walls that will have additional floors resting on them, leave the top portion of the wall unsheathed for now if it is less than 3 ft.. The sheathing overlap from the second floor walls will reach over and fill this space.

When the space is 3 ft. or more, think about installing the sheathing now and letting it extend above the top plate of the wall. Before you do this though, consider marking the layout for the next floor joists (described below). The extended sheathing will make it tougher to grab the top plate of the wall to lift it. But this problem can be overcome by lifting the wall from a window or door opening partway up onto sawhorses; then repositioning it to continue the lift from outside (lifting the wall is discussed below). An alternative would be to lift the walls without installing the last row of sheathing and install the next floor

On end walls that fit between already lifted walls, sheath only the middle part of the walls. After the wall is lifted, cut and nail on sheathing from the outside.

Sheathing between Rafter or Truss Overhang

An alternative to cutting the sheathing flush with the top plate is to extend the sheathing past the top plate to act as an air baffle for the roof insulation. You will have to notch the sheathing to accommodate the rafters or trusses where they extend beyond the face of the wall. Mark the layout for the rafters or trusses on the top plate before you put on the sheathing. Determine the height of the rafter or roof truss at the outside edge of the exterior wall. This can be done by precutting a rafter or drawing a mockup to scale of the rafter or truss tail. Subtract 2 in. from the height and run the sheathing this distance past the second plate. Rip and install the last row of sheathing. Then at each rafter or truss location cut notches 1 3/4 in. wide from the top of the sheathing down to the top of the second top plate. We choose 1 3/4 in. rather than the actual 1 1/2 in. to avoid any binding when installing the roof framing.

deck. Then slide wall sheathing over the edge of the floor deck and down to the sheathing below.

When the next floor cantilevers over the first-floor walls, run your sheathing just to the top of the top plate.

To play it safe, when sheathing a wall that will have roof trusses or ceiling joists and rafters directly above, run the sheathing up to the top plate.

You won't be able to sheathe to the end of the second set of walls that fit between the first set you lifted. On these walls, run out as much sheathing as you can across the studs. Leave 16-in. to 48-in. panels out at the ends of the walls. Precut panels to fill in the voids once the walls are lifted. Remember that the sheathing will cover all the way to the outside corner and not just to the end of the wall.

Planning ahead for other tasks

Before you lift the wall you can do a couple of tasks now while the wall is lying on the deck and easy to access. All of these will save time later.

Install housewrap You can roll out and staple or nail down the housewrap or tar paper on the wall. Flush the material at the bottom edge for

Housewrap or underlayment can be rolled out and stapled to walls before they are lifted. Where sheathing is left out of a wall, roll enough paper back (and onto a stick if necessary) to wrap around the corner of the wall once it's upright and the sheathing is filled in.

first-floor walls or overhang it 6 in. to 8 in. beyond the bottom of the sheathing if it will overlap a wall below. Staple the material down initially and return to nail it down using the manufacturer's recommended fastening method.

Don't staple the fabric on the overhanging area of the sheathing. You'll have to lift the wrap up to nail off the sheathing once the wall is lifted; then you can fasten the material.

Overlap successive courses shingle fashion, so water will be shed properly. We lap courses about 5 in. to 6 in. for good coverage. At the end of a row, we overlap 8 in. to 12 in. Check the wrap manufacturer's specifications for overlap recommendations. You can tape the seams in the material while the wall is down, too.

Extend the wrap over the end studs of the first set of walls you build. Because some of the sheathing will be missing at the ends of the second set of walls, trim the wrap long enough to cover around the corner then roll it back onto a length of furring. When the walls are lifted and the sheathing is filled in, you can finish rolling the wrap out.

Laying out joists or rafters on plates
You can save time laying out for the floor joists of

Mark out the floor joist layout or roof rafter/truss layout on the top plate of walls before raising them.

a second floor or for the roof rafters while the wall is lying down. Observe the procedures you followed for floor joists or look at chapter 6 for roof layout tips. Remember to mark for opening details and move joists to avoid plumbing.

You can even install the rim joist on walls that match flush with the rim joists at corners. Usually these are the first set of walls you build and lift.

Installing a soffit nailer
We're looking way ahead when we install this detail, but it is much

WALL FRAMING **131**

easier to do now. Flat soffits usually need a nailer to hold up the wall edge or install perpendicular blocking to.

Sketch up a full-scale drawing of a rafter tail or truss tail to determine the distance between the top of the wall plate and the bottom of the soffit nailer (refer to chapter 6). Mark that distance down from the plate on the face of the sheathed and housewrapped wall. Snap a chalkline and fasten on the nailer.

Lifting walls

Young framers want to just grab a wall, lift it upright, and then figure out what to do once it's standing. This works fine for short walls, but for long, heavy walls it's safer to plan the lift. And there are ways to lift a wall that are safer and easier than grunting and bearing it.

For safety sake, have a clear area all around the wall. Air hoses, electrical cords, and excess lumber are all hazards you don't need in the way when lifting walls.

Check the bottom of the bottom plate to make sure there aren't any nails protruding or debris on the subfloor that can hold the bottom plate off the floor once the wall is lifted. Remove the nails you drove through the header into the floor to keep the wall square. Gather up braces to hold the wall upright once it's lifted and put them within arm's reach on the floor deck.

Just before lifting, run a bead or two of adhesive or caulking to seal the joint between the bottom plate and subfloor and between the wall sheathing and the mudsill. This will help stop drafts at a common leaky area.

Finally, lift the top plate of the wall up on some scrap 2x blocks to get hands or lifting jacks under easily. And put a couple of sawhorses nearby to use as a resting support in case there's any difficulty lifting the wall.

We've lifted hundreds of walls with brute force and are no worse for the wear, but we've heard some horror stories of broken legs, arms, backs, and death from wall-lifting operations gone bad. Now we use mechanical lifts and try to stay out of harm's way. Here's how to handle both methods. And no matter the method, be extra cautious on windy days.

Manpower If you opt to lift by hand, have plenty of manpower. Don't reach for the limit of your strength to lift a big wall. There's no margin for error when you're maxed out.

Review an escape plan and signal with your crew on each lift. It's very hard to lower a wall that's halfway up when you're out of energy. The natural reaction when it's obvious the wall is coming down is to let go. It's important to have a place to go and to let go as a group. Otherwise someone will get caught under the wall. Window

In preparation for wall raising, clear the floor deck, raise the wall onto blocks to make it easier to lift, have wall braces ready, and bring sawhorses nearby for safety.

and door openings make good escape routes but two guys in a hole may not fit. Make a plan.

Have a set of sawhorses close by and perpendicular to the wall. In a pinch you can hook a foot on the horse and get it under the wall either as a safety stop or in a bailout situation.

The hardest point when lifting a wall is when you have to change your hand and arm position from a lift to a push. Sometimes it's safest to plan a stop point and bring the sawhorses in to hold the wall a little above waist height. Rest and reposition into the push mode. Lock your arms and use your legs to bring the wall upright.

Lifting jacks The other option is to lift the wall mechanically. There are several manufactured systems for lifting walls; but remember, overloaded jacks are as dangerous as overloaded workers. Play it safe and have enough jacks for the job at hand.

Block up the top plate of the wall high enough by hand to get the jacks under. Set the base of the jacks on a floor joist. If you have to position the jack base on the subfloor between joists, use a wide 2x block to spread the load; you don't want the jack to punch through the subfloor during the lift.

Be careful when raising walls by hand. Use a pair of sawhorses to rest the wall on and reposition yourself so your legs do most of the work during the lift.

Mechanical wall-lifting jacks take stress off crew members' backs.

WALL FRAMING 133

Fasten and back up the jack base with some blocks nailed to the floor to prevent a kickout. Have a method to stop the wall from toppling over once it's lifted. Some jacking systems have retainers built in. A couple of heavy ropes tied to the top of the wall and fastened to the floor will suffice, too.

Lift the wall slowly and keep everyone away until the wall is safely up.

Fastening the wall

Once the wall is lifted doesn't mean the work is done. You still have to keep it standing, make all the final connections, check it for accuracy and straighten it in preparation for a second floor or the roof.

Nail adjustable wall braces or spring braces to the wall after it's tilted up. Have one worker eyeball the wall for plumb while another sets the brace.

Bracing the wall Immediately after lifting a wall, attach some braces to hold it upright. Set the wall plumb by eye or make a quick check with a level. Keep the braces about 10 ft. back from the ends of the wall if it is one of the first ones up. You'll need the space clear to build the walls that fit between the first walls lifted.

The braces should be about 10 ft. long so you can nail them to the wall about 7 ft. high and have them angle back at about 45° to the floor. We use adjustable braces to make the wall-stringing process easy, but you can use spring braces too (see the sidebar above for a descrip-

Use a level to plumb exterior corners before fastening corner studs and top plates.

Spring Braces

Spring braces are simple site-built tools used to straighten walls. One end of a long stud or ledger board—about 10 ft., depending on the height of the wall—is nailed on the flat, usually at the top plate. The other end is nailed to the deck with a 2x kicker block nailed against it. A smaller stud, 4 ft. to 5 ft., is placed upright on the underside of the long spring brace, and its bottom end is secured to the deck. The short piece is then tapped toward the floor end of the brace causing it to bend and spring in, pulling the wall in with it. When the wall reaches the desired location, a nail tacks the spring brace to the top of the short stud.

Spring braces are used by most framers to straighten walls. But if you're going to frame more than one house, invest in adjustable wall-aligning braces. (See chapter 1 for more information about wall aligners.)

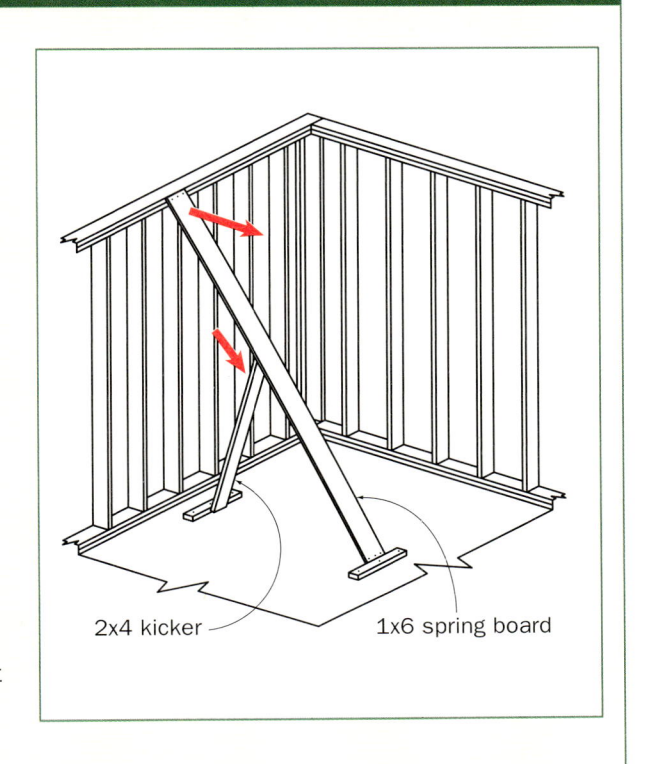

2x4 kicker   1x6 spring board

tion). Space the braces 8 ft. to 10 ft. apart along the wall. We'll come back to the braces when straightening the wall.

Nailing down the bottom plate After the wall is raised into position and braced, adjust the plate to the chalkline it was tacked to. It's easy to drive the wall out away from the floor deck with a hammer blow, but pulling it in is a little more difficult especially on a second floor. You can lean out a window if there is one close by and pound the wall back in to the chalkline. You can also make or buy a peavey, a tool that can dig into the bottom plate and the subfloor to draw the wall in (see sidebar on p. 136).

Once the plate is on the line, drive a spike or two through the bottom plate and into each floor joist on walls that run perpendicular to the joists. On parallel walls, nail close to the outside edge of the wall to catch the rim joist below.

Check for plumb at the end studs of the first set of walls you lift. When the other walls that meet at the corners go up, flush up the top plates and tack nail the corner studs together. Check the plumb in both directions. They should be accurate because of the effort you've made thus far to keep the mudsill, floor deck, and walls level and square at each stage of the framing. If they are off a bit, you can knock the wall in or out a little to make the correction.

Where interior bearing walls meet the exterior walls, tie the top plates together with a sheet-metal plate or strips of lumber banding strap. Nail the wall's bottom plate to the floor first and then plumb up to the top plate. The metal holds the

Peavey (a.k.a. Wall Puller)

When sheathed walls are constructed on the deck then lifted upright into position, more often than not the bottom plate has to be pulled in to meet the layout line. Instead of moving a ladder along the outside of the wall and working the bottom plate in with spikes, we made a simple lever-type device that allows us to do the whole job from the inside. It can be made from just about any type of scrap heavy-gauge steel, but tools like this are also commercially available.

The tool is made up of two pieces of steel. One piece is 8 in. to 10 in. long with some type of hook or sharp point at a 90° bend at the end. The other is about 1 ft. or so long with one sharp end. The dull end of the hooked piece is fastened to the straight piece about 3 in. up. They are fastened loosely with a nut and bolt that allow the pieces to move.

To use the peavey, hold it so that the sharp hook end falls on the bottom plate 1 in. or so from the outside. Pound the hook into the plate then drive the straight piece into the subfloor deck. The leverage of the tall straight piece makes it easy to pull the bottom plate inward into position.

Here, a peavey is used to pull the bottom plate inward until it matches the chalkline. Once adjusted, the plate is nailed to the floor.

wall in place and isn't thick enough to cause a problem with rim joists or blocking above.

Once you're satisfied that the corners are plumb, nail on the sections of top plate you left out when framing. Fit pieces of wall sheathing in place and nail them off. Also, finish spreading out and fastening the housewrap so the wind doesn't get hold of the roll and damage the material.

Stringing the walls It's good practice to straighten walls the same day they are lifted up. Kinks can develop in top plates when temporary braces are left on a wall for a day or two before you string it. The kinks will be harder to straighten out later. Stringing a wall is a process similar to what you did when straightening built-up beams (discussed in chapter 3).

Nail metal straps to secure interior bearing walls and beams to the top plates of exterior walls.

Nail spacer blocks to the top plate about 3 in. away from the inside corner of exterior walls. Run strings between the blocks for each wall or section of wall. When a bump-out interrupts a long wall, string the entire wall as if it were continuous. This ensures that the corners at the bump-out will be straight with the plane of the wall.

Some walls will have interior bearing walls butting into them that interfere with the string. You can either set the blocks and string on the outside face of the wall or let the spacer blocks rise about 1 in. above the top plate so the string will clear the perpendicular wall plate.

Move the temporary braces if you have to so they are spaced 8 ft. to 10 ft. apart along all the walls to be straightened. Work one wall at a time, adjusting the wall braces until your gauge block indicates the wall is parallel to the string.

Leave the strings up so you can recheck and adjust the walls just before and after installing the next floor's joists or the roof framing.

Straighten a wall by gauging the top plate to a string line stretched over furring spacer blocks nailed to the plumb corners of the wall. Use a furring gauge stick to check the plate to string space.

WALL FRAMING

Installing Shear Wall Bracing Details

Wall bracing is installed to resist racking (also known as shear or lateral) forces from wind, seismic activity, and off-center loading. Some areas have very strict requirements regarding corner bracing, and there are a few methods to meet the requirements. This is a good time to consult your building code book. It'll be a lot easier to build a compliant wall the first time around rather than to rebuild after a failed inspection.

Let-In Brace

One method that's built into the exterior wall framing process we described is the structural sheathing that covers the walls. When walls aren't fully sheathed or they're sheathed with a non-structural material, you can use one of the other methods. Check your local building code to determine which method(s) will comply.

A let-in brace is one of the oldest methods of bracing a wall. A diagonal 1x4 wood brace is cut into the exterior (sometimes interior) face of the studs in a wall from the top plate to the bottom plate. This forms a stable triangle with the bottom plate and the studs as the legs and the 1x4 as the hypotenuse. Usually these braces are installed at the corners of walls, but that's not necessary; they can go anywhere along a wall.

To install a let-in brace, first adjust the bottom plate of the wall to the subfloor line before you lift it and square the wall as we described earlier. Snap a pair of diagonal chalklines from the top plate to the bottom plate at a 45° to 60° angle. Space the lines apart to match the exact width of the 1x4. Set the depth of your circular saw blade about $1/16$ in. deeper than the thickness of the 1x4. Cut along the chalklines and then cut a series of saw kerfs between the lines on each stud, jack, or cripple. Use a chisel to knock out the wood between the kerfs.

Lay the 1x4 in the slot and trim the excess at the ends flush with the top and bottom plates. The brace must be continuous and relatively knot free to perform well. Drive two 8d nails through the 1x4 into each stud, jack, or cripple and into each plate.

Install a brace at each end of a wall and again every 25 ft. along the middle of walls.

Metal Strap

There are new versions of let-in braces, made of metal, that are easier to install than wood braces. Metal braces come in T and L profiles.

Install metal braces after you square a framed wall while it's still flat on the floor. Snap only one diagonal chalkline from top to bottom plate and cut a kerf across each stud and the plates. The slot should be $1/16$ in. deeper than the leg of the strap. Fasten the strap into the studs and plates according to the manufacturer's instructions. Again, multiple braces will increase wall stiffness.

Shear Panels

Structural sheathing can replace diagonal braces. Rather than sheathing entire walls you can install one or two panels oriented vertically from top plate to bottom plate on the wall starting at the corner of the wall. This is often done on walls that are sheathed with nonstructural sheathing or insulating foam board. An additional layer of thin foam board may need to be installed over the shear panels to match the thickness of the non-structural sheathing or foam board that covers the rest of the wall.

You can run shear panel sheathing horizontally, too, but some regions subject to extreme conditions may require solid blocking at all horizontal joints between panels. There are also specially engineered shear panel wall sections available that incorporate sheathing, studs, and metal connectors into one unit. These shear panel sections can be incorporated into your wall framing to meet seismic and wind condition requirements.

Bracing Options

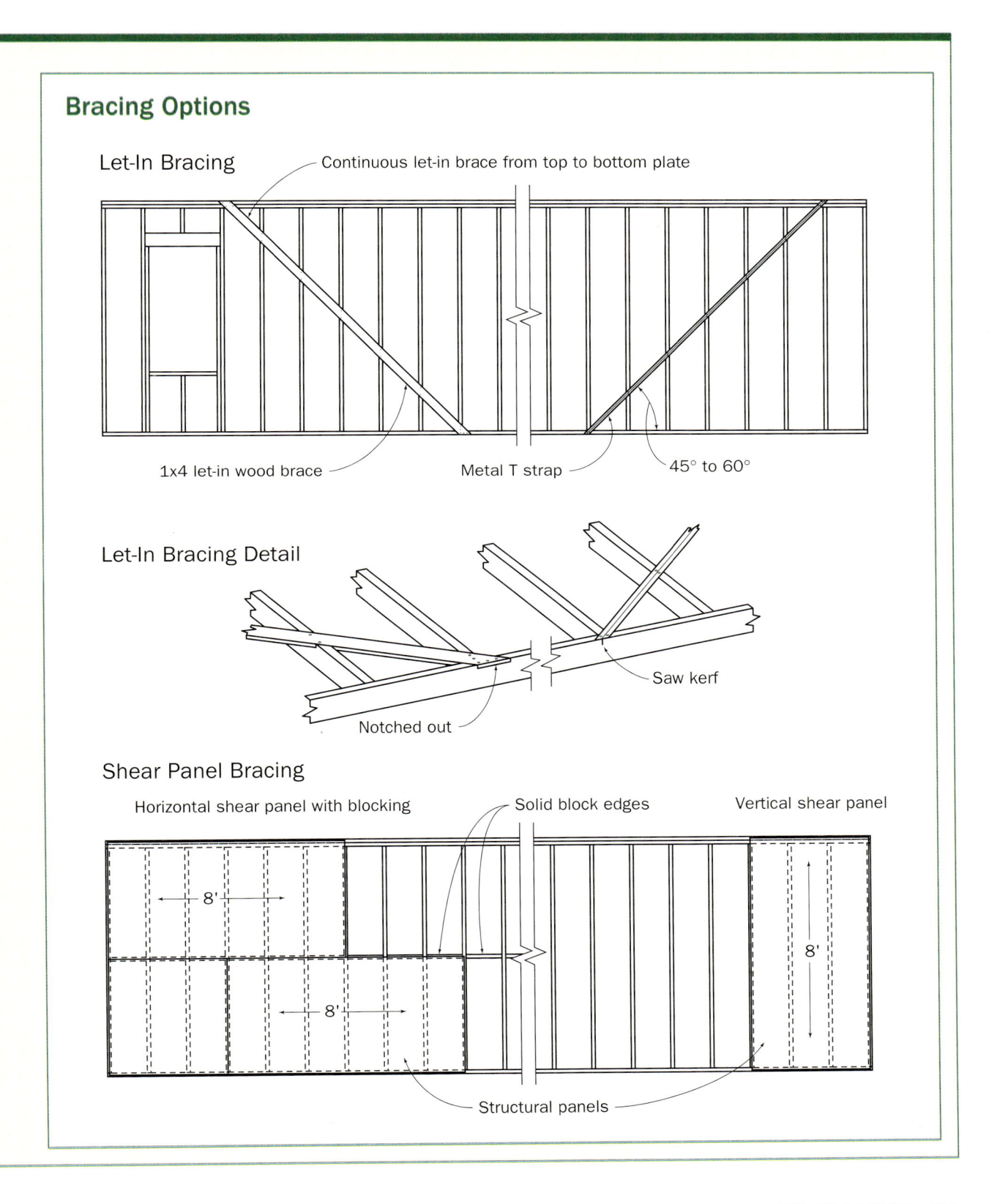

Let-In Bracing

- Continuous let-in brace from top to bottom plate
- 1x4 let-in wood brace
- Metal T strap
- 45° to 60°

Let-In Bracing Detail

- Saw kerf
- Notched out

Shear Panel Bracing

- Horizontal shear panel with blocking
- Solid block edges
- Vertical shear panel
- 8'
- 8'
- 8'
- Structural panels

WALL FRAMING

Framing Other Bearing and Exterior Walls

There are a couple of situations in which you'll have to frame walls without the benefit of a floor deck to work on. The structure and layout of the walls are the same as for a simple wall. You just have to adapt to the limits of your work platform. These walls can still be framed production style.

Other walls, like gable end rake walls, have a different configuration from conventional walls. Again, plan for production wherever possible and treat the details separately.

Framing garage walls

Frost-wall garage foundations usually extend above the surface of the concrete slab and present a variation to the wall-framing process we described for working off a floor deck. Unfortunately, there is no work surface, and you may have to account for an out-of-level foundation wall as well. Both of these problems can be overcome and the wall can be framed production style.

Start by installing and bolting down a single or double 2x6 mudsill on the garage foundation. Cut off the excess bolt so it won't interfere when you lift the wall. When the walls will be framed with 2x4 studs, snap chalklines on top of the mudsill to indicate the inside edge of the garage wall; 2x6 walls won't require this step.

Determine the stud height you need to have the walls match the house plans. Check the top of the mudsill for level to the control line you snapped in chalk around the perimeter of the foundation when checking for level.

Install shim layers where needed on top of the single mudsill plate to match level and don't let the shims extend behind the wall chalkline. If you used a double mudsill, the shims can slide between the plates. Leveling the top within a 1/8-in. tolerance is adequate.

Lay out the wall plates and tack nail the bottom plate up to the chalkline you snapped on the mudsill. Install a pivot strap every 6 ft. to 8 ft. to keep the wall from kicking out during the lift. Spread the top plate away from the bottom plate and prop it up on blocks or tack nail it to short posts so it is nearly level with the bottom plate.

Cut and spread out the studs ready for nailing. Frame the studs between the wall plates. Drill 1-in. or larger holes on the underside of the bottom plate to accept the mudsill nuts and bolts when you lift the wall. Recheck the bottom plate and adjust it to the chalkline.

Check the diagonal measurements of the wall and rack it square. You won't be able to tack nail the wall to the floor deck to keep it square so you'll have to be careful when working on the

Garage walls can be framed, sheathed, and lifted even though there's no floor deck to work off of. Set the bottom plate on the mudsill and prop the top plate on blocks.

wall after it's squared up not to jar it out of alignment.

Measure up the studs from the bottom plate and snap a chalkline for the wall sheathing. The garage-wall sheathing can be planned to link into the house-wall sheathing when the two line up. If you do so, plan to leave a sheet or two out for now and install them after the walls are raised. Nail off the rest of the sheathing and be sure to straighten the end studs of the wall, just as you did for the house walls.

The studs used to frame garage walls are sometimes 10 ft. or more and are prone to bowing. It's a good idea to gauge the studs to the on-center spacing halfway up the wall just before nailing the sheathing (the same process as used on floor joists) and move them side to side so that the sheathing is nailed on center.

Add the upper layer of the top plate and leave it stepped back to overlap into the top plate of the house wall when the plates match. Roll out housewrap and tack it back in areas where the sheathing has yet to be installed. Lay out for floor joists or roof framing (see below) before lifting the wall.

Lift the wall, tie in the plates, fill in the sheathing, nail to the mudsill, and so on. Brace and straighten the walls in preparation for installing a floor or roof above.

Framing slab-on-grade walls

Monolithic or slab-on-grade foundation/floor systems require that you make adjustments to the wall framing procedure that can slow the production.

First, it's harder to tack nail plates to the concrete, but that can be overcome. An out-of-level slab is more difficult to adjust, because you have to do it with the walls. There is no mudsill per se; the pressure-treated bottom plate of the walls is the mudsill.

Start by preparing the slab in the same way as you would a conventional foundation. Snap chalklines for the mudsill/bottom plate and snap a level reference line around the perimeter of the slab.

Lay out the plates as you would for ordinary walls on a wood floor deck. The difference comes when you cut the studs to length. You will need to cut the studs to different lengths to adjust for dips and humps in the slab so the top plate will be flat and level.

Determining stud lengths Measure the highs and lows in the slab perimeter from the level reference line. Pick the average and decide on a stud height to match average. Now add to the average stud height to account for dips and subtract for humps. For instance, if there's a $1/4$-in. dip in part of the slab, add $1/4$ in. to the stud height in that area. Write the heights on the slab or on the wall plates for each stud. Make a list of stud measurements and quantities. Cut the studs to length.

You won't be able to precut the jacks and cripples below saddles for rough openings the same way you can when framing on a level floor deck; you'll have to custom cut many of them. Add or subtract the same amount to the length of the jacks and cripples as you did for studs in the opening area. Prepare these parts too.

Snapping a chalkline for the top plate You can't nail the bottom plate to the straight chalkline, because it will need to match the undulations in the concrete when you lift the wall. Instead, snap a chalkline for the top plate. Measure up from the bottom plate and snap a line on the stud side of the lower layer of the top plates.

Match the top plate up to the line. You can use concrete nails to secure scrap 2x blocks to the concrete between stud locations and against the bottom side of the top plate every 3 ft. to 4 ft. The blocks give you a way to hold the plate straight. Tack nail through the block and into the top plate.

Nail the cripples, headers, and studs to the top plate first and nail the bottom plate on to the studs second. The bottom plate will vary up and down, mimicking the undulations of the concrete slab.

Squaring the wall and strapping the bottom plate You can't square the wall by just measuring diagonals if the end studs in the wall are different lengths. To overcome the discrepancy, measure the end studs an equal distance from the straight top plate as close to the bottom plate as possible and make a mark. Measure diagonally from the top plate corners to the marks and rack the wall until it's square.

Nail wood blocks to the concrete on the inside corners of the wall's end studs where they meet the bottom plate to keep the wall from drifting. Fasten metal pivot straps every 4 ft. along the bottom plate of the wall to the concrete floor to keep the wall from kicking out while raising it.

Sheathing the wall Snap a chalkline across the wall studs as a guide for the wall sheathing. Measure off the top plate to locate the line, because the bottom plate isn't even. Plan to let the sheathing overlap the slab by $1/2$ in., unless the concrete extends too far out. In that case, you can either break the sheathing on the bottom plate or trim the sheathing up from areas where excess concrete will be a problem. Sheathe the wall in the same fashion as described earlier. After the first row of sheathing is installed, remove the tack nails you put through the top plate into the 2x blocks on the floor. If you don't remove the nails now, it will be impossible to get to them once all the sheathing is in place. (Note: On some slab foundations, preinstalled plumbing pipes will keep you from sheathing an entire wall while it is flat on the slab.)

Preparing and lifting the wall Before you lift the wall, drill holes for the foundation bolts. If you have any input before the slab is poured, ask that tie-down straps be installed rather than bolts. They don't require that you drill the plate and they install quickly once the wall is lifted.

Roll out sill seal material and lift the wall. The waves in the bottom plate should match the slab. You may have to drive the wall down over foundation bolts with a sledgehammer. Don't hammer on the bottom plate to draw the wall down; the blows may only separate the plate from the studs. Instead, hammer on top of the wall.

Fasten down, line, and brace the wall as you would a regular wall.

Alternative sheathing method You can avoid the process of straightening and tacking the top plates to blocks and even avoid squaring these walls. Rather than sheathing before lifting them, you can lift them without the sheathing. Brace the wall plumb and snap a chalkline to guide the sheathing edge after you secure the bottom plate to the slab. This process is sometimes faster than struggling to straighten the wall on the slab. Try it both ways to see what works fastest for you.

Rake walls

Rake walls are the exterior frame walls beneath the gable-end roof rafters. There are two ways to frame them. One way is to fill in the studs beneath the rafters after you raise the roof. The other way is to stud beneath a pair of roof rafters while they are on the attic joists. Then sheathe and lift the whole gable end. This usually saves time and is safer, because you don't have to work off staging to sheathe a tall, gable-end wall.

This process is practical only if you sheathe, either temporarily or permanently, the attic or floor deck that the roof rafters will sit on. If this isn't the case, you'll have to resort to stick framing beneath the rafters.

Cutting the rafters and laying out the plates See chapter 6 for a description of figuring and cutting roof rafters. Pick two of the straightest rafters with the least amount of crown. Cut and nail a top wall plate to the bottom of each rafter. Bevel cut the top and bottom of the plates to match the top cut and seat cut on the rafter before you nail them on. Then turn to the bottom wall plate to start marking the layout.

Snap a chalkline on the floor sheathing, as described for wall framing earlier. Cut a bottom plate to reach from the face of one rim joist to the other. Mark the stud layout to match the studs on the floor below. Any window openings can be built as nonbearing, since the rafters are

Rake Wall Framing

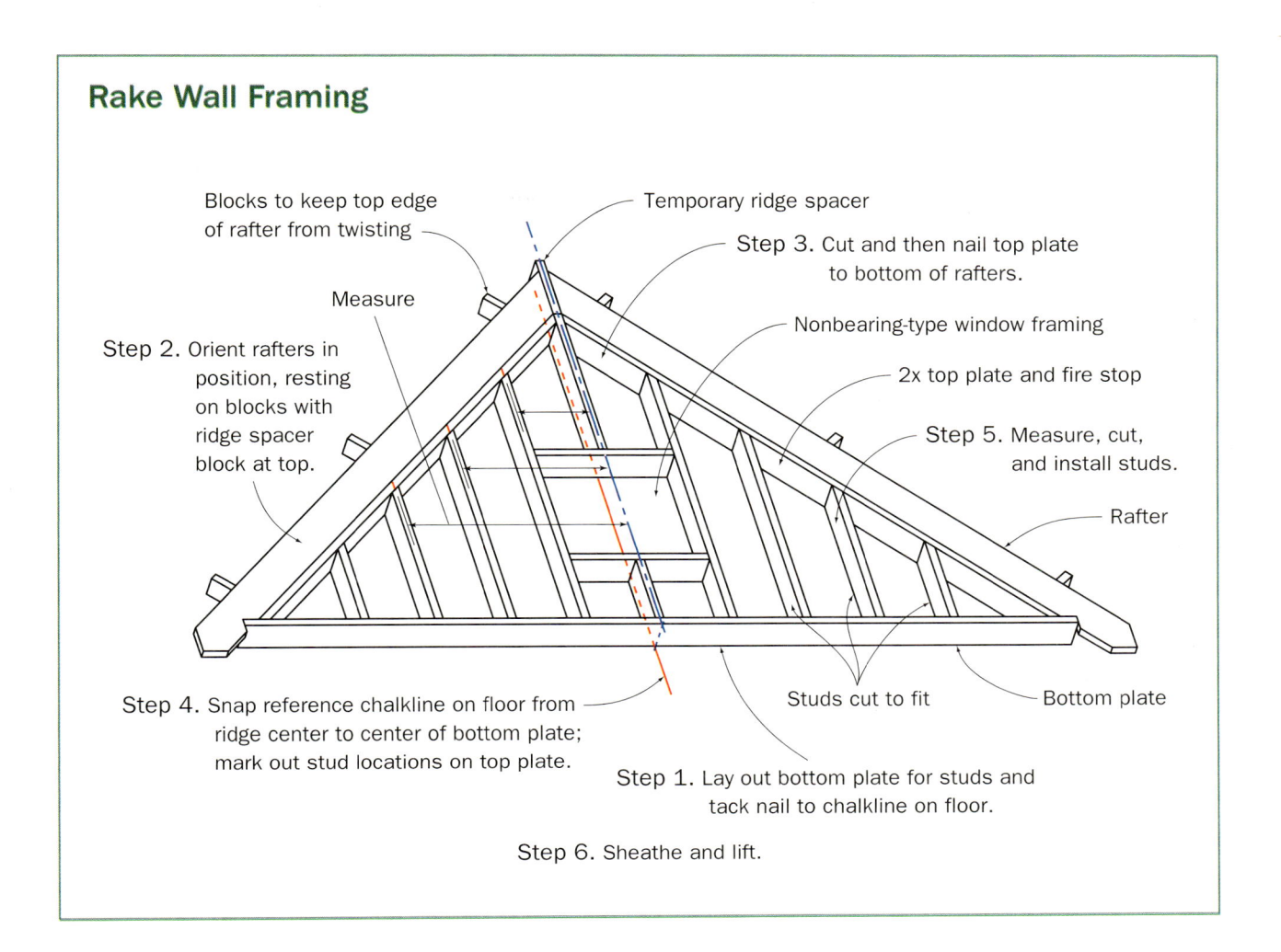

- Blocks to keep top edge of rafter from twisting
- Temporary ridge spacer
- **Step 3.** Cut and then nail top plate to bottom of rafters.
- Measure
- Nonbearing-type window framing
- **Step 2.** Orient rafters in position, resting on blocks with ridge spacer block at top.
- 2x top plate and fire stop
- **Step 5.** Measure, cut, and install studs.
- Rafter
- Studs cut to fit
- Bottom plate
- **Step 4.** Snap reference chalkline on floor from ridge center to center of bottom plate; mark out stud locations on top plate.
- **Step 1.** Lay out bottom plate for studs and tack nail to chalkline on floor.
- **Step 6.** Sheathe and lift.

self-supporting. Tack nail the bottom plate to the chalkline and insert a pivot strap every 4 ft. to 6 ft.

Transferring the layout to the top plate Place the two rafters in place. Match and nail the bottom plate to the seat cut of the rafter at the bot-tom and line up the tops of the rafters at a 2x spacer to mimic the ridge board. The rafters will have a tendency to roll down on the top edge because of the already-nailed-on top plate, so insert some loose blocks to hold them upright. Tack nail the rafter/plate setup to the floor deck every 4 ft.

Snap a chalkline from the center of the ridge to the center of the bottom plate on the floor. This will be a reference line to mark out the stud locations. Measure from the center line to each layout mark on the bottom plate and write each measurement on the plate. With a helper holding a tape measure on the reference line, mark the top plate out for the stud layout. Clearly indicate on which side of the mark the stud will reside.

Square up the marks on the top plate and measure from the bottom plate to the top plate for each stud height. Write the lengths on the top plate and add a note if the measurement is to the long point or short point of the bevel cut. Measure for one stud directly beneath the ridge board even if it isn't on the layout. Insert a crosscut block of ridge stock so you can determine the exact height. Often this stud lands on a window header. That is fine, because the stud will only temporarily support the ridge until you install the rafters.

Framing and sheathing the wall Cut the studs and nail them in place. Nail the bottom plate to the studs first then toenail the stud (with its bevel cut) to the top plate. Be careful not to push a crown in the rafter when you nail on the studs. Check the top of the rafter by eye or with a string line to make sure it stays straight throughout the process.

Measure the overhang of the sheathing to the wall on the floor below. Snap a chalkline across the studs (as described for sheathing walls earlier in this chapter) and fasten on the sheathing. Trim the sheathing back to the top edge of the rafters.

Any rake overhangs (see chapter 6) can be ladder framed on top of the rafters and sheathed top and bottom to keep the gable straight.

Install housewrap and, if you are ambitious, install the siding and trim on the end leaving the nails on the bottom course high enough to slip the wall courses in from beneath.

Lift the gable end the same way you would an ordinary wall. Wide gables with steep pitch roofs can be very heavy. Take extra safety precautions when lifting them.

Modified balloon-framed walls

There are instances when balloon-framed walls make a lot of sense even in the world of platform framing. Take the case of a farmhouse-style Cape Cod, in which the second-story walls may be only 3 ft. tall. Framed in the platform manner, you would have to rely heavily on the collar ties to resist the thrust force of the roof rafters pushing the walls outward. But a modified balloon-framed wall, in which the studs extend all the way from the first floor deck to the bottom of the roof rafters will be stronger. On balloon-framed walls, the floor joists of the upper floor rest on a ledger let in to the wall studs. The floor joists are fastened to the ledger and to the sides of the studs on opposite walls. This framing structure can help resist roof thrust by keeping the walls from spreading apart.

Measuring and cutting studs to length Frame and lay subfloor on the first-floor deck in the

Balloon-framed walls are useful in special circumstances. Floor joists sit on top of a ledger that is notched into the floor joists. (Photo by Roe A. Osborn, courtesy *Fine Homebuilding* magazine, © The Taunton Press, Inc.)

manner described in chapter 4. Calculate the exterior wall stud height from the first-floor deck to the top plate of the second-floor portion of the wall that the rafters will rest on. Account for the second-level floor joists and subfloor in your calculation; the studs will have to pass through this space.

Cut one stud to length after you make your calculations. Draw the various measurements for the first-floor wall height, ledger, floor joist, and second-floor wall height to be sure you have the stud length correct before cutting all of them.

Notching studs for ledger The second-floor joists rest on a ledger board that is recessed into notches in the studs. To cut the notches quickly and precisely, line the studs up on edge on the floor deck flush at the top and bottoms. Nail a block to the floor at the ends to keep the gang of studs from moving.

Balloon-framed walls can be mixed into platform framing to achieve certain details.

Select the ledger board you are going to use and measure its height and thickness. The type of floor joists you use may affect the thickness of the ledger. Minimum bearing surfaces for engineered-wood I joists often require a 1½-in. surface, for instance. We generally select 2x6 kiln-dried (KD) lumber for good results. This works only for walls framed with 2x6s; a 2x4 wall with 1½-in. notches wouldn't have enough wood left to support the wall. On 2x4 walls, use ¾-in. ledger material.

Measure and mark the first and last stud in the group for the bottom of the floor joists. This corresponds to the top of the ledger. Measure from those marks to the bottom of the ledger. Snap chalklines across the gang of studs. Set the depth of a circular saw slightly deeper than the thickness of the ledger. Cut along the lines across the studs and then make additional saw cuts about every ½ in. between the first two to make clearing out the wood easier. Chisel out the notches in the studs while they are still ganged up and relatively stable.

Laying out and framing the wall Lay out wall plates in the conventional fashion. The stud layout must be offset from the joist layout by 1½ in., so each stud can benefit from the thrust support that the joists will add when nailed alongside. Precut the ledger board sections so joints break at stud locations. This is easy to do with the plates laid out. Mark the plate layout onto the ledger board so it can act as a gauge to keep the middle of the studs straight between plates.

Tack nail the bottom plate to the chalkline, just as you would to frame a conventional wall, and position only the studs at either end of the wall, with the let-in notches facing down. Lay the ledger board on the floor with the layout marks facing up. Slide it into the notches of the end studs. Install each stud that falls on a ledger board joint to fix the ledger in place. Now you can lay all the other studs in position.

Nail the bottom and top plates to the studs first, then toenail the studs to the ledger board with one nail only. After you sheathe and lift the wall, you can drive spikes through the ledger into the studs. Check your building code for fire-stopping requirements when building balloon-framed walls. Some codes require solid wood blocking at the first-floor ceiling level and the second-floor deck level. Other codes consider wall insulation sufficient if the spaces between joists are blocked with gypsum or wood panels.

Installing the joists The joists support the walls best if continuous from exterior wall to exterior wall. When this isn't practical, glue and nail the joist lap. Extend the joists within ½ in. of the wall sheathing and drive spikes from the studs into the joist and vice versa. Construction adhesive can also help strengthen the joint.

Chapter 6

ROOF FRAMING

A STICK-BUILT ROOF

ROOF TRUSSES

Framing the roof puts you in the home stretch of the framing project. After the roof, the rest is just "filling in the missing pieces."

There are two types of roof framing common to modern residential construction. The cut roof and the manufactured truss roof. A lot of builders still swear by the cut roof. They, and many owners, like the look and feel of the large dimensional wood (usually 2x10s or 2x12s). They also like the immediacy in that they are able to start cutting the roof the same day they order the materials.

Trussed roofs, however, have become the standard for the majority of builders. Computer-aided drawing (CAD) programs for truss engineering that have come into use in the last decade have enabled manufacturers to design and fabricate almost any type of roof system easily. Some roof designs can only be accomplished with a truss system.

We substitute a truss roof in place of a cut roof whenever possible for a number of reasons. Trusses are made of smaller dimensioned wood (2x4s or 2x6s) that is always kiln-dried (KD) and, therefore, less apt to shrink. A 2x10 or 2x12 of a cut roof can shrink ½ in. or more and is prone to twisting and buckling. The structure of a truss allows it to span the entire width of the building, leaving the entire floor area free from the re-strictions of bearing walls needed to support the ceiling joists of a cut roof. Also, the labor saved by using trusses, particularly on a complex roof, can shave days off a schedule. As

This house uses a combination of roof systems. It has a manufactured truss roof for the main house and a roof system made from cut-on-site rafters for the garage.

for price, both roof systems are comparable when figuring in the labor.

Whether your roof is cut or trussed, you should be working with a square and level bearing surface. From the mudsills on up, if the techniques we've discussed in the previous chapters are followed, the end result will be dimensionally accurate and level walls. This ensures easy installation and alignment of the roof system.

Because there are so many different types and intricacies of cut roofs, we cover only the basics of a simple gable roof layout and construction in this chapter. The detailed formulas and techniques needed to design and frame complex cut roofs would fill an entire volume on their own and are beyond the scope of this book.

The trussed roof discussion is more complete, because the procedures for ordering and installation are much the same for all truss systems, from simple to complex.

A Stick-Built Roof

The discussion of cut roof framing focuses on a simple gable roof layout.

Planning the layout

There are four basic framing members to a gable roof: rafters, ceiling joists, collar ties, and the ridge board.

Most plans give you the size and spacing for the parts, but if they aren't specified or they are questionable, check the tables in your code book or consult with an engineer.

There are occasions when you may want to change the dimensional size of the framing members for reasons not addressed on the plans. For example, you may plan on future use of the attic as living space so you want to upgrade the ceiling joists to support a 30-lb. or 40-lb. live load instead of the 20-lb. load typical for attic floors. Or you may have to increase the rafters of a cathedral ceiling from 2x8s to 2x10s to accommodate the proper amount of insulation plus a vent space.

Make a lumber list Once you have determined the size of the ceiling joists and roof rafters, figure the rough lengths of the members needed. Dimensional lumber is sold in 2-ft. increments, so accurately gauging the length of the members will minimize waste.

Use an architect's scale on the cross section of the plans and measure the length of the rafters and ceiling joists. You'll need to order lumber to the next-larger full-dimensional length. If you scale a rafter at 12 ft. 9 in., for example, you'll have to order 14-ft. stock. And when you're figuring ceiling joists, don't forget to account for at least a 3-in. overlap over the bearing wall if you can't order full lengths to reach between the

ROOF FRAMING 147

Basic Gable Roofs

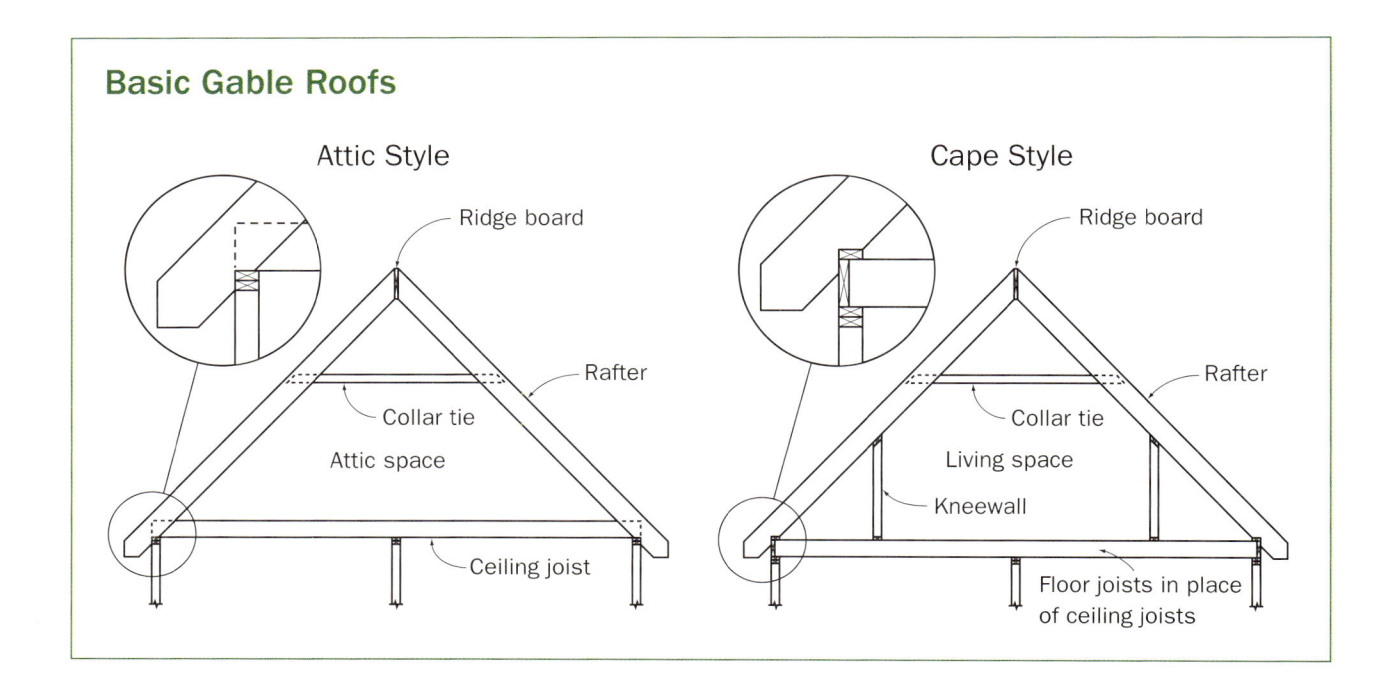

Attic Style
- Ridge board
- Rafter
- Collar tie
- Attic space
- Ceiling joist

Cape Style
- Ridge board
- Rafter
- Collar tie
- Living space
- Kneewall
- Floor joists in place of ceiling joists

---

exterior walls. You can also get a rough count by using the architect's scale, as described in chapter 5.

Once you get a final count, increase the rafter and joist count by at least 20 percent. You'll need the extra stock so you can be fussy when selecting the rafters. Because ceiling joists and rafters are usually exposed to extreme temperature and moisture variations, they are more prone to movement than the other framing.

If the length of the ridge of the roof is short enough, order the ridge board as one member. And unless you're going to go to the lumberyard to select the ridge stock, order twice as much as you need. You want to use the straightest ridge board possible so that the rafter installation is not slowed down because the crew has to fight to adjust warped or bowed lumber.

Marking the layout

Similar to the floor layout, mark up an extra set of plans with a framing plan, including all critical openings and measurements. The most common openings are for the chimney, attic access, and skylights. These are not usually detailed to exact dimensions on the plans so it may be up to you to make a final determination. Be sure to check

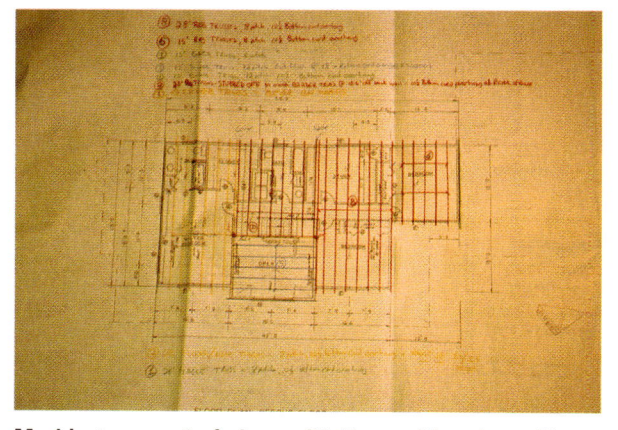

Marking up a set of plans with the roof framing will address important details and eliminate a lot of on-site head scratching.

with individual tradesmen when you make up your plan so they have enough space to work inside or around your framing.

Because the ceiling joists do not line up directly beneath the rafters but sit to one side or the other, the opening sizes will indicate the placement of the rafters. Plan to install the ceiling joists on the outside edge of the rafters making up the opening. This will leave the opening between the joists 3 in. wider than the opening in the

Rough Opening Details

Exterior Wall

Ceiling joist to the outside of the opening

Skylight RO

Cripple rafter

Cripple rafter

Cripple rafter

Rafter on this side of line

Ceiling joist on this side of line

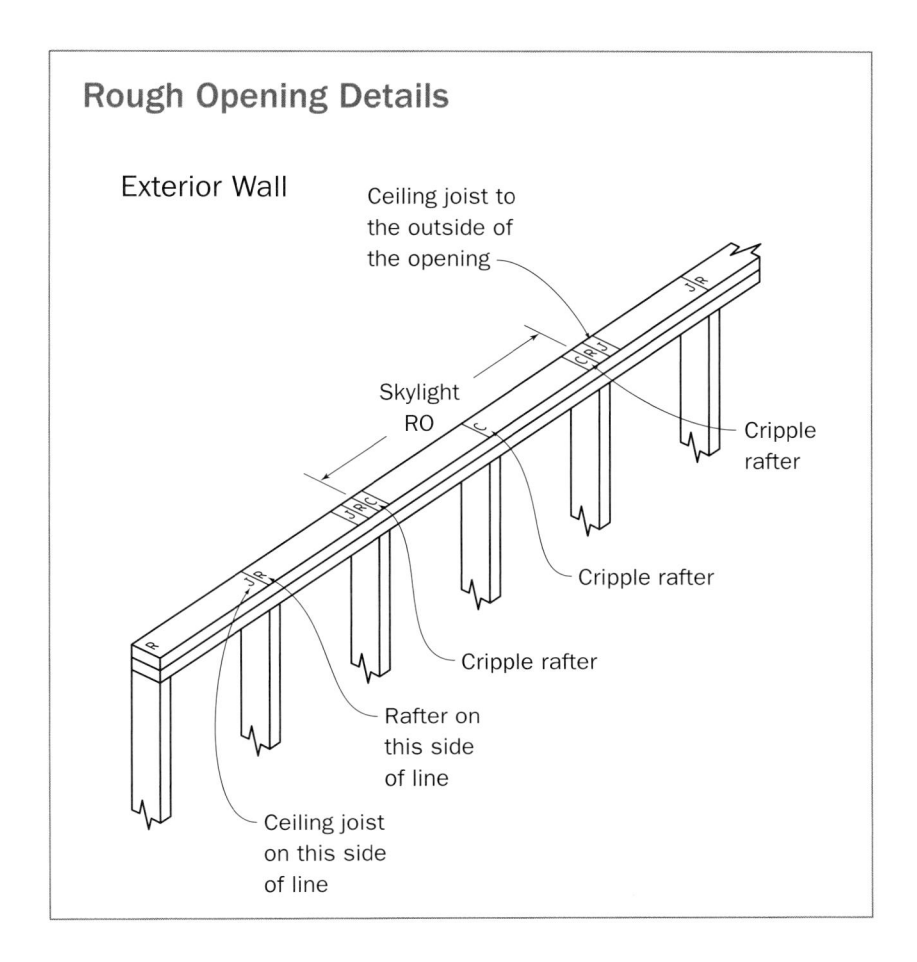

rafters. The length of the opening, however, will be consistent between ceiling joists and rafters (see the drawing above).

The size of the chimney rough opening (RO) should be determined by the mason. He knows what types of materials will be used and what is required by code for the rough openings. He can also help locate the rough opening on the floor plan.

The minimum size and head room for the attic access is dictated by code, but the placement is more appropriately made with common sense. It should be located toward the center of the attic so there will be plenty of head room when climbing up. If you will be installing a pull-down staircase unit, it must be located to ensure there is enough clearance to swing it down and unfold it all the way.

Rough openings for skylights are manufacturer specific. The location is determined by the architect or owner. You might want to ask if there is any leeway in the exact placement. A couple inches one way or the other can save labor and material. If there is any question with a rough opening, frame it bigger than necessary, you can easily close it in. Also, for any of the rough openings that are 4 ft. or wider, add two members to your total lumber count because you'll have to double the rafters and joists on both sides of the opening.

Once the framing layout plan is complete, you can generate a cut list for the ceiling joists. But unless you're proficient at figuring how the opening on the level plane of the ceiling joists will relate to the sloped plane of the roof rafters, don't bother with a rafter cut list. You'll be creating a

ROOF FRAMING **149**

roof template using a quick, on-site method that increases productivity. We'll cover it shortly.

Laying out the roof plan before the walls are lifted Just before lifting the walls into place, mark the layout on the top plates for the roof rafters and ceiling joists. Begin marking the layout from the same end as with the floor joist and wall stud layouts to maintain the stacked framing.

First mark out all of the rafter rough opening details, drawing a line to indicate both sides of the rafters and marking them R or X. Then write J (ceiling joist) next to each rafter mark on the side outside of the rough opening. Within these rough openings, write down the lengths of the ceiling joist headers and tails from your layout sheet (see the drawing on p. 149).

Next mark out for all of the common rafters (see "Marking Layout Spacing" on p. 66 for on-center marking directions). Any on-center marks that fall within the rough openings are marked as cripples. Mark the rafter cripples directly on the on-center mark, then the joists are marked on the side of that mark. This maintains on-center rafters along the entire layout, including the rough openings, ensuring that the sheathing joints always fall on a nailing surface.

For a roof that is too deep to have a full-length ceiling joist but has two joists that meet over an interior bearing wall instead, the layout is a little different. The two opposing exterior walls get the common on-center joists marked on different sides of the rafters. For example, the front wall would have the ceiling joists marked on the trailing side of the rafters whereas the back wall has them marked on the leading side of the rafters. Then mark out the interior bearing wall with the combination of marks from both outside walls. Use an R to denote where the rafters are located and J's on both sides of the R with an arrow to indicate which wall they reference. When installing the joists, you'll have to nail a 2x block to the interior bearing wall over the R mark; then nail the joists to the block and toenail them to the top plate of the bearing wall.

> **Ceiling Joist Layout over Interior Wall**
>
> When the ceiling joists are made up of two members, a 2x block is placed between them over the middle bearing wall. This allows them to be fastened together while retaining their proper layout.

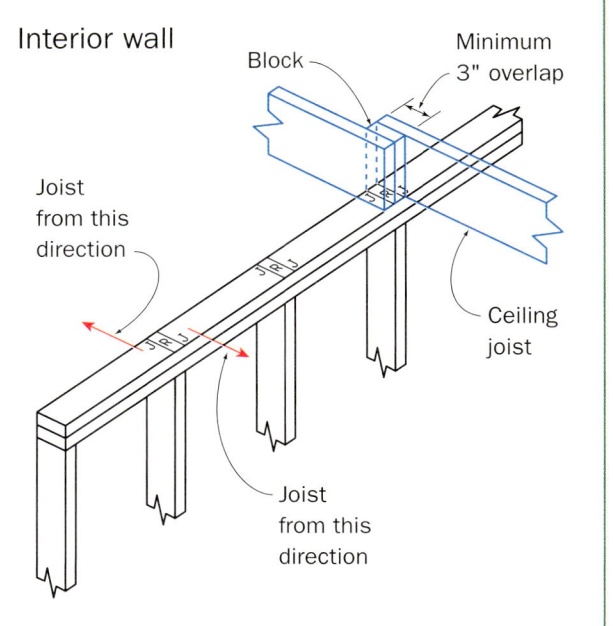

For a Cape-style house, in which the rafters are set right on the floor, the layout is simplified, because the floor joists serve as the ceiling joists and they are already installed and sheathed at this point. The layout is the same as described, except that only the rafters are marked out.

Selecting and laying out the ridge board
Once the layout is marked out on the walls or floor deck, the ridge board is laid out. Select the straightest stock for the ridge and mark the crown side to keep it oriented up.

Following the same layout you've been using, and starting from the same end of the house, mark the top edge of the ridge board for all of the rafters. Square the lines down on both faces of the ridge board and indicate the rafter placement with an X. Having lines on both

Frame the Gable Ends First

It is a lot quicker and safer to build and raise the gable end walls on the floor deck than it is to install the studs, sheathing, and trim while hanging over the edge of the building. You can also put on the rake trim and certain types of siding before the gable is raised in place. The deck provides a nice level work platform.

If the house design uses ceiling joists and creates an attic, you can build the gable walls and the roof gable ends (as for a Cape) as one unit. When the space beneath the roof is framed as a living space, you can build just the roof gable ends on the floor deck (see "Rake Walls" on p. 142).

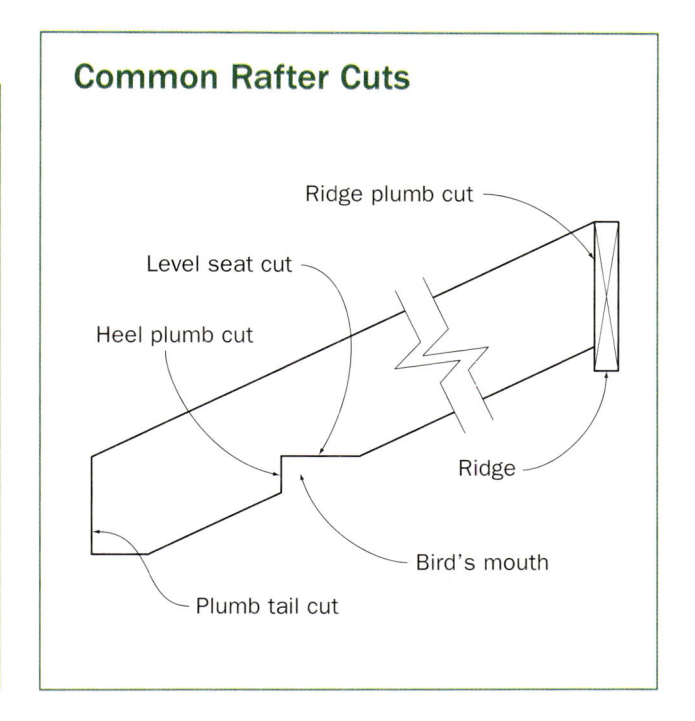

Common Rafter Cuts

- Ridge plumb cut
- Level seat cut
- Heel plumb cut
- Ridge
- Bird's mouth
- Plumb tail cut

faces will make it easier to orient the rafters as you nail them in place.

Be sure to put some sort of reference marks on the end of the ridge so you know which way it is oriented to the house. It can easily get flipped end for end while being moved around, and you might not notice it until the rafters start going up. If the ridge is to be made of more than one board, make sure the butt joints fall about halfway in between rafter bays and mark the ends in a way that keeps them oriented in the proper sequence.

Creating a rafter

There are three cuts to a rafter. The plumb cut, which is the cut at the top of the rafter and lines up against the ridge board. The bird's mouth, which is the notched cut that sits on the top plate or floor deck. And the tail cut, which is the plumb cut at the end of the rafter that determines the size of the fascia and depth of the soffit.

There are many different ways to determine the cuts of a roof rafter, such as rafter tables on the framing square, construction calculators, and triangular rafter squares. We use different methods for different types of roofs. For a gable roof, we use a method that is a little unorthodox but it is simple and easy to understand. It also lends itself very well to the physical layout we perform on the deck

Basically, the sheathed deck becomes a life-size drafting table for the rafter layout. The following procedure presumes a 28-ft.-deep, Cape-style roof in which the rafters will be fastened directly to the floor deck. We will explain the differences in procedures for the attic-type of roof when we complete the sections on rafter and collar tie installation for the Cape.

Snapping layout lines Snap chalklines (bearing lines) on the two lengths of the deck on which the rafters' bird's mouths will bear. Mimicking a 2x4 wall, the bearing line is usually at least 3½ in., but for our purposes it will be 5½ in. Then snap a line for the bottom plate of the gable wall 5½ in. (for a 2x6 wall) in from the gable end edge. Along that line, measure in exactly half of the depth (14 ft.) of the building and make a mark. Now move about 16 ft. or so away from the gable wall and again measure in and mark half the depth (14 ft.); check the measurements from

ROOF FRAMING **151**

Snapping Layout Lines

Diagram labels:
- 28'
- 14'
- 5½"
- 5½"
- End of floor deck
- Bearing line
- Rafter bird's mouth will be set to bearing line.
- Center reference line
- Rafter lines
- 13' 6½" rise
- 13' 6½" run
- 14' reference line

To Calculate the Rise

½ of total length − width of bird's mouth = run
14' − 5½" = 13' 6½" (or 13.54')

run × specified pitch = rise
13.54' × 12 = 162½" (or 13' 6½")

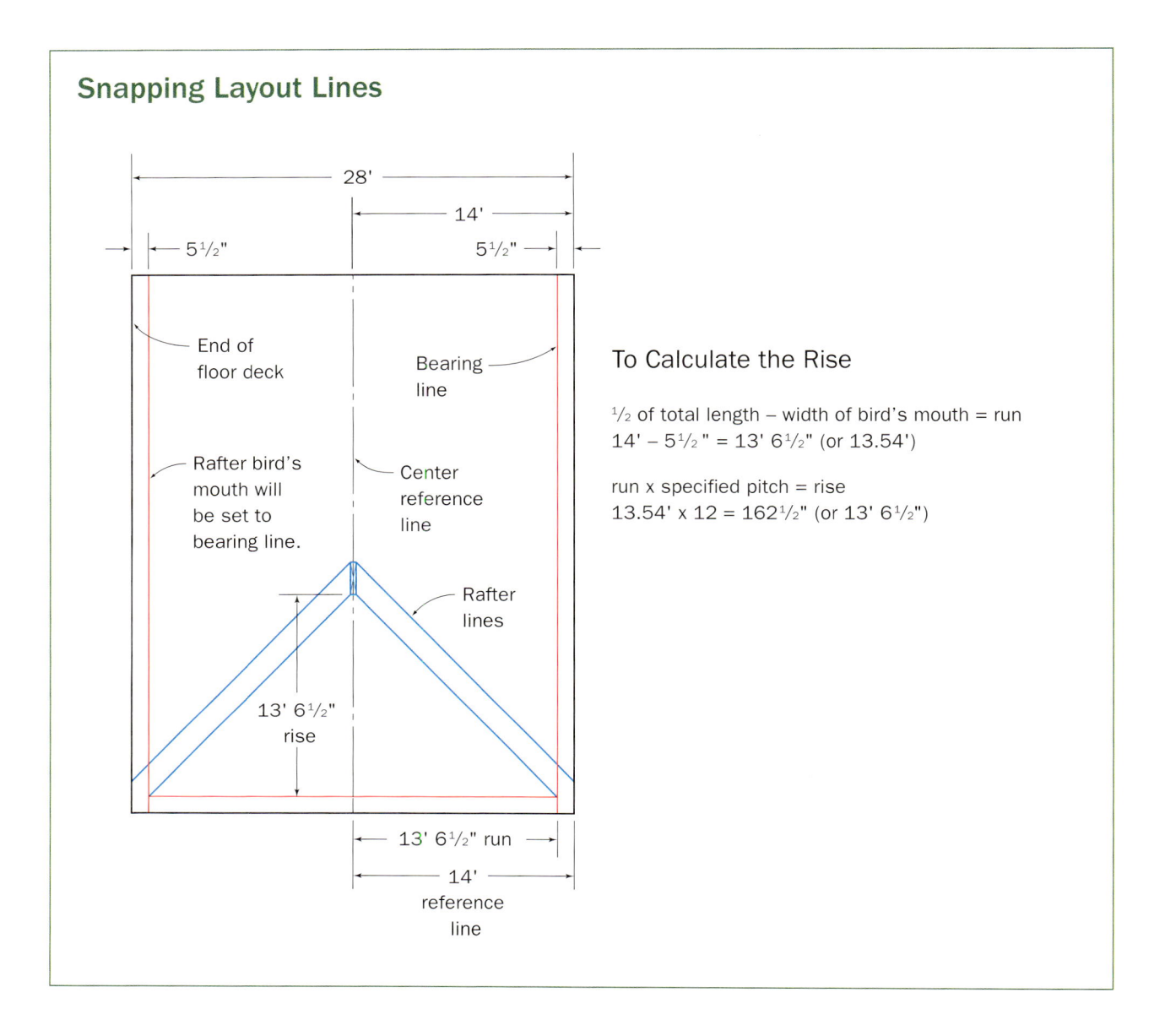

the bearing line to ensure a parallel mark. Snap a line between the two 14-ft. marks. You should end up with a long centerline that is exactly perpendicular to your gable wall lines.

Now pull out your pocket calculator. Subtract the width of the bird's-mouth bearing line from the 14-ft. half depth. 14 ft. minus 5½ in. leaves a rafter run (horizontal measurement) of 13 ft. 6½ in. Determine the decimal equivalent in feet (13.54 ft.) and multiply it by the specified pitch. In this case a 12-in-12 pitch, so it would be 13.54 ft. × 12 = 162.5 in., which is also 13 ft. 6½ in. This is the rise (vertical measurement) of the rafter. For a 12-pitch roof, the run is always the same as the rise. If you had an 8-pitch roof, the rise would be 13.54 ft. × 8 = 108.32 in. (9 ft. 5⁄16 in.).

Snapping rafter lines Now that you have the rise of your rafter, measure from the gable end chalkline, up along the perpendicular centerline, and put a mark on that line at the rise measurement. Snap a line from that mark diagonally to the point at which the gable end wall line and

To mark the plumb cut, lay the rafter along the length of the rafter line snapped on the deck. Transcribe the ridge marks to the top face of the rafter, then connect them to create the plumb cut line.

the bird's mouth bearing line intersect, snap one for each side. These diagonal lines indicate the underside of the rafter. To double-check, measure both diagonals, they should be identical.

Next put a small piece of 2x stock on edge bisecting the centerline, starting at the top rise mark and heading up. Draw a line on either side of the stock and remove it. These lines spaced 1½ in. apart represent the ridge board.

Creating the template rafter Select one of the straighter and lighter pieces of rafter stock and clearly mark the crown on it. This rafter will be the template you'll use to mark and cut all of the rest, so it's important that you are precise when cutting it. Place the bottom edge of the rafter along the diagonal line. Slide the stock along the line so that it falls over the ridge board line. This should leave enough hanging off the tail end to sketch out the desired soffit overhang. If not, your rafter stock is too short.

To mark the top plumb cut, use your square to transcribe the ridge board line you made on the subfloor onto the template rafter. Connect the two marks across the face of the rafter.

Hold a sliding T-bevel on the top edge of the rafter and set the bevel to the angle of the plumb cut. Keep the bevel on the top edge of the rafter and slide it all the way down the rafter until the blade of the T-bevel is beyond the deck and is

To mark the seat cut, slide a framing square along the heel cut line of the bird's mouth until the perpendicular edge overhangs at the wall measurement (6 in. in this case).

flush with the outside of the sheathing of the building. Draw a line along the T-bevel; this is the heel cut line of the bird's mouth. Now place one edge of a framing square along that heel line with the other edge facing the inside of the house. Slide it up or down until the perpendicular edge of the square falls just off the bottom edge of the

ROOF FRAMING 153

Common Rafter

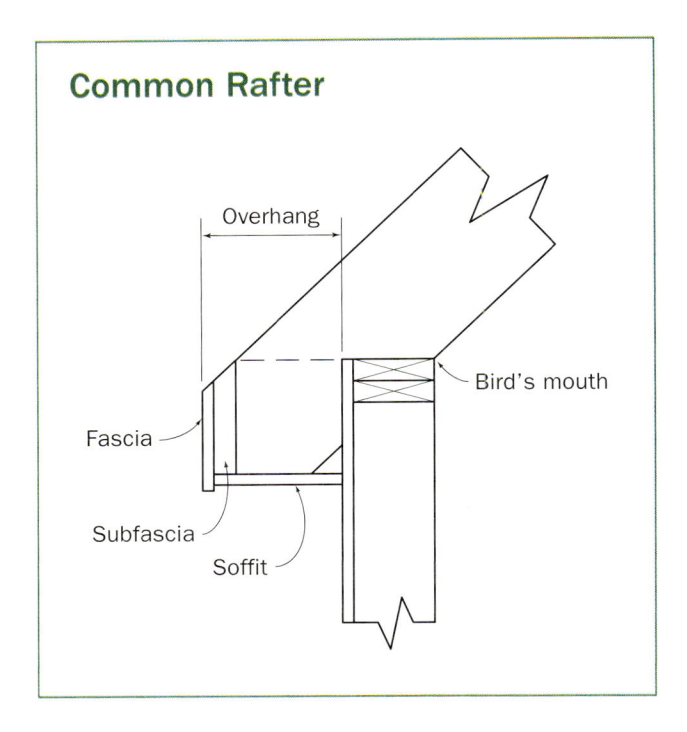

Overhang
Bird's mouth
Fascia
Subfascia
Soffit

To mark the tail cuts, draw the cross sections of the subfacia and the trim on the rafter. This will help determine the proper cuts.

rafter at 6 in. (5½ in. for the framing plus ½ in. for the thickness of the sheathing).

Draw a line along that edge of the square; this is the seat cut line of the bird's mouth. The notch that is created by the two 90° lines—the heel cut line and the seat cut line—at the underside of the rafter is the bird's mouth. It's a good idea to cross out the rest of the line you made on the rafter above the bird's mouth. You wouldn't want to follow that line with your saw and cut through the template rafter by mistake.

To mark the tail cut of the rafter (which is the cut at the opposite end of the rafter from the plumb cut), put the sliding T-bevel back on the top edge of the rafter. Slide it farther down the rafter beyond the heel cut until you reach the desired distance for the rafter overhang, minus the thickness of the subfacia and trim stock if the plans so indicate. (In some parts of the country, especially warmer climates, exposed rafter tails, with no trim, are common.)

For example, if you want a 1-ft. overhang, and you will be using a 2x6 subfacia with a ¾-in. trim board, you would slide the bevel until the blade on the face of the rafter measured perpendicularly 9¾ in. from the heal cut line of the bird's mouth. Now draw that line; this is the tail plumb cut.

Sketch the cross section of the subfacia and finish trim on the face of the rafter beyond the plumb cut line you just scribed. By drawing it out, you can see how to account for the pitch of the roof in relation to the size of the finish trim you plan to use and what size subfacia to plan for. Once you have the subfacia and facia drawn, sketch the reveal between the soffit and the trim and then draw the thickness of the soffit material. The line for the top of the soffit indicates the rafter's horizontal bottom cut. It is perpendicular to the vertical plumb cut line and continues across the face to the edge of the rafter. The vertical plumb cut and the horizontal bottom cut are collectively referred to as the tail cut of the rafter.

After all the layout is done on the template rafter—plumb cut, bird's mouth and tail cut—cut the pattern and lay it back down on the subfloor along the diagonal line opposite to the one you

154 CHAPTER SIX

used to figure out the pattern. The plumb cut should line up with the ridge line on the deck and the bird's mouth heel cut should line up with the outside sheathing. The bearing line you snapped to set the bottoms of the rafters along should match the point where the seat cut of the bird's mouth meets the under side of the rafter.

To prepare the template for marking the rafters you have to fasten a couple of guides to the top of the rafter. The guides make orienting the template to the rafter lumber fast and accurate.

Cut two pieces of $\frac{1}{2}$-in. sheathing 8 in. to 10 in. long and $2\frac{3}{4}$ in. wide. Nail one guide to the top edge of the rafter within 1 ft. of the top plumb, cut even with the face of the template. Leave the extra $1\frac{1}{4}$ in. of the piece protruding down. Nail the other guide in the same fashion just above the bird's mouth. Use at least 8d nails to attach the pieces so they won't come loose as you use the pattern to mark out the rest of the rafters.

Creating a template collar tie

Collar ties can be simple structural members in an attic or they can also be considered ceiling joists for support of a finished ceiling in a Cape-style house. If the collar ties are to be the latter, you must determine the height of the ceiling before the collar ties are sized. The stock you use for collar ties is determined by the span of the rafters, the pitch of the roof, and the height of the ceiling. Check your code or call the building inspector for guidance.

To make a collar tie template, refer back to the rafter lines you snapped on the deck. Measure up from the gable end line along each of the perpendicular bearing lines and mark the height of the ceiling frame. Snap a line between the two marks at the bearing lines. This line indicates the bottom of the collar ties/ceiling joists.

To create the template collar tie, place the bottom edge of a straight piece of collar tie stock (crown up) along the line. Take a 2x block the same dimension as the rafter stock and put it on top of the collar tie, lined up to the diagonal line that indicates the bottom of the rafter. Draw a line along the top edge of the block across the collar tie. Repeat this line on the other end of the collar tie.

To prevent the ends of the collar tie from coming in contact with the roof sheathing, re-mark those lines about $\frac{1}{2}$ in. inside your original line. This will make the collar tie about 1 in. short. Cut the two ends of the collar tie and mark the piece as the template.

Cutting and marking the rafters

The process of crowning and selecting roof rafter stock is the same as the floor joist grading procedure (see the sidebar on p. 70). The only difference is that we try not to use the more severely crowned stock (C grade in our own system) if we can help it. Rafters with large crowns tend to telegraph through the roof system. As you crown the rafters, stack them in neat rows, with the crowns facing in the same direction, on a pair of sawhorses in preparation for cutting.

Marking the rafters with the template
Marking rafters for cutting should be a two-man job, particularly with long rafters. Place the template on top of the first piece of stock. Slide the template so that the guide blocks are tight up against the crown of the stock. Make sure the template is set so that the plumb and tail cuts will not run off the stock. Also, if there is one end of the stock that is not as good as the other, a split or big knot for instance, slide the template to eliminate as much of the defect as possible without sliding the template off either end. Once the template is oriented, draw all of the cut lines on the stock piece beneath. Move the template over to the next rafter and continue the same process.

Be careful not to bump the template too hard against the stock. Even though the blocks are spiked on, they can still work loose. At this point you can also see why the blocks are a little less in width. If they were a full 3 in. or more there's the possibility that they could catch on the rafter stock two rows down and be misaligned with the stock being marked.

ROOF FRAMING

Once the rafter stock is selected, crowned, and stacked with the crowns oriented in the same direction, two crew members can quickly mark and cut a pile of rafters.

You can also see the advantage of marking the rafters this way. By matching the tops of the members to the template you're assured that they will be cut so that all of the tops line up. If the stock varies in thickness (which is not uncommon) the only difference will be changes in some of the lengths of the cuts but the seating in relation to the top of the rafter remains the same.

If you mark and cut all of the rafters at this point, they would have to be stacked somewhere out of the way until the ridge is set. Then they would have to be handled again to get them up to the level of the deck, and then one more time to be installed.

To minimize the labor here is the best sequence to follow:

1. Select the straightest and flattest lumber for the gable rafters.
2. Cut four rafters and use them to build the gable ends.
3. Raise the gable ends.
4. Erect the staging; then set the ridge board.
5. Begin cutting the rest of the rafters.

See "Rake Walls" on p. 142 for a description of building the gable end. The method is the same whether you're placing the gable ends on the deck (as depicted here) or building it on top of a wall.

Installing the ridge board

Either way you frame the gable end, it's important to keep the center stud, which falls beneath the ridge board, cut low enough so that the top of the ridge board is even with the gable rafters when set in place.

A modification to this is to cut the center stud shorter, so that the top of the ridge will end up being about 1 in. down from the top of the rafters. You would drop the ridge board like this to allow air to flow through a ridge vent when it's specified for the job. By terminating the sheathing at the top of the rafter plumb cuts, a 1½-in. gap is left along the top of the ridge to allow venting. This ensures a solid nailing base for the ridge vent by eliminating the need to cut the sheathing back at the ridge to provide the necessary air space when the ridge board is installed flush with the rafters.

Staging the area to assemble the roof is next. Set up your staging at a comfortable work height and make sure the work platform is wide enough so you can work on both sides of the ridge. If the ridge is one piece, you can set it in place, sliding it down on top of the center stud of each gable end.

If the ridge board is made up of more than one piece, you'll need to set up temporary supports out of 2x4s to hold the ridge boards until the

With the proper staging, a one-piece ridge board is easily set into place.

rafters are installed. You can easily determine the exact height of the bottom of the ridge board off the deck by measuring the gable end from the deck to the top of the center stud that the ridge will sit on.

Measure from one end of the 2x4 support and mark the exact height to the bottom of the ridge board. Fasten a 2x4 block, about 1 ft. long, on the face of the support post beneath the mark. Make one of these supports for each butt joint in the ridge.

Measure the length of the first ridge board (starting from the outside of the gable wall framing) and put a mark along the center of the deck. Hold the support post upright and nail the bottom to the mark in the center of the deck splitting the 3½-in. width equally on both sides of the mark. Roughly plumb the top of the support and attach a diagonal brace to keep it in place. A brace with a turnbuckle works well, because it's easily adjusted when the rafters go up.

Lift the first piece of ridge board up and slide it into place in the gable end. The other end will rest on half of the support. Nail a couple of spikes through the temporary support into the ridge board. Place the next piece of ridge board up against the first piece and rest the other end either on the next support or into the second gable end. Make sure the butt joints are tight and nail a couple more spikes through the support into the second board.

Install gusset plates to connect ridge sections

Once all of the ridge pieces are up, cut a couple of pieces of sheathing 1 in. short of the nominal width of the ridge board and about 14 in. long to connect ridge sections. Place these pieces of sheathing on the face of the ridge board over the butt joints flush to the bottom of the ridge. Nail the sheathing to the ridge on both sides of the joint using 6d nails at an angle so they won't protrude through the other side of the ridge. These gusset plates tie all of the ridge pieces together so they won't separate during the rafter installation. You can leave the gussets on the ridge permanently.

Some framers prefer to cut the ridge board to break halfway on a rafter location, thereby eliminating the need for the gusset. This requires a few more hands and involves juggling the rafter installation with ridge setting.

Plumb the gable ends After you have the ridge board temporarily supported on posts and connected with gussets, check the gable ends for plumb. The best way to do this, unless it's very windy, is with a plumb bob.

Measure 1 ft. in from the end of the ridge board and make a mark. Directly under the ridge

ROOF FRAMING

To plumb the gable ends, make a mark on the deck a certain distance from the outside edge of the framing. Hang a plumb bob from the ridge at the same distance from the outside edge of the framing. A plumb bob is suspended from the ridge and the turnbuckle brace is turned, moving the gable wall in or out until the plumb bob is in line with a mark on the deck.

on the floor, measure in 1 ft. from the outside of the framing and draw a reference line. Hang a plumb bob from the mark on the ridge down to the floor. Use a long diagonal brace fastened from the top of the gable end to the floor deck to adjust the ridge in or out until the plumb bob is directly over the 1-ft. line on the floor.

Because the ridge board ties both gable ends together, plumbing one gable end automatically plumbs the other. If after plumbing one gable end, the other is out of plumb, run a tape measure across the top of the ridge board from gable to gable. The top measurement will be different from the bottom floor measurement. Adjust the length of the ridge at the gable ends to correct any difference in the measurements, then recheck both gables for plumb.

Set a dry line to straighten the ridge The final step to prepare the ridge for the rafters is to string a dry line from one gable end to the other. The line should be nailed on top of the ridge flush with either the front or back edge at each gable end. Pull it tight, particularly on the longer ridges, and set a furring block under each end to raise it $3/4$ in. off the ridge. Check the ridge at the support locations. First adjust the braces until the edge of the ridge is lined up with the string (slide a small straightedge up along the face of the ridge to the string), then check the height with a furring gage on top of the ridge to the string. Account for a little dip in the string on the longer ridges.

If you have to raise up the ridge board, pull the nails holding the ridge from the back of the 2x4 supports. Shim between the ridge and the support block and then drive the nails back in. If the ridge board needs to be lowered, place a second block below the first block on the support. Leave a gap of the distance you need the ridge to drop. Pull the nails on the first block, let it drop it down then re-nail it. Now pull the nails holding the ridge from the support. Let the ridge settle back down on the block and then hammer the nails back in. We're only talking about fractions of an inch here. Anything more should be dealt with very cautiously.

Don't worry about the entire ridge not lining up with the string side to side. Installing the rafters will straighten the ridge.

Back to the rafters

Once the ridge board is adjusted, return to the task of marking and cutting the rest of the rafters. After they are cut, lean them up against the house spaced so that there are two about every 16 in. and alternating end for end: one with the tail up and its mate with the tail down. Pull them up and lay them roughly in place on the deck. The ones that are tail up are in the correct position as they get pulled through to the opposite side

Stringing the Ridge Board

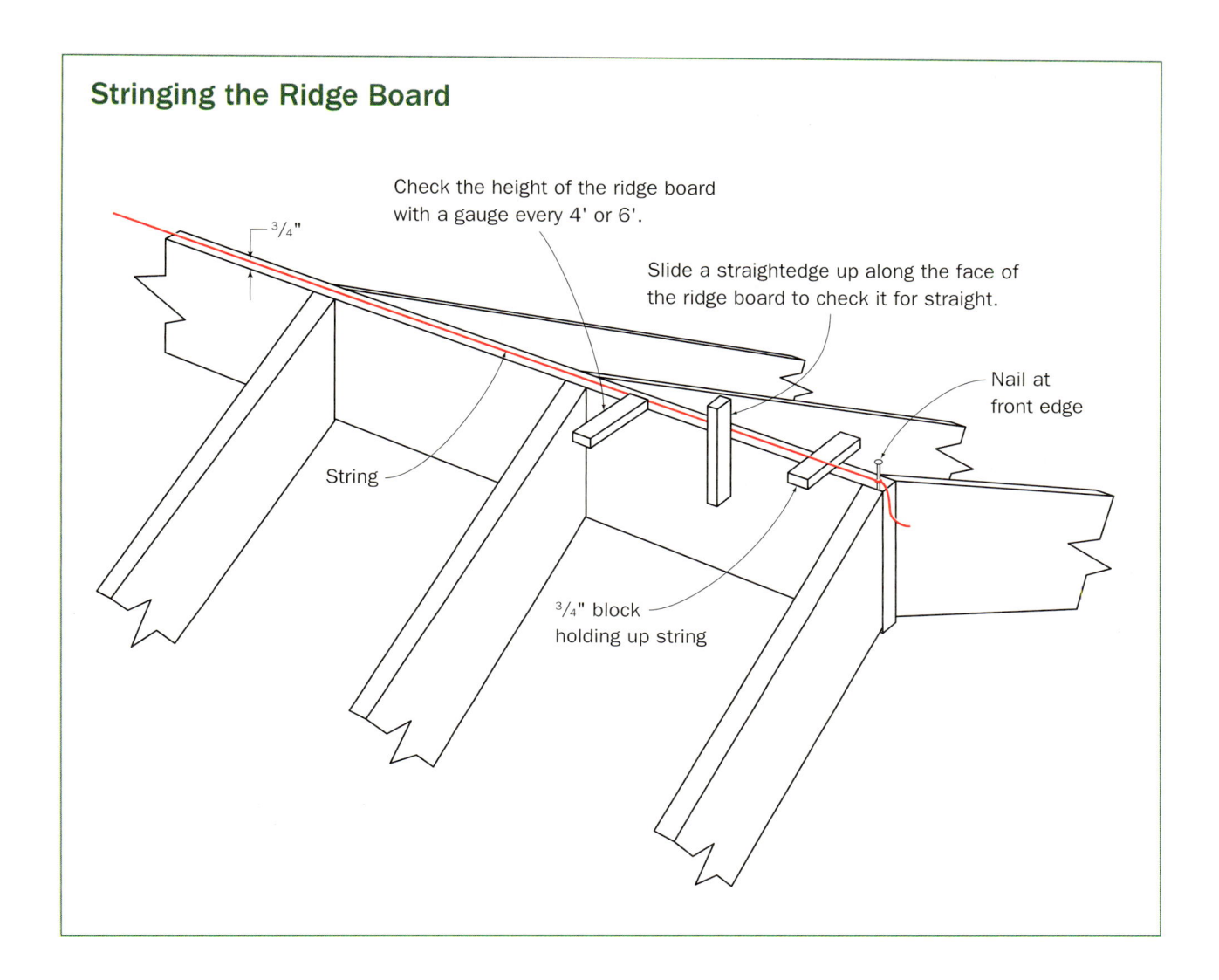

- 3/4"
- Check the height of the ridge board with a gauge every 4' or 6'.
- Slide a straightedge up along the face of the ridge board to check it for straight.
- Nail at front edge
- String
- 3/4" block holding up string

of the house. The ones that are tail down get located to the near side. Cut any headers for skylights, chimneys, etc. and bring them up on the deck as well.

To gauge the rafters into their proper position, set up dry lines from gable to gable at the plumb cut on the rafter tails. Block out each end with a piece of furring.

Start with the fifth or sixth rafter in from a gable end. With two guys in position, one at the ridge on the staging and the other down at the bearing location, raise a rafter into place. Gauge the rafter tail to the dry line with a furring block.

Set the plumb cut at the top of the rafter on the layout mark on the ridge. The top of the rafter should be flush with the top of the ridge board. (If you figured for the 1-in. ridge drop for the ridge vent, then before the rafter is lifted, cut a 1-in. gauge block to slide along the ridge as you install rafters.)

Compare the rafter to the dry line over the ridge board. Make sure it lines up with the edge of the ridge. Then the carpenter at the tail end of the rafter can nail down the seat cut of the bird's mouth. The top man can then nail through from the opposite side of the ridge with 16d nails and into the end of the rafter.

Install the rafter directly opposite in the same manner. The only difference will be in nailing through the ridge. You have to angle the spikes

ROOF FRAMING

To align the tails, a string is set and blocked out ¾ in. across the plumb cut of the rafter tails from one gable end to the other. As the rafters are installed, they are set into place using a ¾-in. gauge.

Temporary Collar Ties

When rafters are long, they may need a temporary support until the whole roof system is complete. Nail a temporary collar tie between the two rafters. Use a smaller piece of stock than the permanent collar tie stock and nail it above the permanent collar tie location, making sure the ends don't extend beyond the roofline. Continue installing the rafters and collar ties every fifth or sixth location, depending on the layout.

Once complete, the ridge will be lined up and secured. Now install the rest of the rafters by starting from one end and putting up opposing members before moving to the next pair. There is no need for additional temporary collar ties.

on either side of the first rafter to go through the ridge to catch the opposing rafter. Continue installing the rafters every fifth or sixth location, depending on the layout.

Adjusting misaligned rafters Occasionally a rafter has to be trimmed to make it fit just right. If the top of the rafter falls below its place on the ridge, cut the heel back to allow the rafter to move toward the ridge. If the top is correct but the tail cut sticks out too far, trim the tail cut plumb. If the top is above the ridge and the tail is correct, trim the seat cut to let the rafter top drop down.

Rafter rough openings Don't double up the rafters of a rough opening as you set the rafters. Install the inside members only. The outside members of the doubled rafters don't get installed until the rest of the opening is framed. This allows you to follow through a nailing sequence to fasten the rough opening parts together.

If the rough opening extends through the deck, such as a chimney chase, the easiest way to transfer the header locations up to the rafters is with a plumb bob. Plumb down along the inside rafters to the opening below. Draw a line along the plumb bob string to indicate the upper and lower positions for the headers. Because the header will be nailed along that plumb line, it will require taller dimensional lumber than the rafter stock. Measure the plumb line and determine the width of the stock, making sure it won't extend above or below the rafter. Often you will have to rip the wide header stock to the correct width.

If the opening is going only through the rafter, like with a skylight, the location can be scaled in place off the plans (unless there are written measurements). Sometimes a client of ours will come on-site to eyeball a skylight's desired location.

Skylight headers can be framed in different ways. Typically, the top header of a skylight is placed perpendicular to the top of the rafter and the bottom header is plumb. As with the previous type of opening, the plumb header will be of a different dimensional size than the rafters. The perpendicular header is cut from the same stock as the rafters. Cut the headers to the lengths needed. If an opening is 4 ft. or more, double the header pieces. Also be sure to check your building code.

Position the headers to the marks of the rough openings and through nail them from the outside of the rafters. If the headers are doubled, measure 1½ in. back and install only the outside pieces. They will be doubled up after the rafter cripples are installed. Transfer the cripple layout marks from the deck and ridge to the headers.

Measure the length of the rafter cripples above and below the headers. For the top cripple, measure from the top of the plumb cut to the top of the header. For the tail cripples, measure along the top of the rafter from the header to the tail end. Use the rafter template to mark out the

Installation Sequence of a Rough Opening

Step 1. Inside members of doubled rafters
Step 2. Outside members of headers
Step 3. Cripples
Step 4. Inside members of headers
Step 3. Cripples
Step 5. Outside members of doubled rafters

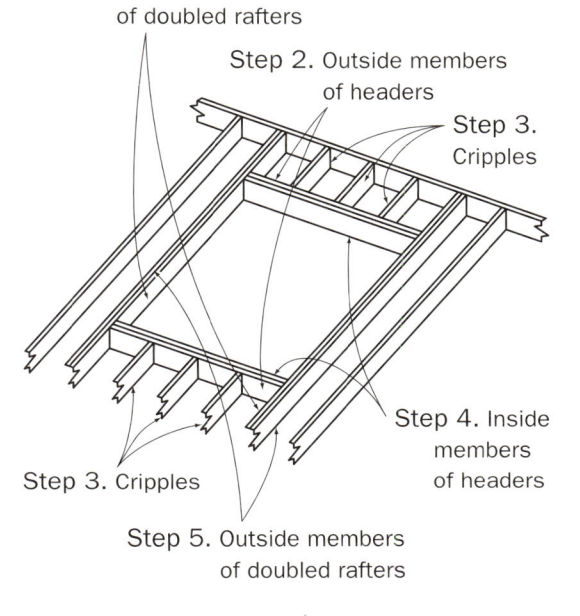

The outside members of the doubled rafters on either side of a large rough opening are installed to complete the assembly.

ROOF FRAMING 161

cripples on the appropriate length stock. Match the angle of the header at the header cut.

Install the cripples, making sure to through nail them at the headers. If the headers are double units, install the second members after the cripples are fastened. Once the headers are complete, install the second members of the doubled rafters on either side of the openings. Once all the rough openings are complete, set them in place and nail all the remaining rafters.

Subfacia

We use a 2x subfacia to tie the rafter tails together and to provide a solid surface for the trim and for attaching the gutters.

The size of the subfacia has already been determined when figuring out the rafter tail cuts. There are two ways to deal with the top edge of the subfacia. One is to rip the top edge of the subfacia to the same angle as the roof pitch so it provides a continuous surface to support the sheathing. The other is to leave the subfacia's top edge square and slide it down the plumb tail cut until the outside corner is at the same plane as the top of the rafter. To do this, simply place a straightedge along the top of the rafter extending beyond the tail. Slide the subfacia up until the outside edge contacts the straightedge. This leaves a small void that is bridged by the sheathing. Either way, adjust the size of the stock so that the bottom of the subfacia is even with the bottom of the tail cut.

Nail the subfacia on to the rafter tail plumb cuts. Cut the lengths so that the butt joints fall on the rafters.

Sheathing the roof

Roof sheathing is an integral part of the roof system. It connects all the rafters or trusses together laterally and helps transfer loads between adjacent framing members. The sheathing also provides a solid nailing base for the roofing. Roof sheathing is installed in a similar fashion to floor and wall sheathing, with just a few differences. We'll describe the process and a few variations you may find useful in special situations.

Sheathing layout From the top center of the ridge, measure down along the gable end rafters. Measure to the 4-ft. increment closest to the bottom end of the rafters, without going past the ends; add $1/4$ in. and make a mark. The extra $1/4$ in. is to prevent the sheathing from binding at the ridge. Sometimes the building specs will call for H-clips to be installed between the sheathing sheets in the bays between rafters. H-clips are made of metal, and they strengthen the spaces

When necessary, shims are installed between the subfacia and rafters, ensuring a straight solid surface.

between rafters. If you are going to use H-clips between the courses of sheathing, add ⅛ in. for every course. (For example, if there are a total of five courses, add ⅝ in. before drawing the marks.) And if you dropped the ridge board for ridge venting, add another 1 in. to your measurement so the sheathing falls short of the top of the ridge. Snap a line between the two marks.

Check the gable ends to make sure they are still plumb. Then eye up the length of the gable end rafters to ensure that they are close to straight. If any of them bow in or out severely, you have to run a line along the edge above the rafter from the top to the bottom. Nail a brace or two to the worst areas and straighten them to the string.

Installing the sheathing Start sheathing with a full sheet flush to the outside edge of the gable end rafter and the bottom edge lined up on the chalkline. Continue the course with full sheets, measuring and tacking the rafters on center using the same sheathing procedure you used to sheathe the floor (see chapter 4). Save all of the nailing until the entire side has been completely sheathed. At that time, snap lines the length of the rafters on top of the sheathing to indicate the center of the rafters; then nail off the sheathing.

If the roof pitch is fairly steep (about an 8 or 9 pitch) it's easier to use a 4-ft. T-square to mark out the nail lines and then nail off the sheets as you install them.

As with the floor sheathing, leave the gable ends just tacked. Begin the next row with a full sheet 4 ft. in from the gable end. Alternate the courses so each row offsets the previous one by 4 ft. Unlike the floor sheathing, you can leave out the end pieces that are not full sheets (unless you are using H-clips). This leaves a 4-ft.-tall gap on the end of every other row. The gaps can be filled in later, because the roof sheathing is not tongue and groove.

If you have rake overhangs framed onto the gable ends, you must account for them in the course layout. The leading sheets have to be cut so that one edge is even with the overhang and the other edge falls on the center of a rafter. The rest of the process is the same.

Straightening the gable end Once all of the full sheets are in place, run a chalkline from the plumb cut at the ridge to the bird's mouth and snap the line on top of the sheathing to indicate the inside edge of the gable rafters. Remove the tack nails from the end sheets and work the gable rafter back and forth until the inside of the rafter lines up directly beneath the chalkline. Fasten the sheathing to the rafter and continue working up

Sheathing Steep Roofs

When the pitch of the roof is 10 or more, we like to sheathe from the top down. This requires a little more staging but it is much safer and saves time.

Set the staging so that you're standing up between the rafters about 6 ft. from the ridge. From the center of the ridge at each gable end, measure down 4 ft. ¼ in. and snap a line across the rafters. Begin the layout as before. After you finish a row, nail it off completely and lower the staging toward the outside of the building. Continue with the process, completing the last course from the outside staging.

It's safer and easier to sheath a steep-pitched roof from the top down.

ROOF FRAMING   163

With strings running from one gable end to the other, a furring block is used as a gauge to place the collar tie accurately.

the rest of the gable rafter until it is straight and secure.

After all of the gable ends have been straightened, fill in the missing sheathing pieces at the ends. And then rip sheets of sheathing to fill in the bottom row.

Installing collar ties/joists

We prefer to put the collar ties on after the sheathing is complete because the sheathing realigns the underside of the rafters a little as it gets fastened from one member to the other.

Reference strings are needed when installing collar ties to ensure accurate placement on the rafters and to ensure a flat and level ceiling. Measure up off the deck to the determined height and make a mark on the gable end wall. Snap a level line across the gable end over the mark. Because installing a full-size collar tie on the line nailed to the gable wall serves no structural purpose, you can use lesser size stock, like a 2x4. You can also use multiple pieces of 2x stock nailed to the studs of the gable wall. Whichever you use, fasten the stock to the gable, matching the bottom edge to the line, and repeat the process at the other end.

On the underside of the gable end collar tie, within about 1 in. to where it intersects with the rafter, string a line from one gable end to the other. Do this at both the front and back rafters so there are two lines running down the length of the building. Place a furring block so the string is held down off the stock at all four corners.

With a helper, place the first collar tie roughly in position above the strings. Slide it horizontally until the gap between the collar tie and the sheathing is about the same at both ends. Gauge

> **ADVICE**
> ### One-Person Collar Tie Installation
>
> *If you want to make the collar tie installation a one-person operation, snap a line across the underside of the rafters about $1/4$ in. lower than the proper placement, on one side only. Tack a piece of furring along that line, across the underside of all the rafters. Now you can rest one end of the collar tie on top of the furring while you gauge the other end. When you have your end gauged, shoot only one nail into it, close to the intersection of the tie and the rafter, so it can pivot easily. Go to the other end, lift it off the support, gauge it, and permanently fasten it. Then go back to the first end and finish fastening.*

the bottom of the collar tie to the string with a small block of furring. When it is in the correct position, spike it to the rafters. Continue the process, completing the installation of all the collar ties.

Rough openings on the collar ties

Collar ties are not expected to carry much weight, so they are usually not doubled like the rafters are at openings. When you come to an opening, place the collar ties on the rafters, outside the opening. Transfer the lines from the opening in the rafters, down to the collar ties. Keep the same angles that the headers were installed to. Cut collar tie headers so that they fit between the two outside ties and then through nail them along the transferred lines, flush with the bottom of the ties.

Fill in any cripples needed from the collar tie headers to the rafters. Measure the last collar tie from the end point to the header. This is the length of the cripples. Nail one end flush to the bottom of the header and use the gauge and string at the other.

Cut two more lengths of stock that fit inside, from one collar tie header to the other, and through nail those directly beneath the rafters of the openings. If the rafters are doubled, flush these pieces to the inside of the opening.

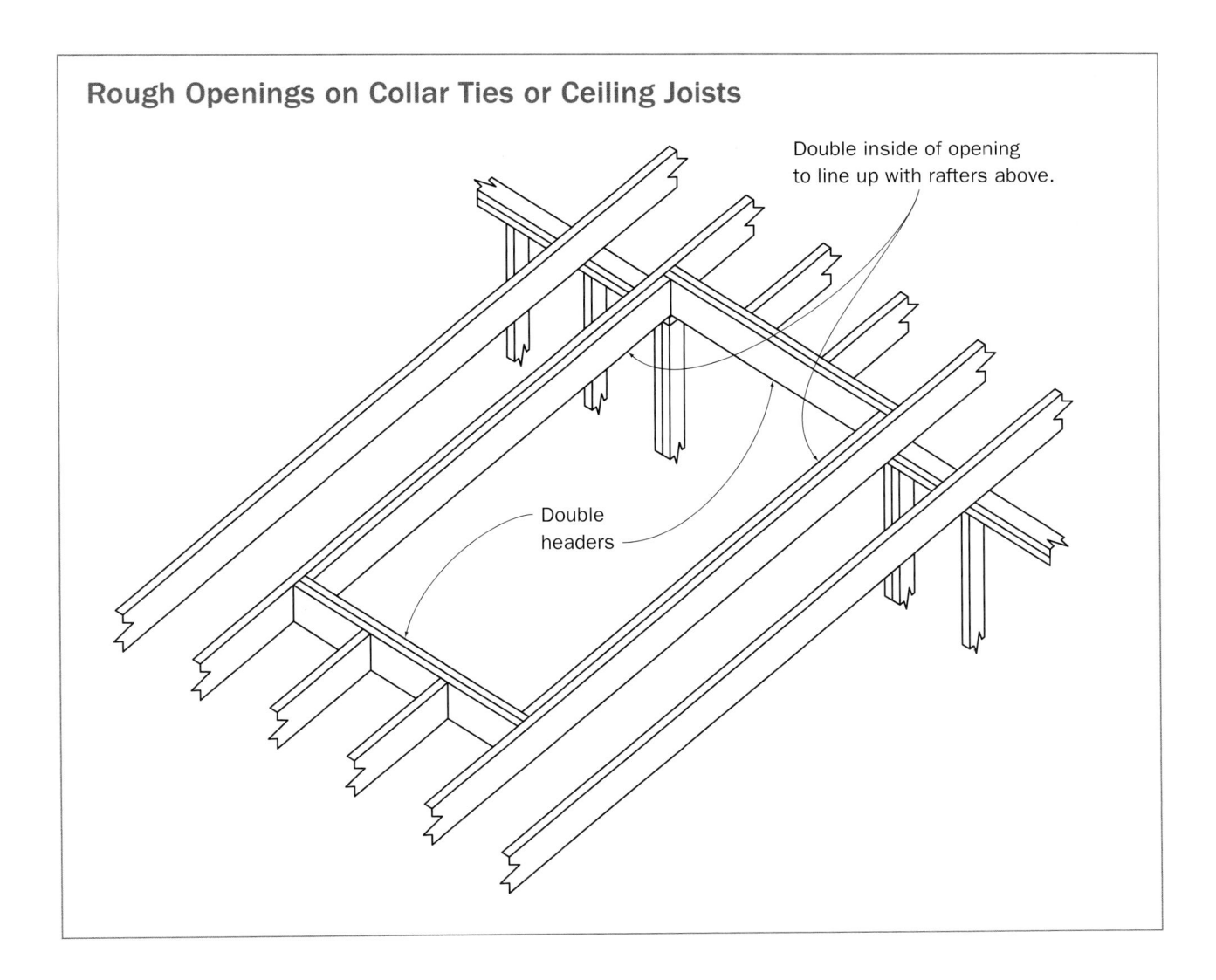

Rough Openings on Collar Ties or Ceiling Joists

Double inside of opening to line up with rafters above.

Double headers

If the opening is to be a finished shaft, fill in 2x stock from the rafter headers to the collar tie headers at each corner. Also fill in between the rafters and the collar tie headers to provide sufficient blocking for nailing the finishes to (see the drawing on p. 165).

Laying out an attic-style roof

There are a few major differences when you're framing a roof that will create an attic space rather than a living space. The gable layout is completed in the same way, except that it is started as far away from the gable end as the wall is high. For example, if the wall that the gable will sit on is 8 ft. high, the layout of the roof starts 8 ft. in from the gable end. The entire unit—the wall and roof gable—can be snapped and laid out at the same time or the wall can be framed and then the gable laid out.

It is best to lay out and build the wall and gable end as one unit (balloon framing). By doing so, you can use continuous studs that go from the bottom plate to the rafter. This eliminates the weak point created at the joint of the top of the wall and the bottom of the gable.

Ceiling joists are cut and installed in a similar manner as floor joists with a couple of differences. First, there is no rim joist across the butt ends. The outside ends of the joists flush up to the outside of the framing. Second, the joists do not touch at the overlap across the bearing wall. They are separated by, and fastened to, a 2x piece of stock, because they are located against opposite sides of the opposing rafters.

When measuring and cutting ceiling joists, the lengths do not have to be exact because they will be overlapping across the center wall. In most cases, however, the outside ends have to be trimmed at the top to prevent them from extending up beyond the top edge of the rafter.

The easiest way to determine the cut is to lay a ceiling joist in position across the rafter layout that is snapped on the deck. Mark the angle of the top edge of the rafter along the top of the ceiling joist. Mark the same angle an extra $1/2$ in. down from the first. There is no need to have the ceiling joist touch the underside of the sheathing, the joist may not shrink the same amount as the rafter, creating a visual defect at that point.

As with floor joists, install all of the ceiling joists, nailing them to the outside walls only. Check the walls to the lines to make sure they are still in place, then fasten the ceiling joist at the overlap to a 2x block set between them and down into the bearing wall. Next construct any rough openings, as described earlier.

Once the ceiling joists have been installed, lay down sheets of roof sheathing across the joists to provide a temporary work platform. The ridge and rafters are installed as described earlier.

The collar ties do not have to be as carefully installed as they are in a living space, because they are structural members only and not supporting a finish ceiling. Measure and mark the desired locations of the collar ties on the gable ends. Snap a line across the underside of the rafters, where the ties meet the rafter, from end to end. Install the ties to the lines as called for by the plans and to code. One collar tie every 4 ft. is most common in our experience.

Roof Trusses

This section covers roof trusses. It applies to all types of truss systems, whether large or small, simple or complex. We have broken down the roof truss operation into four phases. Ordering, handling, truss and site preparation, and truss installation. Each phase varies a little, depending on the type of system; but the basic premise remains the same.

Ordering

One of the biggest mistakes made by most builders is not getting involved with the ordering process of the trusses. The order usually goes from the builder to the lumberyard salesperson, to the truss manufacturer rep, to the truss designer/engineer, to the assembly floor. In any of the connections, the information can (and frequently does) get transferred incorrectly or is misunderstood.

The important thing is to get involved with the ordering yourself and go directly to the truss designer. That is not to say that the lumberyard is getting left out. The purchase order can still originate from them, but the lumberyard salesperson should take a back seat at this point. In some regions, there are truss manufacturers that will sell directly to the customer, others will only sell to a retailer. Either way, you should still

(continued on p. 171)

The gable end is lowered into place to complete the installation of the trusses on the main roof. (Photo by Roe A. Osborn, courtesy *Fine Homebuilding* magazine, © The Taunton Press, Inc.)

ADVICE: Choosing Roof Trusses

There are many different specifications that can apply to any type of truss. Become familiar with what you want for a final product in all of the areas that the roof truss affects. Make sure that you are complete in your specifications because many times the designer will assume that a missed detail is not important and use a default specification. Most often, by the time it's discovered, the trusses are up.

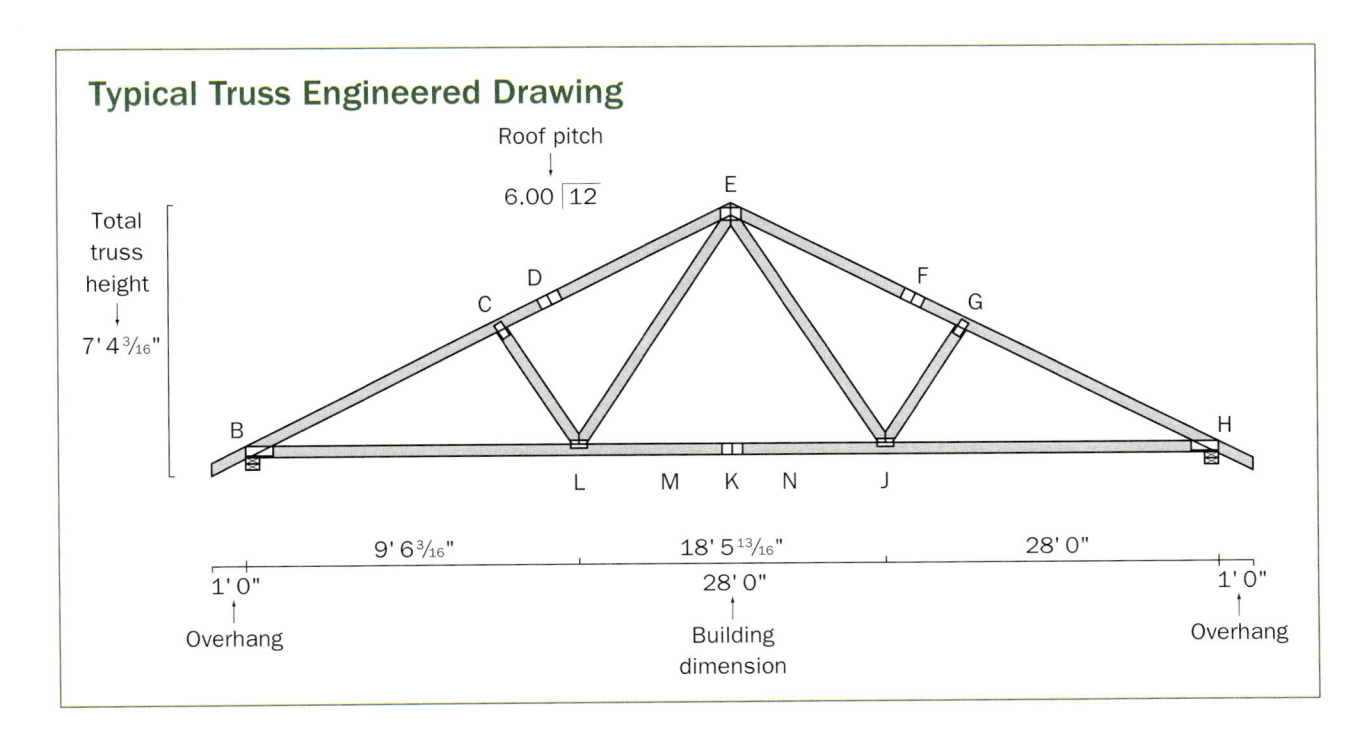

Typical Truss Engineered Drawing

Roof pitch
6.00 | 12

Total truss height
7' 4 3/16"

B C D E F G H
L M K N J

9' 6 3/16"   18' 5 13/16"   28' 0"

1' 0" Overhang   28' 0" Building dimension   1' 0" Overhang

Roof Truss Specifications

The following is a list of specifications that must be determined before the trusses can be designed.

Truss Span

Truss span is the length that the trusses will extend. If the depth of the building is 30 ft. then that is considered the truss span. But for engineering purposes you must also supply the width of the exterior bearing walls so that the "true" span is used in computing the design. If 2x6 walls are being used then the true span is 29 ft. 1 in. (30 ft. minus two walls of 5½ in. each). Don't determine and submit the true span, use the dimension of the building as the truss span and then indicate the wall thickness.

Pitch of the Roof

The pitch of the roof is indicated on the blueprints on a small triangle next to the roof on a cross section or a side elevation. It determines the angle and height of the roof. Be very careful if you change the pitch to alter the appearance of the roof. Follow the change in the rooflines in all aspects of the house to make sure it won't interfere with the existing features. For example, changing an attached garage roof to make it steeper, and therefore higher, might cause it to run through a second-floor gable window of the main house.

Overhangs

The overhang is the part of the truss that will extend beyond the building and become the soffit. It's mainly a function of design. The plans may specify the exact amount of overhang required or the overhang might be drawn on the elevations but with no actual measurements. Either way, determine the desired overhang and subtract the thickness of the subfacia (if the house design calls for one). That number is the overhang of the truss. For example, if a 12-in. overhang is called for on the plans, a 1½-in. subfacia will be used. So the trusses should be ordered with a 10½-in. overhang.

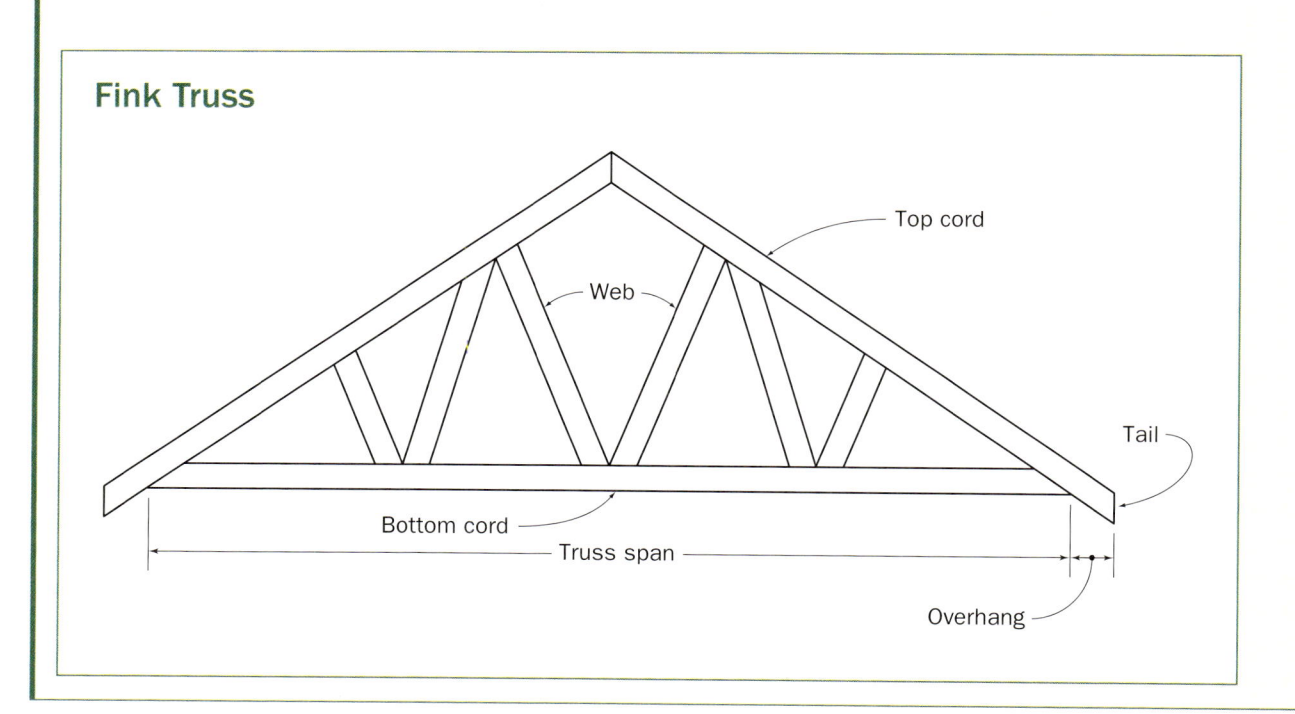

Fink Truss

Overhang Type

The two members of the truss that come together at the ends are the bottom cord and top cord. The top cord is the rafter and the bottom cord is the ceiling joist. The design of the house will dictate what type of overhang is used. If a flat soffit is called for then a bottom cord overhang is specified. But if a flat soffit is called for and it is dropped below the top plate of the wall so that there is a smaller reveal between the tops of the windows and the soffit, then a top cord overhang is specified and the horizontal framing is built on site after the trusses are installed. If an angled soffit is needed, then a top cord overhang is specified and the soffit follows the underside of the top cord.

Ceiling Details

The inside ceilings of each room can vary greatly, especially with a truss system. Vaulted, coffered, tray, or cathedral ceilings can easily be designed into the truss system. It's important with these types of details to identify to the truss designer exactly where they start and stop within the building. Thicknesses of walls and their exact locations should be pinpointed and marked on the plans.

Attic Use

What is the attic going to be used for? Storage, HVAC equipment, or a future room? A factor in design of the trusses is the use of the attic. The design load must be adequate for the intended use. If the heating or air-conditioning unit is to be located in the attic, then its location must be specified so that the affected trusses are designed for the point loads needed to support the equipment. If the attic is to be used for storage, then an attic design is used that keeps the webs of the truss opened away from the center to provide a larger accessible area. If a future room is planned, then an attic type truss with a live load (30 lb. to 40 lb.) designed on the bottom cord is used.

Precut Tails

There are times when trusses are to be supported by truss hangers, flush to a girder truss or a

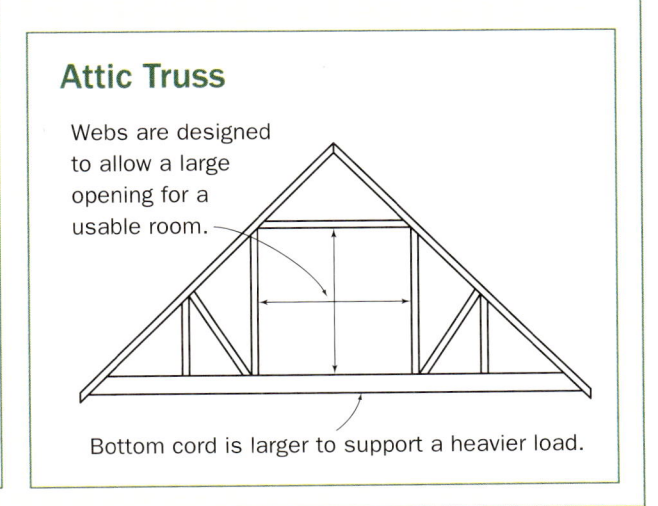

Top Cord Overhang

A top cord overhang drops the soffit well below the top of the wall, as required for certain architectural details.

Attic Truss

Webs are designed to allow a large opening for a usable room.

Bottom cord is larger to support a heavier load.

Roof Truss Specifications *(continued)*

Each truss is specifically engineered and manufactured. This one is lowered into the hanger system it was designed for.

support beam. In this case, the overhangs have to be cut off so the trusses seat properly. Instead of cutting the truss tails on site, which usually involves cutting through the metal truss plate, specify the location of the girder or beam on the plans and have the trusses cut to fit by the manufacturer.

Rough Openings

The size and location of all openings through the ceiling and roof must be accurately identified. The placement of any skylights, chimneys, or chases, have to be marked on the set of plans so the manufacturer can design the truss system accordingly. Any rough opening not accounted for will have to be fit in between the truss bays, because the trusses cannot be cut or altered in any way once they are built.

Energy-Efficient Details

Typical attic insulation height is 9 in. or more. To continue the insulation across the top plate of the exterior wall without its getting crushed by the roof sheathing, a raised-heel truss or a bottom cord overhang truss should be specified. Either configuration provides sufficient room to allow the insulation to continue all the way to the outside

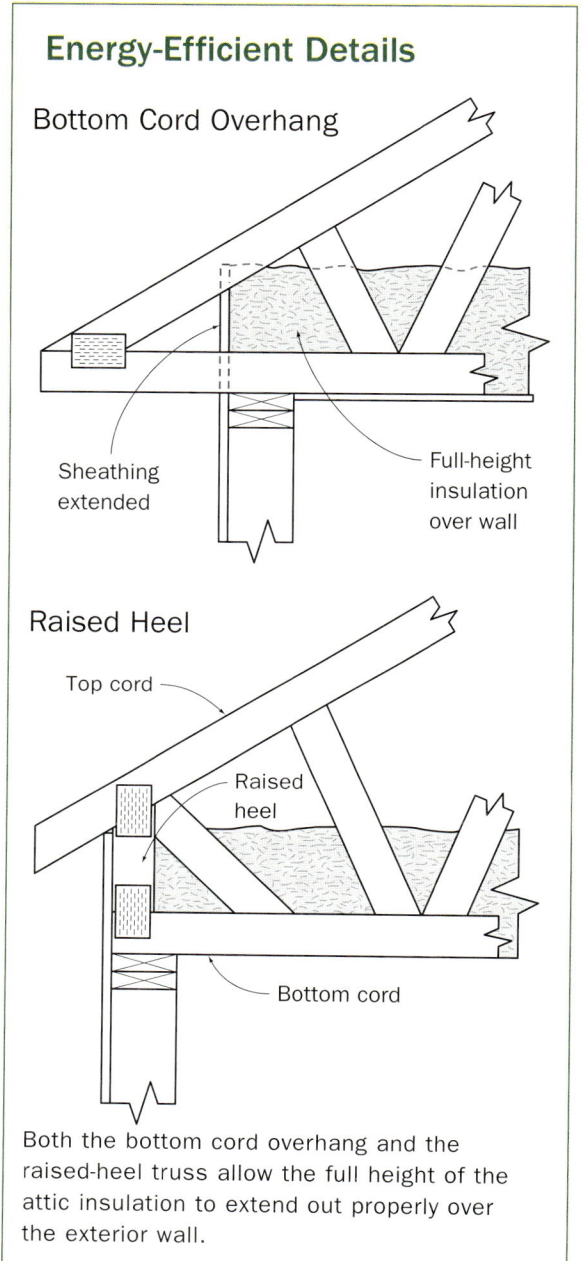

Energy-Efficient Details

Bottom Cord Overhang

Raised Heel

Both the bottom cord overhang and the raised-heel truss allow the full height of the attic insulation to extend out properly over the exterior wall.

edge of the exterior wall. In cold climates, this eliminates the chance for a warm area to develop over the top plate and potentially form ice dams.

170 CHAPTER SIX

communicate directly to the truss designer. There are different ways of putting together a truss order, depending on the complexity of the roof design.

Simple or "stock" order Many times the design of a truss is so common that the trusses are pre-built and stocked. This is sometimes the situation for a simple gable roof with no special details. In this case, you can draft the order yourself and fax it off to the truss designer. Here is the ordering process:

1. Write up a spec sheet that includes the specification and ordering details just covered.

2. Count the number of trusses you need by dividing the length of the building by two (assuming 2 ft. on center) and then adding one to that number. Remember, two out of that total count will be gable end trusses. A 40-ft. building will need 21 trusses: 19 common trusses and two gable end trusses.

3. After the designer receives your order, have him send you the truss design. The truss design is the engineering of the individual trusses; it contains all the details of the roof.

4. Review the design, making sure it includes the correct specifications, such as overhang type and length.

Custom-ordered trusses A custom roof is a little more involved than a simple gable. It can be a gable roof with not-so-simple details, such as raised heels or 4-ft. rough openings for large skylights. Another type of roof in this category is a hip roof. It is not complex, but the roof must be engineered and built to order. The ordering process is a little different:

1. Write up a spec sheet with the necessary information.

2. Send or fax the top floor plan to the truss designer.

3. Get a truss design and a truss plan from the designer. The truss plan is the layout of the trusses. Because there will be a variety of trusses in this design, the plan specifies the location of each truss in relation to the layout of the building and labels each one on the plan to coincide with the label on each truss.

4. Review both the design and plan for accuracy before telling the manufacturer to proceed with the fabrication.

Complex order A complex roof is usually made up of multiple hips and valleys and/or different ceiling details (tray, cathedral, etc.). Here's the procedure:

> **ADVICE: Simplifying a Detail**
>
> Sometimes it helps simplify a detail if you order an extra truss to be "sistered" to another truss at a point where roof or ceiling planes change. Ordering an extra gable truss to fall even with the outside edge of a firewall eliminates the extra labor required to build the wall up to the underside of the sheathing. For gable trusses, make sure they are stacked for delivery with both gable ends on top of the stack. They need to be prepped before they are raised.

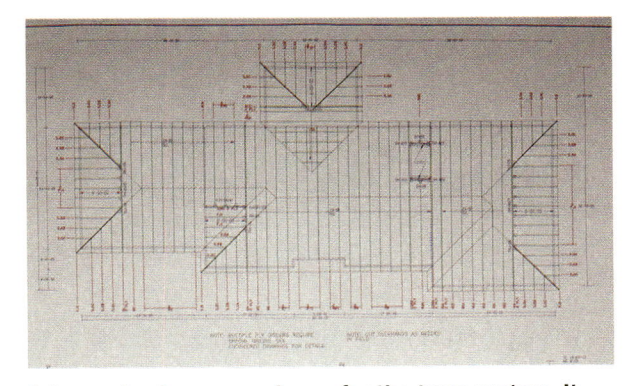

A truss plan is your road map for the truss system. It identifies and pinpoints the location of each individual truss. (Photo by Roe A. Osborn, courtesy *Fine Homebuilding* magazine and Trussco, Inc.)

1. Write up a spec sheet and meet with the designer to review a full set of plans. It may take more than one meeting to iron out all of the details, because the other subs (for example, HVAC and mason) become involved.
2. Once the design is complete, review the truss design and plans. Also ask for an isometric drawing of the truss system to help identify the layout of the different trusses.

Handling trusses

Until the trusses are installed, braced, and sheathed, they are weak individual units, especially when laying down flat. It's important to handle the trusses properly to ensure a smooth installation and to avoid any truss failures.

Be at the site when the trusses are delivered to direct the placement of the stack of trusses. They should be dropped in a flat area that will not interfere with the crane truck location. A delivery with a boom truck is best, because it makes exact placement easy and the trusses are not slammed to the ground. As the trusses are placed by the boom, use 2x stock on the ground to make the stack lie flat.

If a roll-off truck is used, you have to slide the 2x stock underneath to get them flat. Sometimes restacking is necessary if the stack is too heavy to adjust. When moving the trusses by hand, keep them flat and avoid flexing them so you don't put stress on the connector plates.

Cut the banding straps right after they are delivered. The trusses can warp where banded, even within a few days. A warped truss is difficult to straighten during installation, particularly the gable end trusses.

Cover the trusses to keep rain-splashed dirt off. A fine layer of dirt makes walking the trusses during the installation extra dangerous. Also, dirt gets bumped off while being swung overhead and falls down into the eyes of the crew. During the winter, covering protects them from snow and ice and helps keep the frost off the surfaces.

Schedule the delivery day close to the installation day. The less time they spend on the site exposed to the elements, the better.

Preparing the trusses and the site

There are many procedures of a truss system that can be accomplished on the ground before they are raised. Doing these things on the ground makes the whole process easier, quicker, and safer.

Begin the truss prep by organizing the trusses by size, location, and lifting order. This may involve some moving around and restacking by hand. You want to end up with the trusses stacked in the order that they will be installed,

Avoid bad truss drops. These roof trusses have been dropped on an uneven surface, and they are tightly banded together. They will become more difficult to use with each passing day that they are left like that.

with the exception of the gable ends. They are to be left on the top of the stack for now.

Make sure the stacks are flat by using 2x stock on the ground as shims. Then, using a sledgehammer, gently tap the trusses into alignment matching the peaks, seats, and tails. With the trusses flat and aligned, begin the layout marks.

Marking the trusses The seats of the trusses (where the top and bottom cord meet) are not always cut exactly to a point. This makes it difficult to use them as a reference for truss location and alignment to the outside edge of the walls. We use the inside of the walls for truss location. It eliminates the possibility of installing the trusses out of alignment to each other.

Measuring the bottom cord of the trusses end to end, locate and mark the center of the top and bottom trusses. Measure back half the width of the building minus the thickness of the wall and make a mark.

For example, if the house is 28 ft. wide with 2x4 walls, measure back 13 ft. 8½ in. from the center point (figuring the walls at 3½ in.). Mark each end on the top truss then repeat the process on the bottom truss. Draw a line with a straightedge between the top and bottom marks. As the trusses are installed, these lines will be lined up with the inside edge of the wall.

Check the actual measurement between the inside edges of the walls to make sure they are true. If the length is different adjust the lines on the trusses.

Measure for and mark the sheathing lines the same way you would for a stick roof (see p. 147). The same method of measuring for the sheathing mark is used in marking the trusses while they're on the ground.

To mark lines for ceiling strapping, start from the wall lines of the top truss at one end of the stack and measure for the 16-in on-center strapping layout (see chapter 7 for a discussion of ceiling strapping). The easiest way is to measure 17¼ in. from the wall mark (16 in. plus half of

With the trusses stacked neatly on the ground, layout lines are drawn on all of them at once. The line closest to the tail will be used to position the truss on top of the wall plates. The other lines are for ceiling strapping. The top cords are laid out for roof sheathing. (Photo by Roe A. Osborn, courtesy *Fine Homebuilding* magazine, © The Taunton Press, Inc.)

the 2½-in. width of the furring) and tack a nail. Hook your tape measure on the nail and place 16-in. on-center marks the length of the bottom cord. Repeat the process on the bottom truss and then scribe lines along a straightedge connecting the marks from top to bottom truss. Don't forget the first mark where the nail is tacked.

Use a lumber crayon and make fat marks next to each line toward the end you started the layout from. This indicates which side of the line the furring gets lined up to.

It's important to orient the trusses correctly. Theoretically, they should be the same on both slopes and, therefore, match each other no matter which direction they face. In reality, they aren't and they don't.

Before the trusses are moved, and this should occur at delivery if you have to restack them, mark the tail ends of one side of the trusses so they don't get reversed. A quick spray with orange surveyor's paint makes them stand out the best. Even if the manufacturer fastens red tags to the ends to keep them oriented correctly we still mark the ends ourselves.

ROOF FRAMING **173**

The gable end is sheathed, sided, and trimmed before being lifted into place.

Gable end prep You want to complete as much of the gable end as possible before lifting it into place. Applying the trim and siding on the ground is a lot easier than doing it two or three floors up when you're working off of staging.

To sheath the gable, place the gable truss flat on the stack of trusses to use as a work surface. If there are more gable ends than truss stacks, put the extra gables on the ground and shim flat with 2x stock. Try to keep them within reach of the crane.

Start by snapping a line from end to end along the bottom edge of the bottom cord. If there is any part of the bottom cord that extends down below the line, trim it off. Usually it's only a matter of 1/4 in. or less. This lets the truss sit firmly on the top plate of the gable wall without rocking.

The sheathing has to hang down below the bottom cord the same distance that it was left shy from the top plate of the gable end wall. So if you left the sheathing 2 in. shy from the top plate of the gable end wall, hang your tape measure 2 in. below the bottom cord of the gable end. Mark 4 ft. up on the tape at each end of the truss (in far enough to make a mark along an upright member). Snap a line between the marks and start the sheathing at this line.

Apply the sheathing in full sheets, letting the extra hang off the top cord and leaving the smaller areas void. Snap a line on the sheathing to mark the top edge of the top cord and cut off the excess. Use these pieces to fill in the smaller areas. Make sure to angle the sheathing nails to keep them from protruding through the flat of the truss stock.

Apply building paper or housewrap over the entire gable. Leave enough wrap to extend down and overlap the course below. If you are using wood shingles or clapboard, you can install the siding on the gable at this time.

Because a course of siding should fall over the tops of the window trim, the layout of the gable siding must coincide with the top of the windows. Depending on the type of window you use, determine the location of the top of the trim in reference to the top of the wall plate (which is also the bottom edge of the bottom cord). Now hang that measurement on the tape measure down below the bottom edge of the bottom cord of the gable end and extend the tape up. The beginning of the tape is the bottom edge of a siding course. Figure about three or four courses high so you're well up onto the truss and mark near both ends. For example, if you are figuring shingle courses at 5 1/2 in., you would mark at 16 1/2 in. or 22 in. Snap a line at the marks and begin the siding. As you come to the ends of the truss, let the siding hang out beyond it. Keep the fasteners away from the last few inches of the ends. Once the siding is complete, measure down from the top edge of the top cord along the slope and mark 2½ in. for the strapping build-out of the trim (or the width of whatever other stock you intend to use). Make a mark at the ridge and at the tail of the top cord and snap a line on top of the siding. Set the saw depth and trim the siding along the line.

Next fasten the build-out for the gable trim and then the finish trim. Use a small piece of roof sheathing as a gauge along the top of the build-out and install your rake board flush with the top of the gauge.

If you are using gable vents, tack the vent and side around it. Once complete, remove the vent. The hole is used for the straps to lift the gable. After the gable truss is installed, the vent is replaced and permanently fastened.

To finish the process, snap a line along the bottom edge of the bottom cord. Tack in common spikes about 16 in. on center, just above the line at an angle. At the correct angle, these will be driven through the sheathing, bottom cord, and into the top plate of the gable wall when placed in position.

Wherever there is a change in the roof or the ceiling profile, you need to prep the trusses. If the roof profile changes, stack the two types of trusses on top of each other, oriented in the same direction with the smaller one on top. Draw a line along the top cord of the smaller top truss onto the larger truss beneath. If you did not order an extra, so as to be able to sister two trusses at the point where the roof changes height, nail a 2x nailer on the larger truss along the line to catch the roof sheathing. Install sheathing along that line up to the top cord. You may have to add some backers, depending on the size of the profile change.

At this point, you can also side the gable change as described above, except you have to account for the thickness of the roof sheathing, ice and water barrier, felt, shingle layers, and flashing along the bottom edge.

If the ceiling profile changes, stack the trusses in the same manner, then scribe a line along the

To facilitate setting the gable truss, nails are started along the bottom cord. When the truss is in position, a crew member on a ladder will drive the nails into the top plate of the gable end wall. (Photo by Roe A. Osborn, courtesy *Fine Homebuilding* magazine, © The Taunton Press, Inc.)

bottom cord of the top truss to the truss beneath. Nail a 2x nailer along the line to catch the strapping or finish of the ceiling.

Prepping for a hip end roof The end of a hip roof system consists of many different types of trusses, all of which get assembled and sheathed together on the ground.

The first step is to organize all of the different pieces of the hip truss system. The truss design identifies the pieces, and the truss plan tells you where they go.

Arrange the different pieces in small stacks near the area where you will be constructing the hips. Make sure they are all accounted for before beginning the assembly.

ROOF FRAMING 175

The entire end of a hip roof is lifted into position after first being assembled on the ground. (Photo by Roe A. Osborn, courtesy *Fine Homebuilding* magazine, © The Taunton Press, Inc.)

Hip Roof Truss

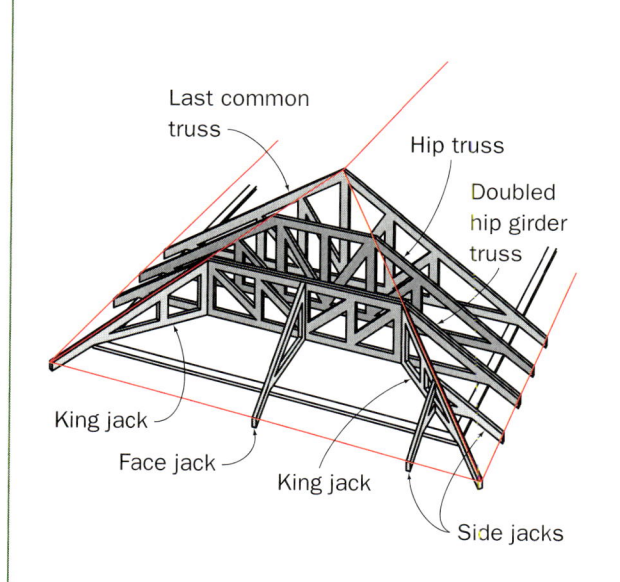

- Last common truss
- Hip truss
- Doubled hip girder truss
- King jack
- Face jack
- King jack
- Side jacks

The hip is formed by a series of flat-top trusses with progressively wider top chords. The lowest truss in the sequence, the hip girder truss, is doubled to support the jack trusses that complete the roof.

The girder is the main member and runs the entire width of the building. It usually has a heavier bottom cord than the other trusses to accommodate the extra weight of the trusses that will get attached to it. Generally, two girder trusses are nailed together and work in tandem.

The face jacks go perpendicular to the girder, sloping to the tail end. The king jacks shoot out 45° from the girder, forming the hips. Both the king and face jacks are secured with special hangers. The side jacks get fastened to the king jacks, finishing the hip frame.

A large, flat area must be cleared to assemble all the trusses that make up the hip. As with the gable trusses, keep them close enough to where the crane can get to them.

Start by locating the exact vertical center of the girder truss, top cord to bottom cord. Locate the middle of the top cord of the truss; then, from the ends of the top cord, measure equal distances diagonally to the bottom cord. Halfway between the diagonal marks is the midpoint of the bottom cord. Draw a line between the top and bottom midpoints. That is the vertical center from which the rest of the trusses are positioned.

Locate the king and face jack locations on the bottom cord of the girder truss using the

On a hip roof built with trusses, a jack truss holds the girder upright. The center face jack is tacked to the girder truss to keep it vertical while the rest of the face jacks are installed. (Photo by Roe A. Osborn, courtesy *Fine Homebuilding* magazine, © The Taunton Press, Inc.)

wall lines as a reference and the truss plan as the guide.

Tack the metal hangers in position on the bottom cord with a couple of nails. They will be nailed in permanently with spikes after the second girder truss is mated to the first. The king jack hangers are different from the face jack hangers. They are fabricated to hold the king jacks at a 45° angle from the girder truss and so are easily distinguished from the face jack hangers.

Prop the girder truss upright on blocks. Set the center face jack into its hanger and tack it to the top of the girder truss to hold them both upright. Make continuous blocking out of 2x stock that's long enough to support the tails of all of the face jacks. Raise the blocking until the girder truss is fairly plumb. Slip the rest of the face jacks in their hangers and tack them at the top. When they're all in place, nail them off through the cords and the webs of the girder truss.

Now tack the second girder truss in place behind the first. Run string lines along the top and bottom cords with the ¾-in. furring gauges, (as you did when straightening walls and beams). Straighten and temporarily brace the girder trusses.

Run lengths of furring along the tops of the bottom cords of the face jacks, near the tail ends. Mark the furring according to the layout of the wall plate (on which the trusses will eventually rest) and fasten the ends of the face jacks in their proper spacing.

Measure diagonally from the top corner of the outer-most face jack to the tail end on the other end. Move the entire tail end assembly until the diagonals from each end are the same. Check the lines to make sure the girder is still straight, then tack a piece of furring diagonally across the top of the face jacks to keep them square. Permanently nail the two girder trusses together along the top and bottom cords as well as the webs. Also nail the hangers permanently to the doubled girder.

Install the king jacks in place on either end of the girder. Measure from the king jack tails to the tail of the girder and again to the nearest face jack tail. Move the king jack tails until the measurements are the same. Secure both king jacks in position temporarily with pieces of strapping.

Run a string along the tails of the face jacks extending over to the king jack tail. Mark the king jack tail where the string falls, scribe the line down the side of the member, and trim the tail at

ROOF FRAMING **177**

Diagonal measurements square the truss-made hip roof system. Measurements are taken between the two outermost jack trusses, and the tails of the trusses are moved in unison until the measurements are equal. (Photo by Roe A. Osborn, courtesy *Fine Homebuilding* magazine, © The Taunton Press, Inc.)

The king jack truss forms the corner of the roof hip. The top cord of the king jack is cut to the pitch of a hip rafter and functions similarly. It is held in place with a special hanger, and the tail is positioned equidistant from the girder truss and the outer-most face jack. (Photo by Roe A. Osborn, courtesy *Fine Homebuilding* magazine, © The Taunton Press, Inc.)

a 45° angle. Trim the other side of the tail to 45° so that a 90° corner is formed on the edge of the tail. This makes the corner of the roof hip.

Nail the subfacia from the face jack tails to the end of the king jack tail. Continue the subfacia, returning it back toward the girder truss tail, and fasten it. Let the subfacia extend past the girder tail so that it can catch the next truss tail.

The side jack truss is a simple monotruss with just a top and bottom cord joined together with a truss plate at the splice joint. The manufacturer cuts the side jacks to the proper lengths but without the 45° angles needed to seat it correctly to the king jack. Cut the 45° angles on the butt ends of the top and bottom cords. Be careful not to alter the lengths and be sure you make left and right cuts as needed.

Mark the subfacia and king jacks with the proper 2-ft. on-center marks following the truss plans and referencing the face jacks and girder truss. Hangers are generally not used for the side jacks, simply install them in position according to their proper size and through nail them into the king jack. Then fasten them to the subfacia.

Start the sheathing 4 ft. up from the subfacia and stop the rows at the last full sheet increment.

Side jacks fill in the framing beside the king jack. Side jack trusses consisting of just a top and bottom cord are nailed into the king jack and subfascia. (Photo by Roe A. Osborn, courtesy *Fine Homebuilding* magazine, © The Taunton Press, Inc.)

Cut the bottom row to fit, but don't nail it in place. Rather, just tack it up on the next course of sheathing. This allows you to access the ends of the trusses that sit on the walls so they can be positioned and fastened to the walls without interference.

Truss layout The truss layout on the walls is best done before the walls are lifted. Follow the truss plan to lay out the location of the trusses on the top plate of the exterior walls. Each truss is labeled, so match the label on the truss to its equivalent on the truss plans. Mark the location on the top plate with the label of the truss. Check all of the details of the truss plan and make sure they are transferred to the layout. Double-check all of the on-center locations and watch out for small changes in centering. For example, many times the girder trusses do not follow the exact 24-in. on-center layout of the common trusses. Sometimes they are offset by ¾ in. or even 1½ in.

Installing trusses

Handling the trusses by hand can weaken the joints, even causing some of the metal truss plates to pop loose and fail. A crane is a better option, because it lifts the truss vertically, putting no lateral strain on the truss plates. Except for narrow, one-story buildings, it pays to use a crane. Not only do the trusses go up quicker and safer but all of the material needed for the second floor can be lifted at the same time. While the crane is on site, you can lift the roof sheathing, interior wall studs, furring, roof shingles, and tarpaper. The cost of the crane is more than saved in on-site labor.

Prepping for the truss installation String and brace the exterior walls using a furring gauge and diagonal wall bracing. Set up staging along the length of the building on the eaves ends. The staging should bring you about waist high to the top of the walls. Set up staging along the gable walls on the interior. It should be about even with the top of the gable wall. On the day of the installation, set up a ladder on the first gable end high enough to reach the preset nails in the already sheathed gable end trusses.

Layout lengths of long strapping and mark them with 24-in. on-center marks for spacing and bracing the trusses after they are lifted in place.

Ready the material to be craned to the second floor. Stack the interior wall studs in bundles of 75 to 100. Keep the stacks up on blocks so the straps can slide underneath.

Have the lumberyard band the roof sheathing together in bundles of 25 to 30. Ask them to use extra banding straps. When they are delivered to the site, make sure they slide off the truck gently so the bands don't snap. Slide them down on top of blocks for strap access.

Also have the lumberyard send extra pallets for the roof shingles. Stack 21 to 24 bundles per pallet. Cut 2x stock the width of the stacks to use as spacers to keep the lifting straps from compressing the shingles when they are raised.

ROOF FRAMING

Use the crane to save labor. Studs, shingles, and prepackaged bundles of roof sheathing can be brought up to the second floor with the truss crane. (Photo by Roe A. Osborn, courtesy *Fine Homebuilding* magazine, © The Taunton Press, Inc.)

A metal clip fastened to the end of a long rope allows the crew member on the staging to easily release this tag line from a truss as it swings into place.

When you're ready to install the trusses, choose an area on-site that is clear enough for the crane to set up and close enough to the building and the trusses to reach both without moving. This should have already been determined before the trusses were delivered.

Review hand signals with the operator because once the job begins, the crane is too noisy to understand voice commands clearly. Make sure the crew knows the signals, but designate one member to do all of the signaling. Always have this crew member in the crane operator's sight.

Plan the areas where the different materials will be dropped. Estimate where the diagonal bracing for the gable ends will be secured to the floor and avoid putting any materials there. Place the roof shingles near the windows, so they can be loaded onto the staging with less effort. Make sure to use the 2x stock to keep the straps from crushing them together. Place the sheathing and studs along the exterior walls or over the bearing wall beneath. Keep the concentrated loads off of individual joists.

Tag line with clip When roof trusses are raised by a crane and swung into position, someone must control the rotation of the truss from the ground with a tag line connected to one end of the truss.

Untying the line from the truss tail requires two hands and is an awkward task for the guy up on the staging who is setting the truss bottoms. To make the job safer and quicker, we attach a small quick-release safety hook to the end of the nylon line. With the thumb of one hand, the clasp can be released and the tag line freed from the truss.

Setting the first gable Before you send up the first gable end, the gable wall must be prepped with a nailer. Round up all of the small blocks of 2x stock to use as nailers. On the top plate of the gable wall, use 2x stock on edge as a gauge and install the blocks 1½ in. in from the outside edge of the framing. Run the blocks end to end, creating a solid nailer overhanging into the inside

The first gable truss is sent up with two regular trusses. By sending the first three trusses up together, the crane will be able to hold the gable truss steady while the other trusses are set and the braces are attached to the gable truss. (Photo by Roe A. Osborn, courtesy *Fine Homebuilding* magazine, © The Taunton Press, Inc.)

of the wall. This provides the base on which to nail the ceiling strapping on the inside and serves as a stop when the gable is placed against it and nailed down to the top plate on the outside.

Send a gable end truss up with two common trusses, but put a separate strap around the common trusses. Lower the gable into position. The front staging crew member directs the truss back or forth until the wall mark lines up with the inside of the wall. When the truss is in the correct location, the crew member who was handling the tag line climbs the ladder leaning against the building and nails the gable from the outside with the spikes that were tacked in earlier. The crane operator should still be keeping a little tension on the straps.

Slide two long diagonal braces through the webs of the common trusses (that were lifted with

Truss Crew

A five-man truss crew is sufficient for most residential jobs. Review each crew member's job as it is assigned.

Tag Line
One crew member is in charge of the tag line. His job is to send the trusses up in the correct order while keeping them from spinning by using a tag line. He also transfers the wall lines on the underside of the bottom cords up along one side to make it easier to see when placing the truss. And he nails the outside of the gable to the wall once it is positioned.

Front Staging
Another crew member stands on the front staging and works the tail ends of the trusses. He signals the crane operator and positions the trusses according to the wall lines on his end of the truss. He fastens the trusses permanently to the front wall.

Rear Staging
The crew member at the rear staging guides his truss end into position but doesn't fasten it. Instead, he drives a couple of tacks into the top plate on either side of the truss to keep it in position.

The front and rear staging jobs are interchangeable, depending on which side of the building the crane sets up on and which end of the trusses are to be fastened first.

Peak Walking
Two crew members stand in the middle of the trusses on the webs and top cords and work the top of the trusses. They direct the job, space and secure the peaks, and instruct the signaler (front or rear staging member).

ROOF FRAMING

the gable truss) and attach the braces near the top of the gable truss. The braces must go through the webs, or the common trusses will be held out of position by their bottom cords hitting the braces.

Use a long straightedge and a level and set the gable truss plumb using the two long diagonal braces. Make sure the bottom of the braces bites into the floor joists below. If the ends fall between joists, spike a 2x block on the floor catching two joists. Then nail the bottom of the brace to the 2x nailer. Release the tension of the crane and remove the gable end strap.

Setting the common trusses Increase the tension of the strap around the two common trusses and slide the trusses into the next position. Again, the front staging member directs the exact placement of the truss. Once in place, nail the front end of the truss into the top plate of the wall. On the other end, tack a couple of nails into the top plate next to both sides of the truss to keep it from drifting. At the peak, use a small furring stick spacer and nail the first common truss at the correct distance from the gable end. If the layout is 2 ft. on center then the distance is 21 3/4 in. inside edge to inside edge. Nail a spacer on both sides of the roof near the peak.

Make sure one of the crew members is holding on to the second common truss and have the crane release tension. Remove the lifting straps and throw them to the ground so the tag line guy can get the next truss ready to fly. Use either a manufactured mechanical truss spacer or long pieces of furring premarked for a 2-ft. on-center layout. Slide the second common truss into position. Wait until the front staging member locates and starts nailing the truss to the wall; then hold the peak of the truss at its on-center location and fasten it. The mechanical spacer or furring stick starts back at the first common truss and continues forward. Keep the spacers near the peak, so they won't interfere with the sheathing installation later.

Repeat this process with the rest of the common trusses, either one or two at a time, whatever is more comfortable. Make sure not to signal for the release of the crane until one of the peak members at the peak yells out that he's got it. After five or six trusses are installed, run diagonal bracing across the top cords from the peak to the tails. Every fifth or sixth truss after that, stop and run more diagonal bracing. If it is a particularly windy day, add extra gable bracing before continuing. When you near the end of the peak spacers, begin another set one truss back, creating an overlap of spacers.

The other gable After all of the common trusses have been installed, swing the other gable into position. If you are swinging two trusses at a time, hold off on the gable to swing it individually.

Set, plumb, and brace the gable as you did on the first gable. Check the overall length of the building at the peak. It should equal the wall length. If not, check the gable end wall. It may have moved a little when the gable was being fastened to it. Tie the gable into the rest of the trusses with truss spacers.

Finishing the installation

Tweak the walls straight again; then nail off the floating ends of the trusses into the wall. Next, double-check the gables for plumb.

Run premarked furring strips along the top of the bottom cord near the center of the building. Nail the bottom cords, matching the layout of the trusses. Install any hurricane strapping as required by local code.

Install the permanent web bracing as required by the truss engineering. If you are not sure exactly what size and where the web bracing goes, contact the designer and have him visit the site to show you.

Subfacia Install the subfacia on the tails of the trusses. Slide a framing square along the side of the building until its corner butts the soffit nailer. Nail one end of the subfacia stock to the first tail so that the bottom of the subfacia rests on the top edge of the square. Have one crew member work the far end of the stock up and down as you move the framing square along, placing and nailing the subfacia into the truss tails. Continue until the entire subfacia is complete.

Run a string along the top outside edge of the subfacia. Tap the subfacia in or out until it lines up with the string. Shim any gaps between the subfacia and truss tails.

Roof sheathing If you have a large enough crew, the roof sheathing can begin at the same time the wrap up occurs.

The most efficient way is to have two crew members up on the roof working together, laying and nailing the sheathing while a third member cuts and feeds the sheets from the floor.

Follow the same procedure for sheathing as explained for a stick roof. Start laying sheets at the sheathing line already established and leave the gable ends tacked until they are straightened. Because the top cords of the trusses are usually 2x4s and can easily move laterally, it's important to check the on-center spacing as you proceed with the sheathing. As you work your way up the roof, remove the truss spacers as you come to them.

Hip roof installation The hip roof installation is a little different from the gable truss system. Because the hip is self-supporting, there is no need for any of the diagonal bracing that supports the first gable truss.

First, strap the hip system with three straps to get it to lift up fairly level. Have the crane operator slowly lift it up to test it. If it's not level, lower the hip back down and adjust the straps. Repeat the process until the hip flies level.

Lower the hip gently into place. Line up the girder truss to the proper location on the walls and nail one end. Lift the flat top hip trusses in ascending order, one at a time. Brace along the flat tops, maintaining the on-center spacing.

Once you finish with the flat tops, install the commons as described previously. When you reach the end of the common trusses, install the flat top hip trusses in descending order. Install the other end of the roof system. Continue with the wrap-up and subfacia installation.

With the outside top edge of the subfacia even with the rafter plane and the bottom edge even with the soffit blocking, the subfacia is nailed and then checked straight along the entire length.

Although not called for in the engineering, we like to beef up the hips. With the flat top hip trusses spaced and secured, measure from hip to hip between the trusses. Cut 2x blocking at compound angles and fasten it between the trusses to create a continuous hip member from the tail to the peak.

Complex roof installation

As with the hip system, become familiar with the complex truss system and restack the trusses in appropriate groups. Follow the truss plan carefully when laying the truss system out on the walls and make sure there is a truss for each one labeled on the plans. Use the isometric drawings to help identify and locate the different trusses. Be careful to maintain the wall layout along the truss peaks as they go up.

Chapter 7

STRAPPING CEILINGS AND FRAMING INTERIOR PARTITION WALLS

MARKING INTERIOR PARTITIONS

LAYING OUT AND INSTALLING STRAPPING

LAYING OUT THE WALL

MEASURING STUD HEIGHT AND PREPPING WALL PARTS

FRAMING THE PARTITIONS

FINISHING UP

Here's a point where our framing practices diverge from those followed by many framers outside the Northeast. We build our nonbearing interior partition walls after the roof framing is assembled. Other framers assemble the interior walls right after the exterior walls but before successive floors or the roof is constructed. The sequencing is a matter of training and personal preference.

One of the steps we take when framing that goes hand in hand with building interior walls is a bit of a throwback to an earlier period of frame construction. To all ceilings we attach rows of 16-in. on-center furring strips, also known as strapping. It used to be that strapping was commonly installed over ceiling joists before nailing on the wood lath that supported wet horsehair plaster. Now strapping ceilings is a regional practice—a practice we think has huge benefits.

Strapping ties the bottom of the joists together and isolates the drywall. This helps reduce screw or nail pops in the drywall caused by shrinking or twisting joists. Strapping also reduces noise transmission between floors by minimizing sound bridging. Plumbers and especially electricians benefit by the small chases created perpendicular

One of the benefits of strapped ceilings is the channels created on the underside of the ceiling joists. Here, an electrician can run wires perpendicular to the joists without drilling holes. Plumbers too, can run supply pipes in the spaces.

to the run of the joists. This means less joist drilling for running wires and plumbing.

Ceiling strapping provides a good base for attaching the top plate of interior partitions. It reduces the framing spacing for the drywall when ceiling joists or trusses are set 24 in. apart. This minimizes drywall ceiling sags in humid climates.

On the down side, strapping may take longer to install and uses a little more lumber than cross blocking floor or ceiling joists for fastening parallel walls.

The sequence of events for laying out and installing the ceiling strapping and interior partitions overlap one another. First we mark for the interior walls on the subfloor; then we lay out and install the strapping. Next we frame the walls. We'll follow this order in our discussion but will jump around a little when describing the details.

Marking Interior Partitions

Interior partition walls don't support structural loads like exterior and interior bearing walls. This gives you a little more freedom in making adjustments to satisfy clients' changes. That's one reason we like to leave the job of building non-bearing walls for the latter part of the framing process rather than building them at the same time the exterior ones go up. Installing them later in the project gives clients the opportunity to feel a space, walk through the layout, and make a final decision about the size and location of the various spaces in their new house. It is often possible to make a room bigger or smaller or to change the location and the dimensions of a closet. And it's much easier to change walls by crossing out a few chalklines than by sawing out studs.

The speed and accuracy with which you can lay out the walls depends a lot on how square and parallel the exterior and interior bearing walls are. You can take all your measurements off any nearby wall, provided you've been checking and adjusting everything as you've framed.

Begin marking out walls that can't be moved, like those along stairways, and then move on to the longest walls. Take the measurements from the reference walls indicated on the plans. Usually, the reference measurements start at the exterior edge of the framing of outside walls.

Some designers mark the interior wall measurements from face to face and designate either $3\frac{1}{2}$ in. or 4 in. as the wall thickness. You'll have to make adjustments in the calculations if the plans are marked for 4-in. walls because your stock will measure only $3\frac{1}{2}$ in. Other designers mark to the center of interior walls and avoid the issue all together. If this is the case, mark the

Mark out the wall location on the floor. Measure from a reference line or exterior wall to determine the center of the wall. Mark half the width of the wall to the left and right of the center mark; for 2x4 walls, this is 1¾ in. Mark both ends of the wall and snap chalklines between the marks to guide wall installation.

center of the wall and then mark 1¾ in. to the left and right of the mark for the edges of the wall. Measure and mark both ends of the walls and both edges of the walls.

Snap chalklines between the marks. Use blue chalk initially and, if you are forced to make changes later, mark the new lines in red. Though it's not necessary to snap chalklines on both sides of the walls, it's helpful on the longer primary walls so you and those who follow can see the bulk of the layout more clearly. For shorter walls, just snap a chalkline at one edge and indicate on which side of the line the plate will go.

Work your way down to the smallest walls in sequence. The pattern of walls builds off of the lines you snap along the way. You'll need to take measurements from previous walls to expedite the process. It's often easier to just use a straightedge and draw lines for the short walls rather than using a chalkline.

Referring to the plans, mark the major details on the floor to help you lay out plate stock later. Indicate the location for door openings (and the direction of the door swing), medicine cabinets, partition backers, and tubs. You don't have to be exhaustive at this point; you'll return to lay out the wall plates later. The highlights you've marked will help you choose where to break joints in wall plates.

There are some walls you should consider making adjustments to during the layout process. Acrylic or fiberglass tubs and showers often come a little larger than the specified size. You should allow an extra ⅛-in. to ¼-in. space in width for them. It's easier to shim out the top of the studs by ⅛ in. than it is to carve them out to fit the fixture.

You could cut and lay out the wall plates now, but they'll get in the way when you install the strapping. We'll jump over to strapping in preparation for building the walls and return to wall plate layout shortly.

Laying Out and Installing Strapping

Strapping is installed 16 in. on center and perpendicular to the bottom of ceiling joists or the bottom cord of roof trusses. Ceilings can be strapped with 1x or 2x stock. Check with your local building code; some jurisdictions don't permit 1x strapping, only 2x stock.

Marking out for strapping

When preparing for subfloor sheathing, you installed blocking on the top plate of the walls running parallel to the joists. This blocking can support the drywall directly, but for our methods you'll use it to attach the strapping.

Start marking the layout for strapping on the bottom of this blocking by measuring from the

186 CHAPTER SEVEN

outside wall or interior bearing wall. Measure and mark out for 16-in. on-center spacing along the length of the wall.

Mark the layout the same at the opposite wall and alongside any interruptions, such as stairways.

With a helper, snap chalklines across the bottom of the joists. (Remember that you have already laid out the strapping on the roof trusses when you were preparing them; see chapter 6.) To avoid confusion make a few X's in crayon on the side of the line to which the strapping will be applied. There's no need to mark X's on every joist; every fourth or fifth one is sufficient.

One of the purposes of strapping is to provide a nailing base for the top plate of interior walls and the ceiling drywall at wall edges. After you snap the chalklines but before you install the strapping, take a look at the wall layout on the floor. Note where the walls run parallel to the strapping. Install more strips of strapping or wider stock to back up these runs.

Roughly mark the wall location on the ceiling joists with a level and straightedge or plumb bob; within $3/8$ in. tolerance is fine. You can use multiple strips of strapping or 1x6 or 1x8 ledger board as the nailer. The ledger gives backing for the wall plate and drywall edges in a single piece. Because you already have chalklines snapped 16 in. on center, you can usually just eyeball the backing strips parallel to the lines rather than snapping separate ones to line the backing material to.

Later, after you raise the interior partitions, you'll see several locations that need strapping or ledger to carry the ceiling drywall. These typically occur at wing walls along side showers, inside closets, and above outside corners where walls meet.

Preparing the stock

Measure and cut the strapping to length so joints land on the center of joists or truss cords. Stagger joints between adjacent pieces of strapping so no more than two or three land in a row on any one joist. Span two successive joists with the joints rather than just breaking on the next one back. This helps minimize drywall-screw pops and it continues the strapping continuity from one end of the building to the other.

A quick way to measure strapping lengths is to make a story stick. Hold a full length of strapping against the top plate of a wall. Make a mark at the center of the farthest joist it reaches. Skip the next joist back and mark the third; skip back again and

Lay out and snap chalklines to guide the ceiling strapping installation. Begin the layout from the inside edge of an exterior wall. Mark for 16-in. on-center spacing at both ends of the ceiling area. Snap chalklines between the marks and make an X on every fourth or fifth joist to indicate on which side of the chalkline to fasten the strapping.

A story pole speeds the measuring and cutting processes of ceiling strapping. Press one end of a piece of strapping against the starting wall and mark the center of three of four truss cords or ceiling joists. Transfer the marks to groups of strapping. (Photo by Roe A. Osborn, courtesy *Fine Homebuilding* magazine, © The Taunton Press, Inc.)

mark the fifth. There's no need to measure more than three or four lengths. Alternating them as starters will be sufficient, more lengths will make the process cumbersome.

Count the total number of starter pieces you will need for a ceiling section and divide by the number of starter lengths you choose. This will give you the quantity of pieces you'll need to cut at each length. Also cut a complement of full lengths for the next group to continue the strapping runs.

It's fast to mark and gang cut the stock when you're using 1x3 material. When you use 2x strapping, gang cutting is more difficult.

Fastening strapping

It's easier to tack on strapping with a helper than to do it alone, especially on taller ceilings. One person can hold each strip of strapping up to the ceiling while the other person tack nails it in place at one or two of the joists. After all the starters in an area are tacked, the full-length companions can be run out across the bottom of the ceiling joists and tack nailed up until a makeup piece needs to be trimmed to fit to the opposite wall.

One person can finish nailing off the tacked up strapping to the ceiling while the other measures and cuts the balance pieces. You can make another story stick to measure off the cuts. Butt one end of a strapping strip to the end wall and make a mark at the joint for each different strapping run. Just mark one each of the three or four different lengths. There's no need to measure each course exactly. Just deduct $1/8$ in. to $1/4$ in. off each so the strip won't bind and push the far wall out.

Drive two 6d or 8d nails or $1/2$-in. crown staples through the strapping into each joist. This is where pneumatic nailers earn their keep. They speed the process and give you several extra inches of reach when nailing off a ceiling.

Blocking between strapping runs There will be a few places where you should nail short pieces of strapping to the bottom of floor joists between the longer lengths of strapping. At stairways, where the ceiling meets the shaft of the stairs, these short pieces of blocking prevent the drywall from being crushed when the corner bead is screwed or crimped on a void. The same goes for skylight shafts and scuttle holes; fill the space between straps with blocks. The blocking doesn't have to be accurately trimmed, within $1/2$ in. short is fine.

Another important place to install blocking between strapping is when you reach the concealed space maximum area limit. The area enclosed between the ceiling of one floor and

Ladder Blocking: Alternative to Strapping

Ladder blocking between floor joists, ceiling joists, or bottom cords to support the top plates of walls is probably a more common practice throughout the country than strapping ceilings. Cross blocking between joists provides attachment points for the top plate of walls and blocking to screw ceiling drywall to.

Start by locating the bays where walls run parallel to the joist direction. Measure the space between the joists at a couple points along the run. Cut 2x blocks to the shortest length you measured, provided they're within ¼ in. There's no point cutting each one exactly for blocking here. This is a good time to look through your scrap pile for material from which to cut blocks rather than cutting full lengths.

Space out the blocks 16 in. to 24 in. apart. It will be difficult to determine exactly where drywall panels will break at this time. This block spacing will be fine for supporting the top plate of the wall and you or the drywaller can install separate blocks for panel joints later.

Sometimes a wall will fall beneath a joist or truss cord. Rather than blocking both sides of the joist, you may be able to block one side and pad out the other edge with 1x or 2x stock to catch the drywall.

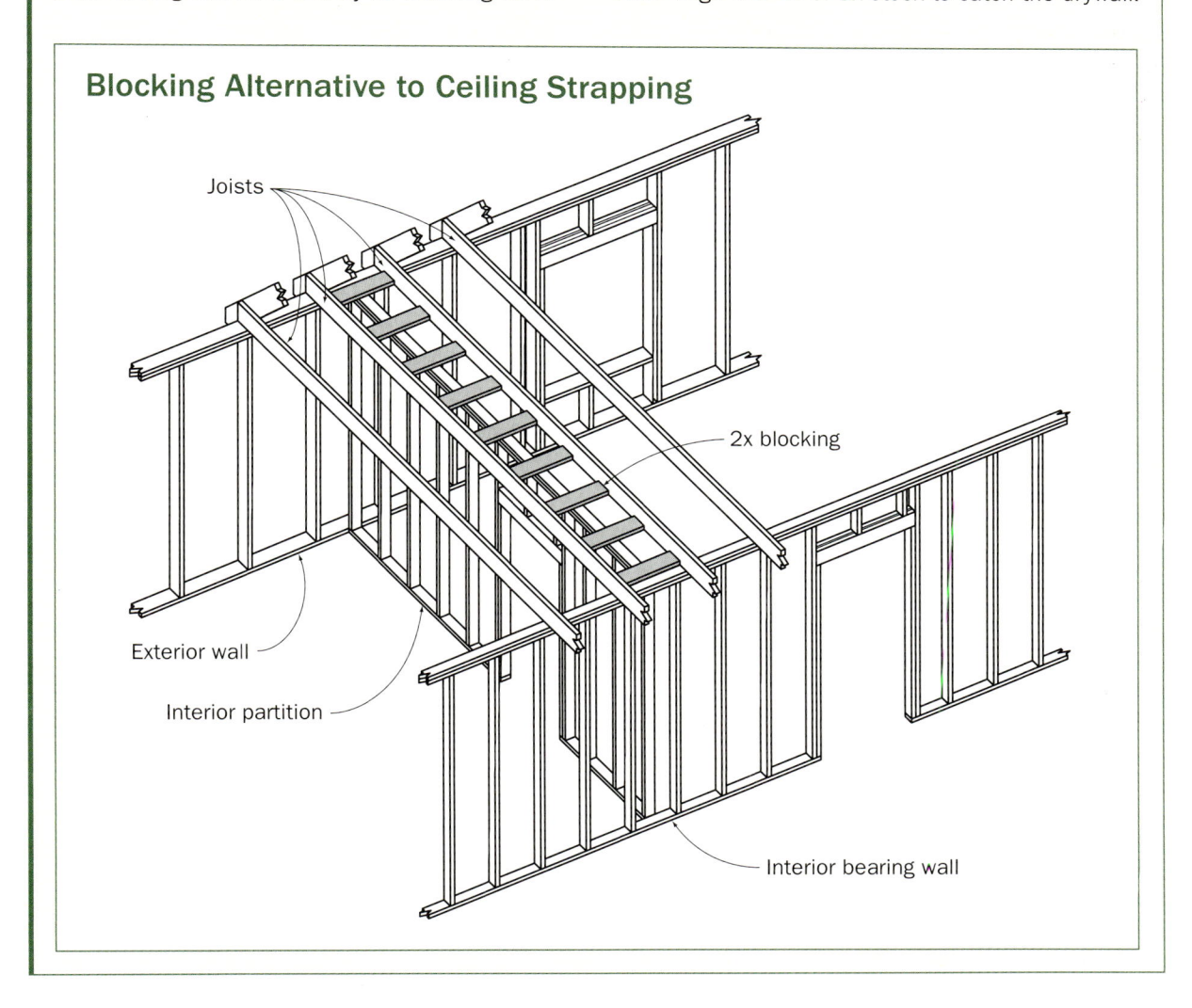

Blocking Alternative to Ceiling Strapping

STRAPPING CEILINGS, FRAMING PARTITION WALLS

While one crew member nails off the strapping, another marks a reverse story pole. Press one end of a furring strip to the end wall and mark to the end of the three or four strapping runs you began with. Make the marks ¼ in. short to avoid pushing the end wall out. Mark off lengths of strapping from the story pole and gang cut. (Photo by Roe A. Osborn, courtesy *Fine Homebuilding* magazine, © The Taunton Press, Inc.)

the subfloor of the next must be blocked to resist fire spread. When the drywall is installed directly to the bottom of joists this usually isn't an issue, because each joist bay is closed. But when you strap a ceiling, you have communicating spaces. The limit is usually 1000 sq. ft., but check your local code.

When you exceed the limit, install strapping blocks cut to fit between the 16-in. on-center strapping. Nail them on the underside of a joist in the middle of the area or at the area limit when you'll exceed the concealed space limit multiple times.

Laying Out the Wall

With the strapping or ceiling blocking out of the way, you're ready to transfer the chalklines for the walls from the floor to the ceiling, then cut and lay out the wall plates.

Transferring lines to ceiling

The most accurate method to plumb the lines from the floor to the ceiling is with a plumb bob but the process requires two people for the best results. One person drops the bob and marks the ceiling, while the other directs him to adjust the bob over the chalkline. In this way, a 1000-sq.-ft. floor can be marked off in 15 to 20 minutes. The alternative is to plumb the lines with a level and straightedge. One person can do the operation, but it's not as precise as with a plumb bob.

With either method, it's essential only to plumb and snap lines for walls longer than about 5 ft. Shorter walls can be plumbed when they are installed by measuring off nearby parallel walls and don't need chalklines to guide top plate positioning.

Preparing wall plates

We use selected plate stock for the bearing walls to make straightening the walls easier. The same holds true for interior partitions. The biggest difference is that for these walls, we use only a single top plate. Grade your stock for top and bottom plate use.

The main consideration when deciding which walls to lay out first is the order of installation. Building interior walls is like a puzzle when there are a lot of them close together. This usually occurs in and near the bedrooms where there are closets, a bath or two, hallways, and plenty of doors.

Start spreading out plates for the longest walls first and work your way down to shorter ones. Don't try to prepare all the plates right away. Do it in stages, so shorter plates don't crowd you out and get in the way while you're building longer walls. Prep and mark out a group of walls, then build and erect them. Move on to the next group and work your way to shorter walls.

When you prep long walls, you'll need several pieces to make up a plate. Plan joints in the bottom plates to break at stud or wall backer locations or in door openings, but not beneath jack or king studs. The small piece left after you cut the plate out of the opening usually splits apart and leaves the studs or jacks floating at their bases. This is where your preliminary door opening marks on the floor will help you plan plate joints.

Seams between top plate pieces can break over any stud. An easy way to determine stud locations without marking the layout is by the joist locations. You'll stack studs over joists, with only a few exceptions.

It is common practice to butt the ends of wall plates against the exterior wall. We use an alternative method that improves the energy performance of the house. Rather than butt interior partition plates to the exterior walls, we leave a 5/8-in. to 1 1/2-in. space. This space permits the insulation installer to wrap the plastic vapor retarder and/or allows the board hanger to pass drywall sheets through and complete the air seal. Though it sounds trivial, it can help make a home more draft proof and energy efficient. Later, when

A plumb bob is more accurate than a spirit level for transferring the partition wall layout up to the ceiling strapping. While one person controls the plumb bob at the top, another can check to see he is on the target line. Once both end marks of a wall are transferred to the ceiling, snap a chalkline across or along the strapping.

By leaving the wall plates short of exterior walls, the drywaller can slide sheets right by an interior wall, thereby creating a more contiguous air barrier. After the drywall is installed on the exterior wall, the end stud in the interior partition wall can be fastened securely.

STRAPPING CEILINGS, FRAMING PARTITION WALLS   191

you frame the wall, leave the last stud loose and the drywaller can install it after he slips the board through the opening.

Marking the plate layout

In the same way you did for exterior-wall layout, make two passes across the plates when you mark them out. First mark partition backers, door openings, and any details; then mark the stud locations with a second pass.

Partition backers, outside corners, and doors
Partition backers on interior walls don't have to be framed with insulation in mind. You can use backer channels like those shown in the photo on p. 112, ladder blocking, or a 2x6 flat in the wall. Mark out the type you want to use on the plates. Most framers use backer channels on interior walls, even if they use other backer styles on exterior walls. Mark the backer clearly and pay attention to which plate is the top and which is the bottom. Make a symbol to indicate which side of the wall the blocking will face so there's no confusion later.

Where two walls meet to form an outside corner, frame in blocking to support the corresponding inside corner. The most common way is to mark the plates that extend out to form the corner with an X-S-X unit and the intersecting partition plates with a single stud. The *S* stands for "space." A few blocks spaced apart between the two studs strengthens the assembly. Some framers nail three studs together rather than using spacer blocks.

Door openings are typically framed with jacks and king studs to provide extra width for nailing door trim and for added stability when the door is installed. Oversize the rough opening widths for hinged and bifold doors by 2 in. to 2½ in. greater than the door's size. This leaves plenty of space to shim the door jamb within the opening. Bypass doors need a narrower rough opening because the door panels will overlap one another within the door jamb. Make these openings only 1 in. to 1½ in. wider than the door size. Pocket door framing is a special situation and is discussed in chapter 8.

Common stud spacing Once you have all the backers and openings marked out, make a second pass over the plates to mark the studs. You could just pull your tape measure off of the end of the wall plate and mark the stud centers from there; but there is a more practical way that helps plumbers, HVAC installers, and electricians to avoid drilling or cutting floor joists and strapping. Plan the layout to stack interior studs directly over floor joists in walls going perpendicular to the floor joist direction.

To do this, set the plates in position and locate the lines of nails you drove through the subfloor into the joists. Find the edge of one joist to get a precise reference. Drive a nail through the subfloor several times working away from the middle of the joist to locate the joist edge. Draw a line on your wall plates to correspond to the edge of the joist. Using that line as a reference, mark the rest of the studs with the same on-center spacing as the joists.

There won't be any joist centers to match on walls running parallel to floor joists. Instead, mark your stud spacing to match the ceiling strapping. Even though they are obvious, the strapping won't have to be cut when it's in the plumber's way as he installs pipes and fixtures.

When studs are laid out this way, trade contractors can feel freer to cut or drill the top or bottom plates between studs without hitting joists or strapping.

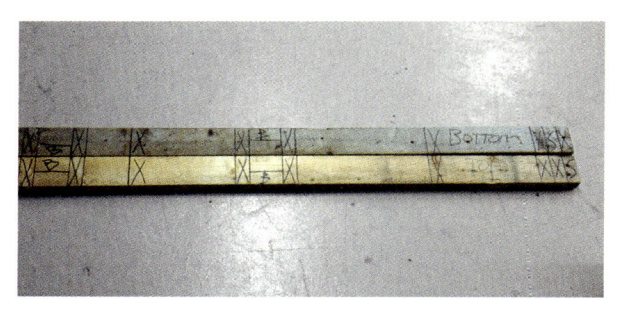

Clearly mark the location of all the details on the wall plates. The blocking in partition backers needs to face the direction of the oncoming wall it will attach to. Pay attention to which of the two plates is the bottom and which is the top plate, so you mark it correctly.

Wall studs that are stacked up over the floor joists beneath make it easier for plumbers, electricians, and HVAC contractors to plan their utility runs. Drive probe nails through the subfloor until you locate the edge of a common joist. Stretch your tape measure from the nail to mark the stud layout to match the joists beneath.

ADVICE: Saving Lumber by Skipping Studs

You can save lumber by skipping studs that fall within 3 in. of a door opening or a channel-type partition backer provided that the overall space between successive studs isn't greater than 24 in. Make sure that the stud you plan to leave out doesn't fall where a drywall sheet will end. This savings can amount to a lot of studs on walls with many doors and backers.

Uncommon stud spacing There will be times when you'll need to space studs differently. Walls that will house rough plumbing stub-outs and shower and tub mixing valves are typical locations where you'll need to make adjustments with the stud spacing. Electric panels and medicine cabinets also need to be considered when spacing studs.

Most plumbers like to stub-out drains and supply piping centered on lavatory sinks. This is of particular concern with pedestal and wall-hung sinks. Identify the precise center of the fixture and make sure there is no stud within about 4 in. Ideally, a 12-in. to 16-in. space centered on the future fixture will make the plumber's work easier. Details like this are discussed during the pre-framing meeting you have with various trade contractors, as noted in chapter 4.

Special stud spacing planned for plumbing and mechanical equipment makes it easier for trade contractors. Here, studs have been spaced 12 in. apart and centered on the tub/shower unit so the plumber can install the mixing valve easily.

Sequence the Layout with Framing

Lay out a few sets of wall plates at a time, build and erect them, then move on to the next group. Don't overcrowd yourself or prepare all the plates and stack them out of the way when you begin building the walls. It's easy to get confused about where a dozen roughly 8-ft.-long wall plates go after they've been turned around and moved.

If you have a crew of three or four working on wall framing, you can mark the layout while others are building the walls. You can leapfrog one another in different parts of a building. Once a couple of walls have been framed, you can swap locations, and the crew can build the walls you've just marked out.

Another place to deviate from standard stud spacing to accommodate a fixture is for shower and tub mixing valves. On the plumbing wall adjacent to shower and tub/shower units where the valve and supply tubing is installed, space studs 10 in. to 14 in. apart to accept the mixing valve. Center the stud space on the fixture's drain at the midpoint of the wall.

Sometimes you have to leave spaces for electric panels and medicine cabinets. Although most of these boxes fit between standard 16-in. on-center spacing, occasionally they have to fit in a precise location. Medicine cabinets are usually centered on a sink, for instance. You'll need to have the studs centered and spaced wide enough for these fixtures.

Measuring Stud Height and Prepping Wall Parts

The stud height for the interior partitions will be different from the studs for exterior walls. To determine the height, measure between the subfloor and the ceiling strapping (or joist bottoms if you are using the blocking method for parallel walls). Check the distance in several spots around the floor in case there is a short spot somewhere. Because the partitions aren't supporting any load from above, it won't matter if there is a little space between the top plate of the wall and the ceiling framing; so go with the shortest height.

The stud length will be $3\frac{1}{4}$ in. less than the height you measured. That's 3 in. for the top and bottom plates plus an extra $\frac{1}{4}$ in. to prevent the walls from binding at the ceiling when you lift them upright. When you frame a 2x6 interior partition as a plumbing wall, you should deduct $\frac{1}{2}$ in. from the height to prevent binding when standing the wall.

Determining door heights and cut jacks

Jack lengths for door openings depend on the interior door heights. The standard rough opening height is $2\frac{1}{2}$ in. greater than the door height. A 6-ft. 8-in. door will need a 6-ft. $10\frac{1}{2}$-in. opening. In this example, the jacks will be 6 ft. 9 in. (the bottom plate makes up the other $1\frac{1}{2}$ in.). Precut two jacks for each opening.

Sometimes bypass-type doors require openings a little taller. It depends on how the supplier prepares the door. Make the openings 3 in. taller to account for the sliding track, if you don't expect the doors to be trimmed down to 6 ft. 7 in.

Prepping door headers and cripples

Precut the door headers and cripples to speed production. The headers will be 3 in. longer than the rough opening width. You laid out the door

Cut the studs for interior walls so the walls will be about ¼ in. shorter than the ceiling height. This makes it easy to tip the walls into place.

Partition channel backers and outside corners

Take a count from the plans or the laid-out plates to prepare the partition backer channels and outside corners before building the walls.

Assemble the partition backers by nailing three to five blocks along the edge of one stud spaced about 1 ft. apart. Drive several nails through the stud into the edge of each block. You can flush the end blocks with the butt end of the stud but it's not necessary. Nail the second stud to the blocks but make sure to flush the ends of the two studs first.

To make up the outside corner blocks, nail three or four blocks flat against one stud. Angle the nails so they don't protrude through the stud. Face the crown of the second stud opposite to the first and nail through it into the blocks. Make sure the ends of the studs are flush and align the edges as you go. Opposing the crowns will make the assembly, and the corner, straighter.

Framing the Partitions

The process of building interior partition walls is similar to assembling bearing walls. The difference comes when it's time to lift the partitions upright.

For long walls, place the bottom plate along the chalkline you snapped on the floor. Face the studs with the crowns up and drive two nails through both the top and bottom plates into the studs. Door openings will have a jack and king stud with a 2x flat header with cripples on top like those in nonbearing exterior walls.

Pay attention to which side of the wall partition backers need to have the blocking on. It's easy to overlook this step and end up with them facing the opposite way. If this happens, you can just nail in blocks once the wall is lifted.

After you have a partition framed, but before you lift it, saw partway through the bottom plates on the inside of door openings. If you're using a 7½-in. circular saw, you can go full depth (about

opening widths 2 in. or 2½ in. wider than the actual door widths. so the headers will be 5 in. to 5½ in. wider than the doors. Cut a header for each opening. Select straight lumber for headers on wide doors. Even a medium crown in a long header will make installing the door and the trim difficult for the finish carpenter.

An easy way to determine the length of the cripples that go over the door headers is to put a jack alongside a stud and measure the difference. From that deduct 1½ in. for the header and you have the length. For now, precut four cripples for each door opening. Wide pocket doors and double doors will need extras, so be sure to plan for them.

Before tilting up a wall, run a circular saw through the bottom plate along the jack studs of door openings. Though the blade won't cut all the way through the bottom plate, it will be easier to finish off the cut with a reciprocating saw or handsaw once the wall is up.

Nail the bottom plate of the walls to the floor with two nails at the base of each stud. There are two benefits to nailing in this location. For walls that run perpendicular to the floor joists, the nails will hit the joists directly beneath each stud. On walls that run parallel to the joists, the nails will be out of harm's way when a sub's drill bit or saw cuts through the plate between studs locations.

$2\frac{1}{2}$ in.) without worrying about cutting all the way through. This will make trimming out the plate piece faster and easier after the wall is lifted.

Long walls are easier to lift when you drive a couple of 6d tack nails through the bottom plate and into the subfloor to act as a hinge and keep the bottom from sliding along the floor. There's no need to straighten the wall to the chalkline before you tack it down. Lift the finished wall upright and use a sledgehammer to drive the top plate to the chalkline if it binds to the strapping on the ceiling. Tap the bottom plate in place along the line and orient the butt ends of the wall to ones already lifted or to the lines for those walls. Drive two spikes through the bottom plate along side each stud and into the floor joists for perpendicular partitions. For walls running parallel to the joists, also drive the nails next to the studs; you just won't be hitting the joists beneath. Nails driven into the subfloor are sufficient to hold the wall in place.

Line the edge of the top plate to the chalkline and the butt ends to the top plate of an already upright wall or to its chalkline. If you snapped only a single line for the top plates on the abutting walls, then there may be a $3\frac{1}{2}$-in. space between the end of the wall you're working on and the line. You can just use a block of 2x4 to gauge the space or measure before you nail the top plate.

When you have the wall in the correct position, drive two spikes through the top plate into each of the strapping pieces it crosses to secure it. For walls running perpendicular to the ceiling joists, drive the nails through the strapping and into the ceiling joists.

Use a reciprocating saw to trim out the bottom plates at door openings as you erect each group of walls. You can use the plate pieces for blocking in backers or to cut up for cripples on walls yet to be framed. Toenail two nails through the bottom plate into the subfloor at the plate cut outs just beneath the jacks. This keeps the plate breaks at door openings secure for door hanging.

Long walls are easier to frame in the location where they go so you don't have to drag them into position, but short walls may be easier to frame away from the action of building and lifting the longer partitions. Just be sure to orient the wall end for end as well as top and bottom before you install it so the partition backers, door openings, and studs end up where they belong.

We didn't transfer the lines for short walls from the floor to the ceiling. When you lift these walls, measure the distance between the bottom plate and that of a nearby wall. Gauge the same measurement at the top plate and the wall will be parallel. Otherwise, you can use a level to plumb up the short walls.

Finishing Up

There are a couple of details to finish up wall and strapping installation. Check the ceiling for any walls that ended up without strapping at the corners or ends. Slip a short length of strapping across the adjacent ceiling joists to support the drywall wherever this occurs.

Secure the miscellaneous wall-to-wall and corner connections. Nail the end studs of walls to backers on the intersecting wall. This secures one wall to another. Angle the nails so they don't protrude through the blocking. Don't nail the end studs of an interior wall to the partition backers of exterior walls until the vapor barrier or drywall has been installed if you left the stud loose to permit the pass-through. Also, nail the end stud of walls meeting at outside corners to the corner stud blocks. All of these may seem obvious, but they can be easily overlooked and the drywall hanger may be left to struggle with loose connections.

Skip short walls when snapping chalklines for the top-of-the-wall location. Frame the diminutive walls last and just measure from a nearby parallel wall.

Pull out any nails you used as pivots to tack the bottom plates to the floor during lifting to keep power cords and hoses from being snagged. And after you sweep up, draw crayon marks on the floor at each stud location to make it easier for the drywall hangers and finish carpenters to find them after the drywall goes up; especially if you happen to be filling those roles too.

Chapter 8

SPECIAL FRAMING DETAILS

SPECIAL DETAILS FOR FRAMING INTERIOR PARTITION WALLS

SPECIAL DETAILS FOR ROOF FRAMING

SPECIAL DETAILS FOR FRAMING FOR SUBCONTRACTORS

In this chapter we cover a number of framing details not covered in the rest of the book because they don't fit conveniently into the framing sequence. These details deserve mention because they're not usually outlined on typical blueprints, and if you frame enough houses, you'll run into them eventually. The details and responsibilities are not always covered by the standard scope of work for a framer, but on a custom frame they add value to your workmanship. If you plan well while framing, you can build in a lot of these details without adding much extra labor.

Special Details for Framing Interior Partition Walls

Many of the interior partition wall details can be easily overlooked and are not discovered until the walls are covered and the finish work begins. Make a checklist for the details you need and do a walk-through just before the drywall goes up.

Half-wall supports

Whenever a half-wall dead ends, we strengthen it by extending some of the studs through the subfloor and securing them to the floor joist system. Dead-end half-walls, such as might surround a stairwell or serve to visually separate two rooms, have no connection to a top plate, and they don't adjoin a wall at both ends. Therefore,

Half-Wall Support Detail

The end stud is secured to the blocking between the floor joists and below the decking.

End stud continues through floor decking.

Blocking

Floor joists below

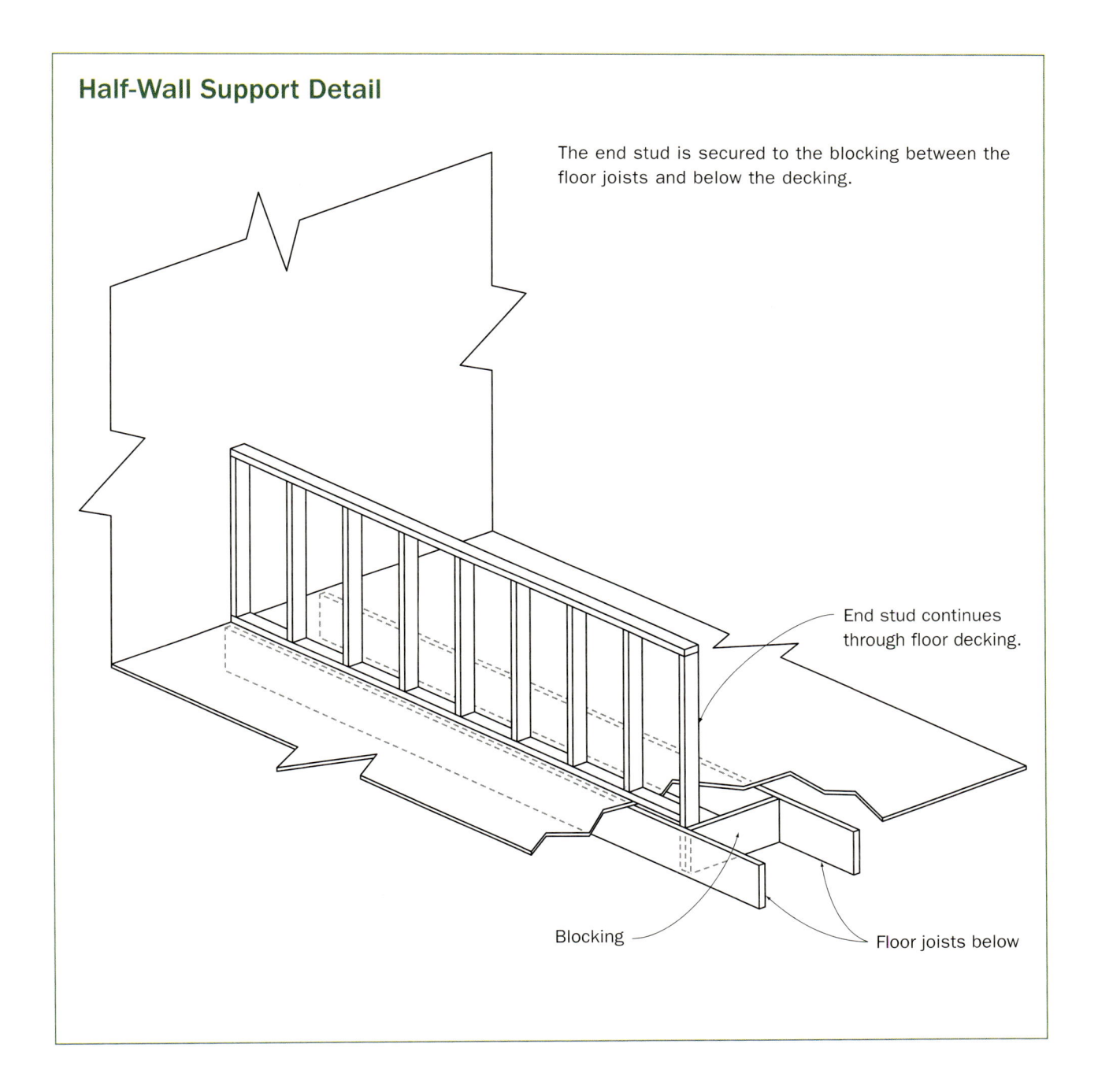

they can tend to wobble after time if the bottom plate is nailed just into a subfloor or even nailed through the subfloor and into a joist.

On short walls, less than 8 ft. long, locate and mark the end of the half-wall on the subfloor. Cut the bottom plate short by 1½ in. but leave the top plate full length. At that end point of the bottom plate, cut out the floor sheathing to the dimension of the end stud. Build the wall and nail the bottom plate to the subfloor but leave the end stud out. Cut the end stud long enough to protrude through the floor to the bottom edge of the floor joists. If the end stud falls on a floor joist,

SPECIAL FRAMING DETAILS

Firestop Installation

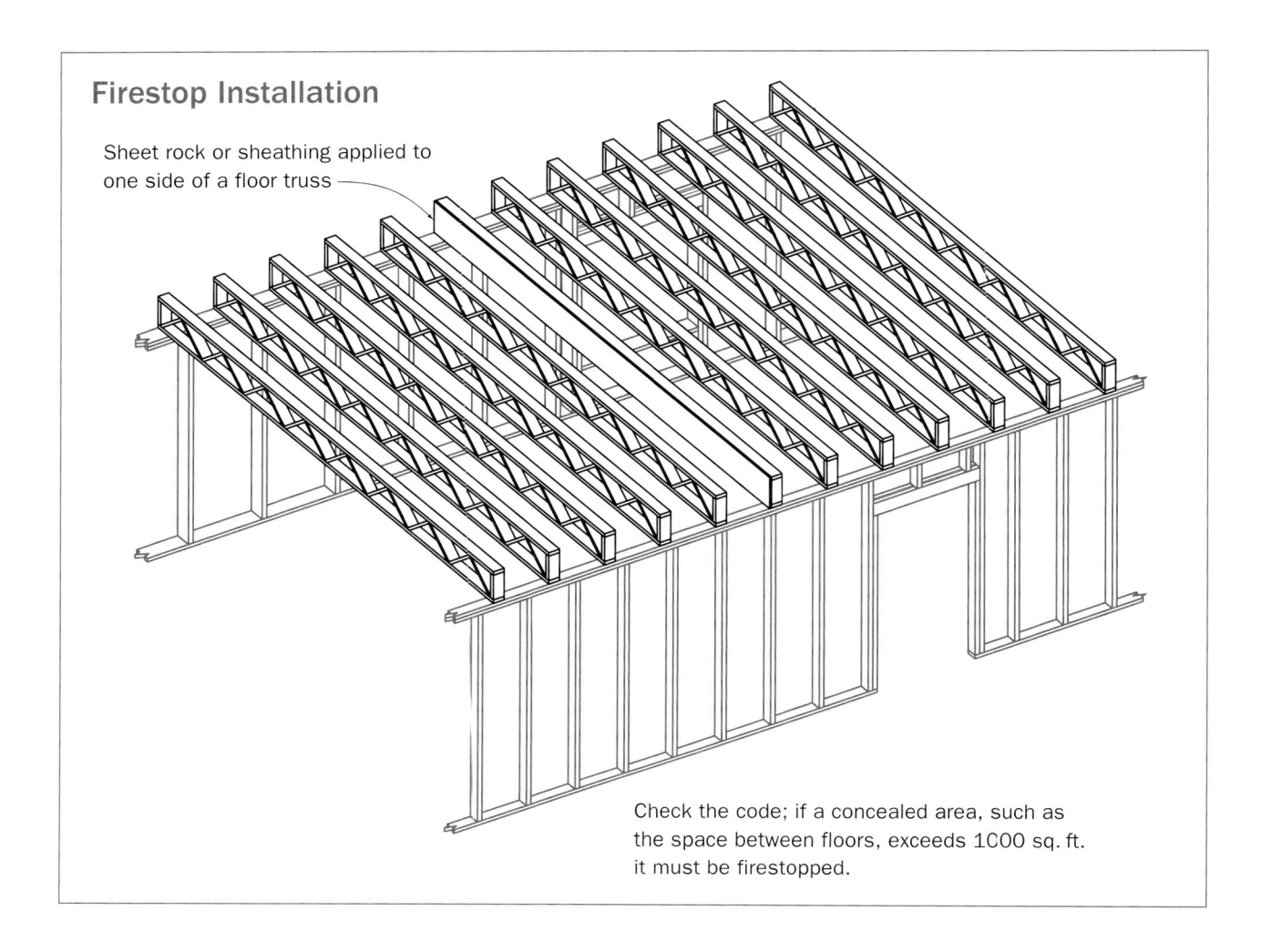

Sheet rock or sheathing applied to one side of a floor truss

Check the code; if a concealed area, such as the space between floors, exceeds 1000 sq. ft. it must be firestopped.

notch the bottom of the stud to fit down beside the joist.

Most often the stud will fall between joists and need additional blocking to secure it. Align the block between the joists and alongside the stud hole. Make sure the block is square and plumb, then nail it to the other floor joists.

Now insert the end stud post through the subfloor hole and slide it until it's flush with the bottom of the floor joist block and meets the top plate. Nail the top of the post to the top plate. Have someone hold the wall plumb and nail the stud to the joist block. Additional blocks or blocking padded between a joist and the stud post may be needed to stiffen the wall.

You may need to install additional stud posts at midpoints along walls longer than 8 ft. Leave a 1½-in. break in the bottom plate of the wall and cut through the subfloor. Install blocking the same way as for end stud posts.

Firestops

Firestops prevent flames and gases from spreading within building cavities and between floors and walls in the event of a fire. Check your local codes to find out where firestops are required. Some of the firestopping is installed during the framing process, but a lot of the firestopping doesn't occur until the mechanical subs have finished and the framers are long gone. Firestop areas to concentrate on during framing are the kitchen soffit and wall connections, the space between floors when floor trusses are used, and areas within tall and balloon-framed walls.

To firestop cabinet soffits, install stud-width blocking between studs at the level where the bottom of the soffit meets the wall. This stops fire within the walls from spreading into the concealed soffit space.

By code, concealed areas are usually limited to 1000 sq. ft. These areas often occur between the first and second floors when open-web floor trusses are used to support the second floor. When a space exceeds the area maximum, you need to install a firestop to reduce the space. One way is to install drywall or structural sheathing (usually ¾ in. thick) on one side of a truss at the middle of the floor.

Tall wall cavities usually can't exceed 10 ft. without firestops. Placing solid blocking between studs at 10 ft. or halfway within the walls is the most common method. On balloon-framed walls, you need to install blocking at the height of the ledger and at the floor level above to prevent the wall space from communicating with the space between the floor joists.

Some building codes permit fiberglass or rock-wool insulation to be used in lieu of blocking. Be sure to consult your code for requirements.

Pocket doors

A pocket door kit consists of a track to hang the door from and thin steel and wood studs to support drywall. The track and wheel assemblies generally work well, but the studs create a flimsy section of wall. We like to improve on the kits by framing the walls a little wider and using 2x4s surrounded by steel track inserted edgewise to support the drywall. The steel track lends extra support to keep the studs from warping, and framing the wall wider gives extra space for some plumbing and wiring to pass through.

Follow the instructions that accompany the pocket door kit for rough sizing the opening, but frame the portions of the wall beyond the opening using 2x6s rather than 2x4s. Attach a 5½-in. steel track to the bottom of the header and to the floor where the door pocket will be. Cut straight wood 2x4s to stud in the pocket area and screw 3⅝-in. steel track around them. Orient the wood face of the steel and wood studs toward the outside of the door pocket and screw them on the inside edge of the top and bottom track.

Framing a pocket door this way provides a much stronger base for the overlaying wallboard and it's easier for the finish carpenter to nail the jamb stock onto the edge of the 2x4. The wood 2x4s will also support cabinetry or other trim-work, if need be; whereas the standard pocket door kit studs may not.

Radius openings

Framing a radius is done after the rough opening is first framed in the normal fashion with headers supported by jacks. Curved openings are often used for Palladian-style windows and interior passageways to add a decorative touch.

First make a pattern of the radius from a piece of cardboard or ½-in. sheathing. Cut the material to fit snugly within the top of the already framed opening and plot the desired profile in place. If you're lucky, the radius measurement will be labeled on the plans. More often than not though, you will have to cut a number of different patterns for the customer to select from.

Once the radius is sketched and cut, make two cutouts from ½-in. sheathing for each opening. Install blocking within the rough opening to support the ½-in. cutouts. Use blocks a full 1 in. narrower than the stock the opening is framed with. For example, if the opening is framed with 2x4s, you need 2-in. by 3-in. blocking. Tack one piece of marked sheathing in the opening, flush to the outside face. Place the 2x block up against it tight to the top corner of the opening and mark the end of block where it begins to extend beyond the piece of sheathing. Do this vertically and horizontally on both sides of the opening.

SPECIAL FRAMING DETAILS

Pocket Door Frame

The "pocket" for the pocket door is framed with 2x4s on the flat and encased with a steel stud track.

- 2x6
- 5½" steel track
- Door track
- Stud

Section A-A

Steel track enveloping 2x4 on inside face

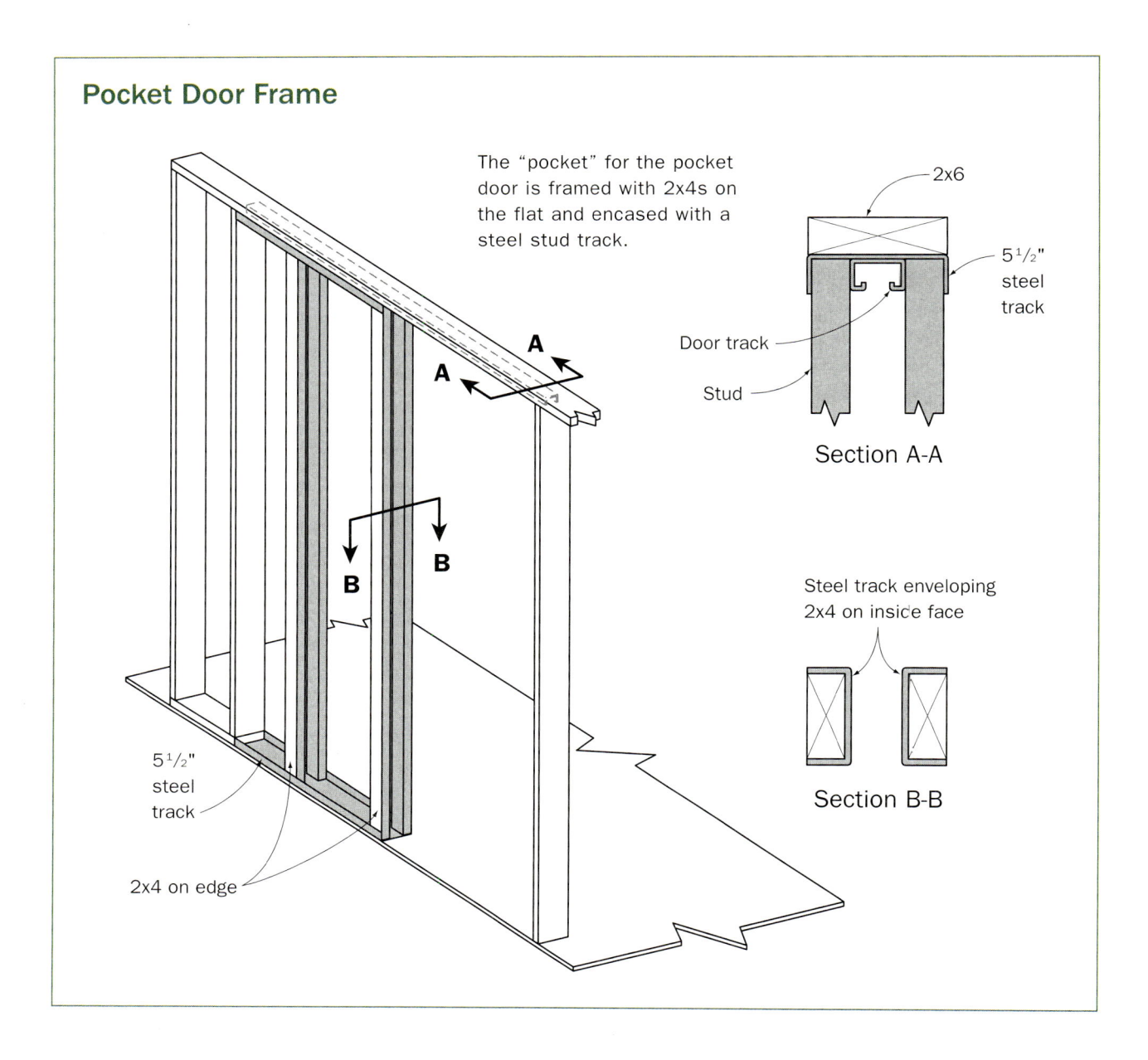

Section B-B

5½" steel track

2x4 on edge

Cut the block just shy of the mark and then cut enough blocks for all of the openings if you have several to finish out.

Nail the blocks in the center of the framed opening. This should leave a ½-in. reveal on both sides of the block. Nail the ½-in. sheathing to each side of the block, flush with the outside edges of the opening.

The radius edge of the panels may be flimsy, especially on large openings. To stiffen the sheets, you can cut short blocks of the same size 2x blocking material just used. Just nail or screw blocks close to the radius edge. Don't worry if there is a 2-in. or 3-in. void between the curved panels and the blocking; you don't have to fill the space completely. Another way to stiffen the panels is to screw steel track around the opening. We use the C-shaped steel track that is made for plate stock for steel-stud framing. Make cuts 1 in. apart through edges of the track equally on both

A radius detail is added to the door opening after it has been framed. (Photo by Tom O'Brien, courtesy *Fine Homebuilding* magazine, © The Taunton Press, Inc.)

sides along the entire length of run. This will allow the track to bend to the curve of the radius. Slip the track over the sheathing panels and screw it on as you bend the track to the arc.

Cabinet soffits

We've found the easiest way to install and build any type of soffit is to use ripped lengths of sheathing. As a guide, start by sketching out the soffit on the floor, just beneath its location. Rip ½-in.-thick sheathing—thicker but not thinner stock will work, too—to fit exactly on the layout. Here's a good place to use some of the leftover scrap pieces from the walls and subfloors. Then rip more sheathing to the desired drop of the soffit minus the thickness of the material of the first rips. For example, if the soffit is dropping 12 in. and the sheathing is ½ in., the rips will be 11½ in.

Transfer the layout from the floor, up to the ceiling joists. Nail a 2x cleat on the ceiling, ½ in. back from the layout lines (assuming ½-in. sheathing is being used). When soffits run parallel to the ceiling joists or furring, you will have to install blocking to fasten the cleat.

Nail the vertical rips to the outside of the 2x cleat. Then nail additional blocking along the bottom inside edge of the vertical face rips to support the bottom of the soffit.

Measure, mark, and snap chalklines on the walls that the soffit will be fastened to. Measure the line down from the ceiling joists the same distance as the vertical rips are wide. Nail the cleats above the chalkline on the walls.

Tack up the bottom of the soffit to the cleat on the wall and flush to the outside edge of the sheet with the vertical face of the soffit. Place a framing square up along the stud wall to the underside of the soffit to check it for square before nailing.

Closet shelves

By considering stud placement as well as blocking placement, you can add additional support for shelving. Most of the houses we frame get finished out with the vinyl-coated steel-wire shelving. These systems are usually fastened into just the drywall with plastic clips and wall anchors, and the shelves are prone to pulling out when they are overloaded. Blocking between studs at shelf height is easy to do while framing.

The back walls of closets usually aren't a problem because the studs provide support for

SPECIAL FRAMING DETAILS

Using Cleats for Soffit Framing

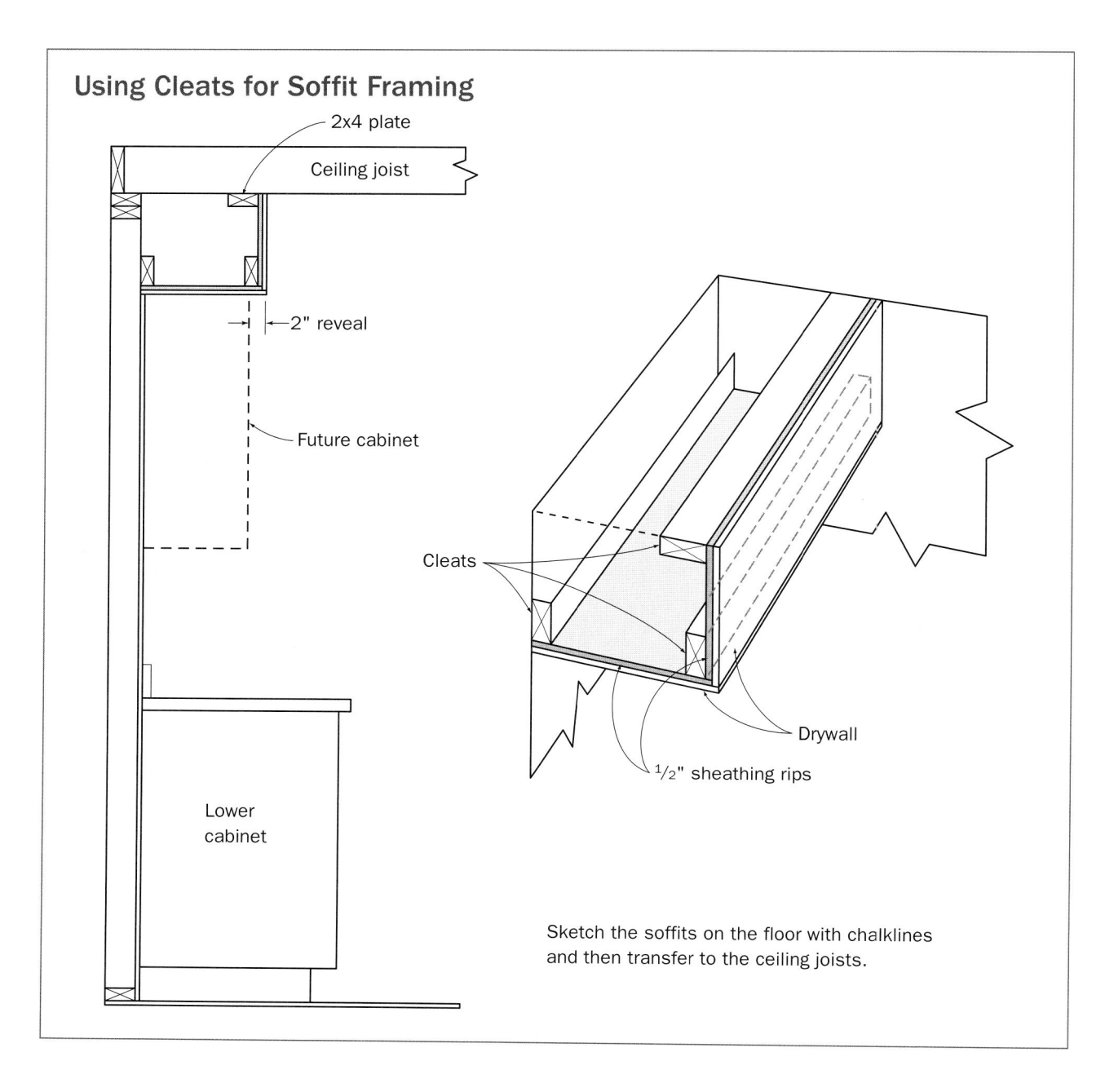

- 2x4 plate
- Ceiling joist
- 2" reveal
- Future cabinet
- Lower cabinet
- Cleats
- Drywall
- 1/2" sheathing rips

Sketch the soffits on the floor with chalklines and then transfer to the ceiling joists.

clips. The side wall vertical location where the shelf cups go can be a problem. Shelf hardware is often the same depth from one closet to the another, so whenever we frame in a closet we install a stud on the sides of each closet 12 in. from the rear of the closet. These studs pick up the cups at both ends of the shelf. Nail an extra piece of furring on each side of the stud where shelf heights are expected to be. This ensures that no matter what height the shelves are installed in that range, there will always be solid blocking to bite into.

Cabinet blocking

Cabinets have to be securely fastened to walls with plenty of screws. This isn't always possible,

Closet blocking is installed during framing to ensure a solid backing when the shelves are installed.

By blocking for all of the cabinets, the cabinet installer doesn't have to rely on attaching the cabinet to just studs, possibly giving the cabinet insufficient support. An upper kitchen cabinet loaded with dishes can be very heavy.

especially when the exterior studs are spaced 24 in. on center. Some wall cabinets are narrow enough to entirely miss a stud. The best way to solve this problem is to install solid blocking for the cabinets at three levels. One level supports the top of the base cabinets, the other levels support the bottom and top of the wall cabinets.

First snap lines across the wall studs at the cabinet support locations. Then cut blocking to size to fit in between the studs in each bay. Use two different widths of blocking and alternate along the wall; 2x4s and 2x6s or 2x8s work well. First install the 2x4 blocks in every other bay, centered on the chalklines. Nail them on the flat, flush with the inside edge of the studs. Next install the larger blocks. By alternating them in this way, you can through nail all of the blocks through the studs instead of having to toenail.

Bath hardware

Have the owner walk through and indicate where the bathroom hardware will be located. Mark the spots, then nail blocking either flat against the studs or across the stud bay, depending on the type of hardware. If there's a question of exact placement, just throw in a few extra blocks. You'll thank yourself when the owner decides to move the toilet paper holder.

Medicine cabinet

A recessed medicine cabinet has to have a rough opening in the wall just like a window. If it's in a bearing wall, a medicine cabinet may need a small header if it's wider than the stud spacing. Have either the unit itself on the job or get the installation instructions for the proper rough opening. This is important to do before the mechanical subs go to work. Because the medicine cabinet is usually over a sink, the stud bay behind the sink is used for the plumbing vent pipe. And, it's not uncommon to see wires running through the same bay, feeding the wall light. Framing the medicine cabinet early, claims that stud bay before the other subs arrive.

Special Details for Roof Framing

Unlike many of the wall details, the roof details discussed in this section should be well planned before the roof framing commences, especially if you are using roof trusses.

Attic access

Building codes state a minimum size for access into an attic. Access can be provided by means of a scuttle hole or by pull-down stairs. Sometimes the location is planned in advance, other times it's decided after all of the walls and ceilings are framed.

If the access is to be the minimum-size scuttle hole, then waiting until the end of the project to place it usually works out. But if the access is going to be large, particularly one with a set of pull-down stairs, then the location should be determined before the ceiling framing is complete. Header off the joists for the ceiling opening, as described in chapter 6. If the access hole will be trimmed with wood, make sure to add the trim thickness to the minimum rough opening.

When the attic insulation is going to be a blown-in type, you should create a tall barrier around the inside of the attic access to prevent the insulation from spilling into the area. Use some sheathing ripped at the height of the insulation plus an inch or so. Nail the rips flush with the bottom around the inside of the frame, extending up into the attic. Don't forget to

An attic skuttle, or an opening for attic access, is installed during framing.

account for the extra thickness of the sheathing when making the rough opening.

Skylights shafts

Skylight shafts can be framed to just about any configuration according to the owner's taste.

Generally speaking, a shaft is framed with the sides at the same width as the rough opening between trusses or rafters. The top of the rough opening, though, is usually framed perpendicular to the rafters; and the bottom is framed plumb. Variations of the top and bottom splays create a wider or narrower shaft, but the framing sequence

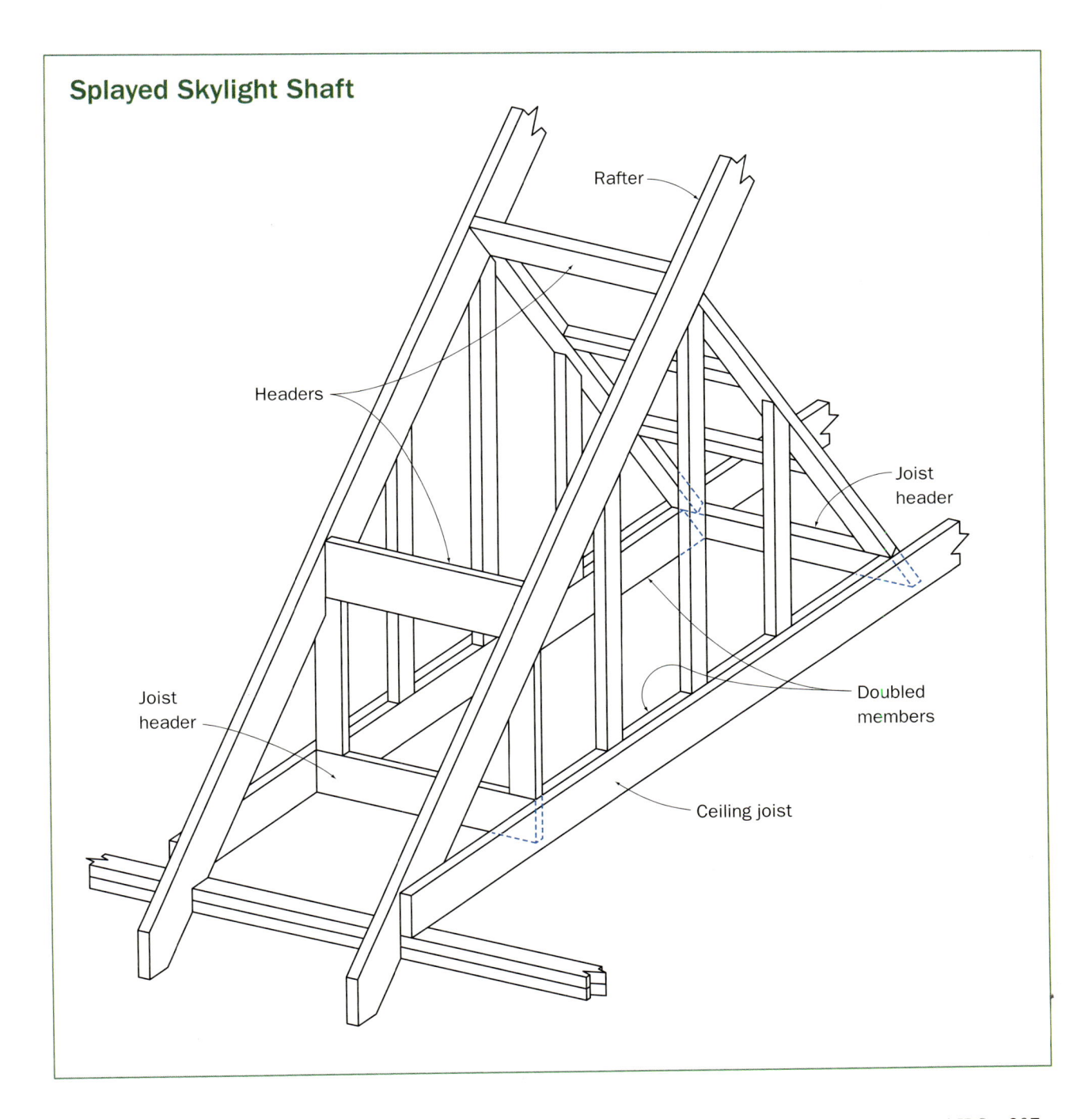

Splayed Skylight Shaft

- Rafter
- Headers
- Joist header
- Joist header
- Doubled members
- Ceiling joist

SPECIAL FRAMING DETAILS 207

Sheet stock is used for backing behind the staircase skirtboard. This prevents the fight with clumps of plaster that usually accumulate there.

remains the same. The ceiling joists should already be framed directly below or wider than the roof rafters, as described in chapter 6.

After the skylight is installed, check the rough opening to ensure that the drywall will fit properly into the slots of the skylight frame. Shim the rough opening as needed. This shimmed rough opening is what you should be referencing the shaft from.

Start at the two corners of the top end of the rough opening and hold a straightedge along the path of the splay. Mark the rafters and ceiling joists along the straightedge and repeat the process for the two bottom corners.

Cut four 2x4s the length and angle of the different shaft ends. Install the 2x4s along the lines drawn on the rafters and joists at the top and bottom corners. Nail 2x stock across the bottom of the shaft ends, flush with the underside of the ceiling joists. If the shaft is wider than 2 ft., install nailers in a ladder effect up the ends of the shaft. If the shaft is deeper than 2 ft., install vertical nailers every 2 ft. along the sides of the shaft.

Blocking for stairways

Although we did not cover stairs within the scope of the book, we'll note a special framing detail for blocking for stairways. We have seen many jobs that did not include this simple blocking, which makes the finish easier to install and much more secure.

Installing skirtboard backers If the house is going to be plastered or drywalled, we install a 7-in.- to 8-in.-wide length of ½-in. sheathing along the walls as a backer for staircase skirtboards. These backers also keep the plaster or joint compound from building up near the edges of the stringers.

Slip the sheathing rips in the $1\frac{5}{8}$-in. space between the outer stringer and the wall. Rest them on top of the 2x4 blocking and nail to the wall studs. Make sure the rips will be ½-in. shy of the top of the future skirtboard. When joints between the sheathing rips don't fall on studs, install a backer block to support the edges.

There are many areas around a staircase that need blocking to accept the finish work: the termination and transition of the skirtboards and baseboards as well as handrail hardware, terminations, and reinforcement. And like the half-wall support, some sort of planning and accommodation should be made for the below-floor support of newel posts.

Special Details for Framing for Subcontractors

Review the plans with the subcontractors before framing to determine their needs. Also keep them informed of any changes that are made to the structure, even if a change does not appear to have an effect on their job.

HVAC contractor

It is important to plan for the HVAC contractor. As throughout, allowances in the framing must be made for the ductwork of the HVAC system. These have the least flexibility off all the utilities and should be given priority.

Install headers in the openings as the framing progresses instead of saving it until the HVAC sub gets there. Stack framing the house really starts paying off at this point. When laid out properly, you can cut out a couple sections of plate stock and floor sheathing and have an instant basement-to-attic chase.

If the equipment is going into the attic, you also need to frame in the necessary supports and platforms.

Plumber

Because plumbers have a reputation for cutting anything in their way, a lot of your labor can be saved by working with them before the frame is complete.

Drains Tub and toilet drains fall in specific spots directly under the fixtures. If the fixture wasn't properly planned for when the joists were laid out or the fixture location has been changed, any joists that are in the way must be cut and headered off. This usually involves difficult nailing and scraped knuckles but it's a popular item with inspectors.

Whirlpool framing If the house is going to have a whirlpool, you should meet with the contractor, plumber, tile installer, and anyone else that will be working on it. If anything goes wrong, they're all going to try to blame the framer.

The height of the platform on which the tub sits can be critical if it's part of the support system. The inside dimension must be exactly what the instructions call for, and the outside

The frame for a whirlpool bath must be carefully laid out and constructed to accommodate all subcontractors who will work on the tub. Plumbers, electricians, and tile setters will probably be involved.

Access panels are framed to size as directed by the particular sub. (Photo by Tom O'Brien, courtesy *Fine Homebuilding* magazine, © The Taunton Press, Inc.)

dimensions must allow the finishes to be applied as laid out by the finisher (usually a tile setter). Setting, supporting, plumbing, electric access, and finish should all be decided on at a single meeting.

After the platform is built and the tub installed, build a cover from scrap 2x stock and sheathing. This protects the unit from the other subs until it's ready to be finished.

Access panels Certain plumbing fixtures may require access panels. Discuss this with the plumber to identify the locations of any access panels he needs. Frame them out before he begins roughing out the pipes. You'll avoid having to skirt around his plumbing, and he'll have more room to work. It's easier for everyone involved.

Tile showers For the bathroom that will have custom tile showers, you have to frame the unit first. Under the direction of the tile setter, frame the shower walls and floor pan to his specifications. The plumber should then have the shower pan made to the floor area you've built. If a copper pan is already built, then you must build the shower to the correct size. Provide perimeter blocking at the base of the shower from 2x stock wide enough to support the tile backer where it meets the shower pan. It's a good idea to screw and glue shower curb framing rather than just

The electrician needs a solid backer on which to mount the electric service panel.

using nails as fasteners. Dimensional lumber can warp and crack tile in these moist locations, so a little extra attachment can help.

Electrician

Some electricians include these details in their scope of work, others do not. If you don't know the electrician, it may be easier to plan to do these details yourself while your tools are out.

Panel backers If the circuit-breaker panel is going to be located in the basement or garage, it needs some type of backer panel to mount it to. We use sheathing. It can be $\frac{1}{2}$ in., $\frac{5}{8}$ in., or $\frac{3}{4}$ in.; the thickness is not as important as the support beneath. Check with the electrician to determine

A backing for the electric meter makes for easy flashing and identifies the exact location in which the meter is to be installed.

Use 2x blocks to hold out the electric work boxes to keep the electric trim covers from interfering with the door casing during the finish work.

the right height and width. He'll probably want it bigger than the breaker panel so that he has enough room to mount other wired services such as telephone and cable TV connections.

Meter boxes On some occasions, most often when the house is going to get vinyl siding, we frame a backer for the meter box. As with the circuit-breaker backer, we check with the electrician for the correct size. We cut it out of 3/4-in.- to 1-in.-thick stock and fasten it to the side of the house. It then gets wrapped in aluminum and flashed before the siding goes on.

Fixture blocking The electrician needs extra blocking in the ceilings for fixtures that are particularly heavy, such as ceiling fans. And we always frame in a small flat block at the inside peak of vaulted or cathedral ceilings to accept a fixture.

Switch/outlet blocking Sometimes a switch has to be mounted on the king stud of a door opening. If the electrician marks all of the locations, we nail a scrap block on the stud to mount the box to. This keeps the switch trim from running into the door trim. This is especially noticeable when 3½-in.-wide or wider casing is used for trim.

SPECIAL FRAMING DETAILS 211

Index

A

Anchor bolts:
   marker for, 37–38
   for mudsills, 26
Arches, interior, forming, 201–203
Attics:
   access to, 149
      by pull-down stair, 206
      skuttle-hole, 206
   insulation barriers for, 206–207
   roofs for, 151, 166
   uses of, determining, 169, 171

B

Baselines, establishing, 26–27
Basements, head room in, and recessed joists, 77
Bathrooms:
   blocking for, 205–206
   framing for, 209
   tile showers in, framing for, 210
   See also Spas; Whirlpools
Bathtubs:
   framing for, 62
   See also Spas
Bay windows. *See* Cantilevers
Beams:
   bracing, 49–50
   built-up,
      assembling, 47–50
      planning, 43–45
   center, 42
   flush with joists, 57, 72
   height of, calculating, 50–51
   installing, 45–47
   joist hangers with, 76, 77
   laminated-veneer, 54
   layers for, adding, 50
   layout for, 59–61
   ledgered, 76
   levels of, rechecking, 56
   locating, 45–47
   parallel-strand, 54
   pockets for, 43
      correcting, 25
   recessed,
      with hangers, 76, 77
      ledgers for, 75–76
   shimming, 51–52
   solid-wood, 53–54
   steel, 55
   straightening, 49
   strapping, 53
   supports for, 45, 46–47, 48
      column, 55–57

Blocking:
   for bathrooms, 204–206
   for cabinets, 204–205
   for drywall, 81–82
   for fixtures, 211
   for interior walls, 94–95
   ladder, 110, 112, 189
   for roof-shaft finish, 166
   for shelves, 203–204, 205
   squash, 80–81, 91, 92–93
   for staircases, 208
   between strapping, 187–90
   for subflooring, 86
   vertical, for heavy loads, 80–81, 92
   See also Firestops
Bolts, nuts and washers for, 26
Breaker junction boxes, providing, 16

C

Cabinets:
   blocking for, 204–205
   medicine, blocking for, 206
Calculators, construction-type, using, 6
Cantilevers:
   parallel to joists, 78
   perpendicular to joists, 78–79
Caulking guns:
   choosing, 9
   using, 9
Ceilings:
   blocking in, for fixtures, 211
   heights of, 103
   joists for, 166
   strapping, 184–90, 196–97
      on truss layout, 173
   and trusses, 169
Chalklines:
   colors with, 9
   dominant, 27
   for floor sheathing, 82–83
   on foundations, 34–36
   long, snapping, 106
   quality, 9
   twine for, 13
   uses of, 8–9
   using, 9
Chimneys:
   and floor layout, 60
   planning for, 149
Closets, blocking for, 203–204, 205
Collar ties:
   installing, 164–65
   solo, 164
   marking for, 166
   openings in, 165–66

spacing, 166
template, 155
temporary, 160
Column cutters, uses of, 13
Columns:
  beam-support, 55–57
  cutting, 56
  installing, 57
Compressors:
  antifreeze for, 19
  choosing, 16–17
  gas, 17
  motors for, 16–17
  pressure regulators for, 19
  repair kits for, 19
  tank sizes for, 17
Corner poles, making, 31
Corners:
  with exterior walls, 115, 116–18
  foundation, marking, 34
  of foundation drops, 33
  with interior walls, 110–13, 195
Cracks, avoiding, with squash blocks, 80–81
Cranes, with trusses, 179–82
Crawl spaces, beams in, supporting, 48
Cripples:
  collar-tie, 164
  defined, 100–101
  for interior doors, 194–95
  rafter, installing, 161–62
  sizes of, 102
Cut lists:
  for floors, preparing, 61–63
  for walls, preparing, 103–105

D

Doors:
  interior, heights for, 194
  "kits" for, 120, 123
  large, heavy,
    headers for, 71
    squash blocks for, 80–81
  pet, framing, 105
  pocket, 201, 202
  See also Arches
Drills, choosing, 15
Drywall:
  ceiling blocking for, 81–82
  clips for, 112–13, 117
Dumbwaiter shafts, and floor layout, 60

E

Electric:
  fixtures, blocking for, 211
  outlets, blocking for, 211
  switches, blocking for, 211
Elevators, and floor layout, 60
Exhaust systems, and floor layout, 60
Extension cords:
  gauge for, 15
  and GFCI breakers, 15–16
  making, 15–16

F

Fireplaces, framing for, 105
Firestops, locating, 200–201
Fixtures, blocking for, 211
Floor plans, for floor framing, 59
Floors:
  cut lists for, 61–63
  details of, marking, 63
  with I-joists, 88–95
  interruptions of, 60
  joist layout for, 59–60, 89
  openings in, 60–61
    and beams, 45
    "kits" for, 72–73
    marking, 63–64, 65
  with open-web trusses, 95–97
  sub-, 82–88
    courses of, 85–86
    end support for, 86
    with I-joists, 94, 95
  successive, 88
Floor safes, and floor layout, 60
Forms, aligners for, 22
Foundations:
  centerlines of, finding, 32
  checking for level in, 33–34
  corner poles for, 31
  drops in, 30–33, 40–41
  inspecting, 25
Framing:
  balloon, 144–45
  books on, 99
  stack,
    defined, 80–81
    squash blocks for, 80–81

G

Gable ends:
  with balloon framing, 166
  framing, 151
  plumbing, 157–58
  siding on, 174
  straightening, 163–64
  trusses for,
    ordering, 171, 173
    preparing, 174–75
    setting, 180–82

vents for, 175
GFCI, wiring for, 16
Girders. *See* Beams
Gluing, of subflooring, 83–88
Ground-fault circuit interrupters. *See* GFCI

H

Halls. *See* Arches
Hammers:
   selecting, 6–7
   sledge-, choosing, 7
   wood vs. other, 6
   See also Nailers
Headers:
   for chimneys, 160
   collar-tie, 164–65
   defined, 100
   floor,
      nailing sequence for, 73
      for sliding-glass doors, 71
      spans for, 60
   I-joist, 93
   for interior doors, 194–95
   layout for, 59–61
      marking, 65
   rim joists as, 71
   in roofs, locating, 160–61
   for skylights, 161
   wall,
      assembling, 123, 124
      full-length, 104
      preassembling, 119–20
      sizes for, 102–103
Heat ducts, and floor layout, 60
Hoses:
   pneumatic, 18
   quick-disconnect ends for, 18
House wraps:
   for gable ends, 174
   before raising, 130–31
HVAC, and floor layout, 60
HVAC contractors, working with, 62, 209
HVAC systems:
   chases for, 209
   supports for, 209

I

I-joists:
   backer blocks for, 94
   bearing surface for, 91
   carrying, 91
   cutting jig for, 91
   flanges of, care with, 90
   handling, 90
   hangers for, 94
   installing, 89–91
   marking for, 89
   planning for, 89
   pre-nailing, 91–92
   properties of, 88–89, 90
   squash blocks with, 91, 92–93
   wall-plate backers for, 94–95
   web stiffeners for, 93
Insulation, attic barrier to, 206–207

J

Jacks:
   beam-lifting, 52
   screw, 23
   wall-lifting, 22, 133–34
   See also Staging, A-frame
Joist hangers:
   with beams, 76, 77
   with I-joists, 94
   using, 72, 76, 77, 79–80
Joists:
   in attics, installing, 164
   with balloon framing, 144–45
   under bathtubs, spas, 62
   cantilevering,
      perpendicular, 78–80
      simple, 77–78
   ceiling, 166
      over interior walls, 150
   cripple, marking, 65
   cuts in, avoiding, 62
   hangers for, 72, 76, 77, 79–80
   installing, 73–75
      over beams, 75–77
   "kits" of, for openings, 72
   lapping, over beams, 67–68, 75
   layout for, 59–61
      marking, 63–69
   opposing, connecting, 75, 76
   rim,
      cutting, 71–72
      as headers, 71
      installing, 69–72
      squaring up, 82, 87
   selecting, 70
   shimming, 75
   spacing of, 59, 66–67
   spans for, 60–61
   squaring up, 72
   See also Blocking; I-joists; Trusses

K
Knives, utility, 8

L
Laundry chutes, and floor layout, 60
Layout, on-center, considerations for, 66–67
Levels:
  builder's, 21
    calibrating, 21
  checking, 11
    of foundations, 33–34
  choosing, 9–10
  electronic, 10
    laser, 10
  laser transit-,
    infrared, 21–22
    visible-beam, 21–22
  magnetized, 10
  reference lines with, 34
  self-stopping, 22
  spirit, 9
  water, 21
    using, 35
Lumber:
  crowned side, marking, 70
  dimensions of, checking, 105
  for floors, estimates for, 61
  green vs. kiln-dried, 70
  for mudsills, 26
  for roofs,
    ordering, 148
    planning, 147–48
  for staging, 20–21
  for walls, estimates for, 99–103

M
Markers:
  for floor layout, 59
  for plans, 6
Measuring:
  scales for, 5–6
  See also Measuring tapes
Measuring tapes:
  care with, 8
  choosing, 7–8
  one, for squareness check, 28–29
  two, for squareness check, 29
Metal, saw for, 14
Metal snips, using, 11
Meter boxes, panel backers for, 211
Miter boxes, power, uses of, 14–15

Mudsills:
  crew for, 24
  drilling, 36–38
    tool for, 37
  fastening, 38–39
  to floor plan, 26–27
  on foundation drops, 30–33
  importance of, 24, 25, 41
  layout for, 26–33
  materials for, ordering, 26
  shimming, 26, 39–40
  single vs. double, 26, 36
  sizing, 26
  strapping, 39
  termite shield and, 26
  as top plates, for drops, 41

N
Nailers:
  nails for,
    coil, 18
    strip, 18
  pneumatic, 18
  staplers as, 18
Nails, concrete, 26

O
Office, setting up, 5–6
Outlets, blocking for, 211

P
Partitions. See Walls, interior nonbearing
Planning. See Office
Plates:
  for bearing walls, 105
  double, cutting, 14
  layout on, 131
    for openings, 108–13
    roof, 150
  lumber for, 99–105, 107
  nailing, to wall studs, 122–23
  for nonbearing walls, 190–92
    marking, 192–94
  preparing, 107–108
  secondary,
    cutting, 115
    layout for, 115–19
  setting, 108
  straps for, 137
  top wall, voids in, 125
Pliers, choosing, 12

Plumb:
    to foundation drop, 33
    transits indicating, 21–22
Plumb bobs, choosing, 9
Plumbers, working with, 62, 209
Plumbing:
    access panels for, 210
    and floor layout, 60
    locations of, marking, 64
    strapping for, 184–85
    stud placement for, 193–94
    and truss planning, 96
Prybars:
    cat's paw, using, 11
    mini-, uses of, 8
    uses of, 10, 11

R

Rafters:
    bird's mouth of,
        calculating, 152
        illustrated, 151
    collar-tie template for, 155
    cripples with, 161–62
    cuts of, 151
    headers with, 160–62
    installing, 159–60
    layout for, 131, 151–53
    long, supporting, 160
    lumber for, grading, 155, 156
    misaligned, correcting, 160
    openings through, 160–62
    rise of, calculating, 152
    setting, sequence for, 156, 158
    shimming, 162
    template for, 153–55, 155–56
Rectangles:
    self-checking, 27
        extending, 30
    with string lines, 32–33
Ridge boards:
    gusset plates for, 157
    installing, 156–57
    laying out, 150–51
    lumber for, 148
    straightening, 158, 159
Roller scales, choosing, 6
Roofs:
    attic, 151, 166
    and attic access, 149
    Cape-style, 151–66
    cut lists for, 147–48
    gable ends of, framing, 151
    hip, truss preparation for, 175–79
    layout for, 147, 148–50
    lumber for, 148
    openings in,
        chimney, 149, 160
        skylight, 149
    openings through, 160–62
    overhangs for, and trusses, 168–69
    pitches of, and trusses, 168
    ridge boards in, 148, 150–51
        installing, 156–58
    sheathing, 162–64
    trussed vs. stick-built, 146
    trusses for, 166–83
    types of, 148
    See also Rafters; Staging

S

Saddles, defined, 100–101
Saws:
    circular,
        amperage of, 13
        choosing, 13–14
        worm-drive, 13
        worm-drive braked, 13
    cordless, 13–14
    hand, choosing, 11
    reciprocating, choosing, 14
    See also Miter boxes, power
Scaffolds. See Staging
Screwdrivers, multi-tip, 12
Sheathing:
    air pressure for, controlling, 19
    delivery of, 179–80
    floor,
        installing, 82–88
        preparing for, 82–83
    for gable ends, 130, 174
    gluing, 84
    with I-joists, 95
    nailing, sequence for, 83–85
    nailing off, 87–88
    nail lines on, with squares, 12
    between rafters, 130
    roof, installing, 162–64, 183
    savings in, 129
    for steep roofs, 163
    wall,
        axis for, 127
        installing, 128–30
        layout for, 127–28
        rake, 144
        squaring for, 126–27
Shelves, blocking for, 203–204
Shims:
    material for, 52
    ordering, 26

Shingles, delivery of, 179, 180
Siding:
   on gable ends, 174–75
   pre-attaching, 151
Sill seal, ordering, 26
Skylights:
   openings for, 149
   shafts for, 207–208
Sledgehammers, choosing, 7
Soffits:
   cabinet, 203, 204
   nailers for, before raising, 131–32
   and truss design, 168–69
Spas:
   framing for, 62
   See also Whirlpools
Squareness, with diagonals, 27–30, 32–33
Squares:
   bevel, 12
   choosing, 8
   combination, 8
   fixed-angle triangular, 11
   4-ft. T-, 12
   framing, choosing, 11–12
   steel, 11
Squash blocks:
   for heavy loads, 80–81, 92–93
   with I-joists, 91
   uses of, 80–81
Squeaks:
   and joist overlap, 75
   minimizing, nailing sequence for, 72–73
Staging:
   A-frame, for beam support, 45, 46, 47, 52
   H-frame, for beam supports, 48
   planks for, wood vs. aluminum, 20–21
   pump jack, 20
      wood vs. aluminum, 20
   for ridge boards, 157
   wall jack, 20
Staircases:
   blocking for, 208
   and floor layout, 60
   gauges for, 12
   newel-post support for, 208
   pull-down, 206
   skirtboard backers for, 208
Stair gauges, using, 12
Staplers:
   hammer, uses of, 12
   pneumatic, 18
Story sticks:
   for strapping, 187–88
   for window layout, 110
Strapping:
   fastening, 188–90
   for interior walls, 184–90
   lumber for, 187–88
   marking for, 186–87
String lines:
   setting up, 31–33
   supports for, 30
Studs:
   aligning, before sheathing, 129
   centers for, finding, 115
   cutting, 119
   delivery of, 179–80
   grading, 119
   heights for, determining, 40–41
   interior, planning for, 192–94
   for interior nonbearing wall, 194
   jack, 100–101, 102
   layout for, 113–18, 197
   lengths of, determining, 102–103
   notched, for ledger boards, 144–45
   sizes of, noting, 105
   skipping, for savings, 193
   types of, defined, 100
Subfacia:
   installing, 162, 182–83
   lumber for, 162
   and truss design, 168
Subflooring. *See* Floors, sub-
Switches, blocking for, 211

T

Tape measures:
   care with, 8
   choosing, 7–8
   one, for squareness check, 28–29
   two, for squareness check, 29
Tilework, framing for, 210
Toolbelts, selecting, 6
Tools:
   battery-operated, 15
   hand, 6–13
   pneumatic, 16–19
   power, 13–16
   See also individual tools
Trim:
   rake, pre-attaching, 151
   See also Soffits; Subfacia
Trimmers:
   defined, 61
   squaring up, 87
Trusses:
   and attic use, 169, 171
   braces for, 23
   ceiling details with, 169
   checking, 173
   choosing, 167
   for complex roof, 183

cords of, 169
energy-efficient, 170
extra, 171
fire stopping for, 97
floor open-web, 95–97
   advantages of, 96
   ordering, 96
gable-end, 174–75
handling, 172–73
hip, 175–79
   installing, 183
   strengthening, 183
installing, 96–97, 179–83
   crew for, 181
layout for, 96
marking, 173
openings in, 170
ordering, 167–72
overhangs with, 168–69
preparing, 172–73
properties of, 95–96
roof pitch for, 168
at roof profile change, 175
spans of, 168–69
specifications for, 168–69
stock, 97
tag line for, 180, 181
tails of, precut, 169–70
web bracing for, 97, 182–83
Turnbuckles, for form alignment, 22
Twine, uses of, 13

V

Vents, and floor layout, 60

W

Walls:
   aligning,
      with peavey, 136
      with string, 136–37
   assembling, 121–32
      sequence for, 106–107
   balloon-framed, 144–45, 166
   bracing,
      with let-in braces, 138, 139
      with shear panels, 138, 139
      spring, 134–35
      with straps, 138, 139
   centers of, finding, 27–28, 29
   cut lists for, 99, 102–104
   on drops, 40
   exterior,
      marking for, 105–106
      planning, 99–105
   garage, 140–41
   half-, supports for, 198–200
   heights of, 102
   house wrap for, 130–31
   interior, marking for, 106
   interior bearing, layout for, 119
   interior nonbearing, 184–97
      backer options for, 110–13, 114, 124–25, 195
      framing, 195–96, 197
      lifting, 196
      line transfers for, 190, 191
      marking, 185–86
      openings in, 192, 194
      plates for, 190–92
      securing, 197
      sequence for, 194
      strapping for, 184–90
      studs for, 194
   intersections of, marking, 110–12
   jacks for, 22
   lifting,
      by hand, 132–33
      with jacks, 133–34
   load-bearing, 101
   lumber for, 99
   nailing, 135, 136
   nonbearing, 101, 103
   openings in, 100–105
      assembling, 120, 123–24
      marking, 110
      radiused, 201–202
      and sheathing, 128
   plates for, filler, 126
   rake, 142–44
   section of, 100–101
   slab-on-grade, 141–42
   soffit nailers for, before raising, 131–32
   squaring, before sheathing, 126–27
   straps for, 122, 137
   truss layout on, hip, 179
   See also Sheathing
Whirlpools:
   consultation for, 209–10
   framing for, 209–10
Windows:
   "kits" for, 120, 123
   layout for, 110–11, 114
   layout stick for, 110
Wiring:
   breaker junction boxes for, 16
   conduits for, and floor layout, 60
   ground-fault circuit interrupters, 16
   service-panel backers for, 210–11
   strapping for, 184–85
   stud placement for, 193–94
   See also Extension cords